RETHINKING JUSTICE IN CATHOLIC SOCIAL THOUGHT

Recent Titles from the Moral Traditions Series

David Cloutier, Andrea Vicini, SJ, and Darlene Weaver, Editors

Radical Sufficiency: Work, Livelihood, and a US Catholic Economic Ethic
Christine Firer Hinze

Tragic Dilemmas in Christian Ethics
Kate Jackson-Meyer

The Fullness of Free Time: Leisure and Recreation in the Moral Life
Connor Kelly

Law from Below: How the Thought of Francisco Suárez, SJ, Can Renew Contemporary Legal Engagement
Elisabeth Rain Kincaid

On Teaching and Learning Christian Ethics
D. Stephen Long

Beyond Virtue Ethics: A Contemporary Ethic of Ancient Spiritual Struggle
Stephen M. Meawad

Growing in Virtue: Aquinas on Habit
William C. Mattison III

Reenvisioning Sexual Ethics: A Feminist Christian Account
Karen Peterson-Iyer

Ecological Moral Character: A Catholic Model
Nancy M. Rourke

Wealth, Virtue, and Moral Luck: Christian Ethics in an Age of Inequality
Kate Ward

RETHINKING JUSTICE IN CATHOLIC SOCIAL THOUGHT

DANIEL K. FINN, EDITOR

GEORGETOWN UNIVERSITY PRESS / WASHINGTON, DC

© 2025 Georgetown University Press. All rights reserved. No part of this book may be reproduced or utilized in any form or by any means, electronic or mechanical, including photocopying and recording, or by any information storage and retrieval system, without permission in writing from the publisher.

The publisher is not responsible for third-party websites or their content. URL links were active at time of publication.

The publisher is delighted to acknowledge the contribution of the Institute for Advanced Catholic Studies at USC in making possible the publication of the book.

Library of Congress Cataloging-in-Publication Data

Names: Finn, Daniel K., 1947- editor.
Title: Rethinking justice in Catholic social thought / Daniel K. Finn, editor.
Description: Washington, DC : Georgetown University Press, 2025. | Series: Moral traditions | Includes bibliographical references and index.
Identifiers: LCCN 2024025459 (print) | LCCN 2024025460 (ebook) | ISBN 9781647125813 (hardcover) | ISBN 9781647125820 (paperback) | ISBN 9781647125837 (ebook)
Subjects: LCSH: Justice—Religious aspects—Catholic Church. | Christian Sociology—Catholic Church.
Classification: LCC BX1795.J87 R48 2025 (print) | LCC BX1795.J87 (ebook) | DDC 261.8088/282—dc23/eng/20250313

LC record available at https://lccn.loc.gov/2024025459
LC ebook record available at https://lccn.loc.gov/2024025460

EU GPSR Authorised Representative
LOGOS EUROPE, 9 rue Nicolas Poussin,
17000, LA ROCHELLE, France
E-mail: Contact@logoseurope.eu

26 25   9 8 7 6 5 4 3 2   First printing

Cover design by Jeremy John Parker
Interior design by Westchester Publishing Services

To James Heft, SM
Visionary and Founding President of
the Institute for Advanced Catholic Studies

CONTENTS

Acknowledgments   ix

Introduction   1
Daniel K. Finn

PART I: SOURCES FOR RE-THINKING JUSTICE

1   African Understandings of Justice   13
Agbonkhianmeghe E. Orobator, SJ

2   Hindu and Buddhist Understandings of Justice   33
George Kodithottam, SJ

3   Justice in Latin American Theology   54
Maria Inês de Castro Millen

4   Scripture as a Resource for Re-thinking Justice
in Catholic Social Thought   78
Anathea Portier-Young

5   Thomas Aquinas's Theory of Justice   100
Jean Porter

6   How Liberalism Can Contribute to Re-thinking Justice
in Catholic Social Thought   116
Francis Schüssler Fiorenza

7   Justice in Catholic Social Teaching   133
Lisa Sowle Cahill

8   Experience, Social Location, and Justice   157
Agnes M. Brazal

9   Justice as a Characteristic of Social Structures   177
Daniel K. Finn

PART II: THREE CONSTRUCTIVE ACCOUNTS OF JUSTICE

10   A Synthetic Statement of What Justice Might Be Understood
to Entail in Catholic Social Thought Today   197
Agbonkhianmeghe E. Orobator, SJ

11   Justice: A Three-Dimensional Account from Catholic
Social Teaching   207
David Cloutier

12   Justice as a Virtue in Catholic Social Thought   226
Lisa Sowle Cahill

PART III: A ROUGH CONSENSUS

13   Toward a Definition of Justice in Catholic Social Thought   243
Daniel K. Finn

About the Participants   249

Index   255

ACKNOWLEDGMENTS

This project is dedicated to re-thinking justice in Catholic social thought and has been five years in the making, and so it relies on the generous contributions of many. As editor, I am deeply grateful to the ten authors. The diversity of their cultural backgrounds, the breadth of their life experiences, the history of their erudition, and their openness to deep engagement with others is what makes this volume so rich and so helpful. I am indebted to Julie Clague (University of Glasgow), James Heft, SM (University of Dayton), Christine Firer Hinze (Fordham University), Alexandre Martins (Marquette University), and Steven Pope (Boston College) for their insightful advice on the steering committee that guided the project at every stage, from planning eighteen months before the first conference to debriefing after the second. I am especially indebted to Alex Martins for his careful work in translation for author Maria Inês de Castro Millen. And most fundamentally, this project arises from the Institute for Advanced Catholic Studies, founded by Fr. Jim Heft, whose leadership and vision have engendered an array of important scholarly projects.

Dr. Rebecca King Cerling, executive director of the institute, has provided essential support to the project, along with her staff, Douglas Morino and Kylie Uyeda. Richard Wood, the president of the institute, began his duties as the project was well along, but his support has been critical to its completion.

I am grateful to two anonymous readers of the manuscript for Georgetown University Press, and to the editor of the press, Al Bertrand, for his steady support, and to Alka Ranjan, who so ably coordinated the production of the book.

At every step of this journey, Mrs. Judy Shank, executive secretary for the Clemens Chair here at St. John's University and the College of St. Benedict, has faithfully typed and retyped plans, statements, and edits of the manuscript. Mr. Owen Haubenschild has been readily helpful in many particular tasks needed in my own work as editor.

Introduction

Daniel K. Finn

Everyone wants to be treated justly, but disagreements about what that means are everywhere. There is broad agreement in the Catholic tradition and beyond with the ancient conviction that justice is a virtue that leads a person to give to others "what is due to them." Yet as a definition of justice, this leaves a lot of room for disagreement about what exactly *is* due. Recent decades have seen hundreds of books and articles addressing justice, particularly "Justice and . . . ," where a critically important issue or group completes the title. Yet as a senior scholar in moral theology recently observed, she was unable even to *find* a contemporary definition of justice in recent Catholic scholarship. She observes that even *Justitia in mundo*, a statement from the World Synod of Bishops dedicated to the issue, does not *define* justice.

Justice has been a fundamental part of Christian theology from the scriptures and early church to the twenty-first century. Thomas Aquinas, the most influential intellectual force shaping modern Catholic social thought, had much to say about justice, both as a virtue and an obligation, incorporating diverse sources from Greek and Christian traditions. However, his views are difficult to summarize briefly. In the 1950s, German philosopher Josef Pieper proposed a systematization of the Thomistic view of justice. His description of three forms of justice has come to be widely accepted within Catholic social thought, particularly in the English-speaking world.

Pieper asks, "When might justice be said to prevail in a community?" He says, "St. Thomas's answer might have run like this: . . . whenever the three basic relations [in a community's life] are disposed in their proper order." The three relations and their corresponding forms of justice are (1) individuals to one another (commutative justice), (2) the social whole to individuals (distributive justice), and (3) individuals to the social whole (legal or general justice).

Still, we have seen developments in human history that complicate the beautiful simplicity of this medieval view and call for a re-thinking of justice. These include democracy, secularism, industrialization, migration, structural injustice, and a host of justice obligations related to the environment, social media, privacy, religious freedom, gender, racism, harassment, war, transparency, and a number of others.

To address this gap in Catholic social thought, this volume provides a record of a multiyear effort to re-think justice, organized by the True Wealth of Nations project at the Institute for Advanced Catholic Studies in Los Angeles. Planning began in 2018. A steering committee of eight scholars met in a daylong session in May 2019 and decided on a multiyear, two-stage, two-conference format. As a result, this book is not "a volume of conference papers." It is a record of sustained conversations, a report on an organic process in which scholars—both the authors and the others on the steering committee—read and discussed each other's work over years, got to know and truly learn from each other, and developed a self-understanding as an ongoing community of inquiry. This was a community capable of coming to a rough consensus on the primary issue they were addressing, a definition of justice. This outcome, never guaranteed from the start, is quite remarkable, given the diversity of approaches represented by the participants.

Because the project aimed for a fundamental reconsideration of justice, a first conference would focus on a variety of sources for insights—often conflicting, at times mutually supportive—out of which a more adequate view of justice might arise. The second conference, to be held eighteen months after the first, would focus on a few constructive accounts of justice arising from the source papers and conversations at the first conference.

The committee identified the topic areas for these "source papers" and, for each, crafted a list of scholars best suited to address the topic.

Constructing such a list of potential sources is daunting, and our list could not be exhaustive. There might have been chapters on Islam, Confucianism, Taoism, Sikhism, Rabbinic teaching, or the indigenous peoples of North or South America. Even within the Christian tradition, there might have been separate essays on the New Testament, the early church (or Augustine himself), the Reformation, contemporary Protestant thought, or the Eastern Orthodox tradition. There might have been separate chapters on ancient Greek philosophy, Utilitarianism, Marxism, or the work of many individual philosophers and theologians of recent centuries from which insight can be drawn.

But at some point, any continued widening of the range of sources leads to a volume that is less accessible to a broad audience. The size of a volume matters for its ultimate effect, and we aim for a book that will be widely read.

Today, one of the most fundamental criticisms of the treatment of justice in Catholic social thought is that it has been so thoroughly rooted in one culture, Western European, and has been largely unaffected by the insights from elsewhere, particularly the Global South.

As a result of these considerations, we decided to engage nine source chapters, giving special importance to voices from the Global South: from traditional African, Hindu, and Buddhist accounts; from contemporary Latin American Catholic approaches to justice; and from the insights of an Asian theologian investigating the role of context and social location in the understanding of justice.

Authors completed their papers six weeks before the first conference, which was held January 3–6, 2022 (after a one-year COVID-19 delay). This meeting was attended only by the authors and the steering committee. With all papers read beforehand, each author's work was discussed and interrogated for ninety minutes. After the conference, authors revised their papers in light of insights they gained from the conversations. Part I comprises these nine essays.

The second conference, in June 2023, aimed to re-think justice, focusing on three papers, each written as a substantive statement about how justice ought to be understood in Catholic social thought today. These make up part II.

Discussions of a possible consensus view of justice at that second conference led to a final chapter, in part III, articulating the rough consensus arising among the participants on a definition of justice.

From the beginning, we have aimed for a conception of justice that, as far as possible, is coherent, comprehensive, faithful to the tradition, responsive to the best of contemporary insight, adequate for confronting pressing injustices, and stated simply enough to be accessible to nonexperts.

Part I of the manuscript, then, comprises nine chapters that examine a variety of sources for deeper reflection in this process of re-thinking justice in Catholic social thought.

In chapter 1, Agbonkhianmeghe Orobator, SJ, outlines several basic elements of traditional African religion concerning justice. He points out that justice is fundamentally social and "prioritizes the relationships of people in community." He identifies three "generative sites" for reflection. The first is *Ubuntu*, an insight that personal identity is only possible within communal relationships. The second is palaver, the traditional conversation in African communities, the social locus "where justice is discoursed, practiced, and dispensed." The third concerns rituals of forgiveness and reconciliation that constitute the embodiment of justice realized. Concrete examples from Uganda, Rwanda, and Burundi illustrate the practices. Orobator includes an identification of shortcomings of traditional African approaches to justice, including the problems of tribalism and traditional patriarchy.

Chapter 2 is a presentation of Hindu and Buddhist understandings of justice provided by George Kodithottam, SJ. For more than 3,000 years, Hindu insight has seen justice and righteousness as reflections in this world of the harmony and natural order of the universe. The notion of "dharma" is central to any consideration of justice in Hinduism because it sustains the moral, social, political, and economic order and eventually came to refer to the rights and duties of individuals and groups. "A just life is rooted in dharma." Karmic retribution—that one's current station is the inevitable result of one's own behavior in an earlier life—makes the individual fundamentally responsible for justice. Unlike Hinduism and Catholic moral theology, the understanding of justice in Buddhism does not rely on a divinely created order. And for the Buddha, "there is no metaphysical self; the idea of an 'individual self' is an illusion." Compassion is the most basic human value. Following *dhamma* (different from dharma) is the way to avoid suffering and reach happiness. Justice is that which promotes mutual self-interest. "As a rational person, one cannot expect others in the community to respect one's interests unless one is prepared to respect the interest of others." Everything that occurs is caused—the doctrine of "dependent origination"—so there can be no sharp dichotomy between humanity and the natural world, a conviction that leads to a robust environmental ethic.

Chapter 3 presents a Latin American, and specifically Brazilian, approach to justice by Maria Inês de Castro Millen. Because no comprehensive account of Latin America is possible, she avoids "homogenizing differences." Instead, she recounts a variety of organizations and movements that have arisen in Brazil in response to colonization and the abuses of indigenous groups, people of African descent, and many of mixed races who have been marginalized and oppressed. Whether affiliated with the Catholic Church, governmental efforts, or spontaneous developments from marginalized people, the essence of the creation of justice is the gathering and empowering of people, conscientizing and enabling the voices of the poor to speak and work for justice in an unjust world. Because of the importance of the Amazon ecosystem, Brazilian justice movements have long insisted that ecological issues are central to making justice a reality. Events like the Synod for the Amazon, convened by Pope Francis in 2017, point to a more hopeful future.

In chapter 4, Anathea Portier-Young begins her overview of the Hebrew scriptures as a resource for re-thinking justice with a reminder that "context shapes our understanding of justice." She calls for a "hermeneutic of justice," one that is committed to self-criticism and mutual accountability, whatever the particular biblical tools one employs. She calls for greater care in realistically recognizing the shortcomings of even biblical exemplars of virtue. Although the texts do not portray examples of democracy, she cites several that entail a limitation on the authority of those in power. Her chapter engages an ongoing conversation with contemporary Christian activists committed to living out the conviction that "God requires God's people to *do* justice." The chapter helpfully recounts a number of biblical teachings on economic justice and others concerning ecological justice. "It shifts focus from classical protagonists to marginalized characters and expands attention from individual action to broader systems and structures," providing significant assistance for efforts to re-think justice today.

Chapter 5 is a summary of the understanding of justice in the work of Thomas Aquinas, written by Jean Porter. Aquinas accepts Justinian's definition of justice as "a constant and perpetual will rendering to each that which is his right." Porter clarifies Aquinas's views on distributive, commutative, and general (or legal) justice. She explores the central place that the common good has in the conception of general justice and the conviction that "society exists for the sake of its members." Porter investigates whether Aquinas has an understanding of personal rights (i.e., rights "possessed" by individuals), concluding that he "does not seem to think of rights as discrete moral powers" but "that the individual possesses the authority to determine the course of their own life in certain critical ways." Although Aquinas does not have any treatment of social structures or structural justice, his work nonetheless implies that today, "a truly just individual would be disposed to preserve and promote equality through institutional structures," in addition to respecting claims of right in individual actions.

Chapter 6, by Francis Schüssler Fiorenza, examines the ways that the tradition of liberalism in the West can be an asset to the project of re-thinking justice in Catholic social thought. Fiorenza sees a lesson in John Rawls's granting priority to "the right" over "the good." That is, unlike Aristotle and the Catholic tradition, Rawls argues that contemporary deliberations about the character of justice should bracket debates about the good (because modern societies cannot agree on exactly what *is* good for people) and focus instead on justice itself ("the right"). Fiorenza emphasizes this insight of Rawls because there are problems with too great an emphasis on the common good in Catholic social thought. For example, is it not futile to appeal to the common good to resolve the choice between the construction of an interstate highway (that makes national cohesion easier) and the destruction of city neighborhoods required in the process? Even the emphasis on communitarianism implies distinguishing those who are within the community from those without. Fiorenza argues that Rawls's second principle accomplishes much of what Catholic social thought has aimed for in its appreciation of the common good and the preferential option for the poor.

In chapter 7, Lisa Sowle Cahill presents the view of justice in papal social teaching, the most influential "source" for this project on re-thinking justice. She examines the most fundamental notions employed in the treatment of justice in this tradition: the common good, the dignity of the person, the preferential option for the poor, solidarity, and other commitments such as the rule of law, just participatory political institutions, and reciprocal rights and duties. She highlights the influence of the notion of social justice introduced into Catholic teaching by Pope Pius IX in 1931. She carefully recounts the history of the development of modern papal teaching, coming to adopt human rights, the preferential option for the poor, and the notion of sinful social structures. Among the challenges she sees for the future are the calls for decentralization of authority and the problem of gender bias.

In chapter 8, Agnes Brazal examines the role of experience and social location in any effort to explain the demands of justice. To make her argument more concrete, she focuses on issues of gender in church and society, and she criticizes the use of "gender complementarity" in the magisterium's approach to just relationships. Brazal presents the work of Martha Nussbaum, "justice within a politics of sameness," to note Nussbaum's claim of the universal characteristics of human dignity that any just society will further. Similarly, she examines the views of Iris Marion Young, "justice within the politics of positional difference," to better understand preferential treatment and "role exclusion" as remedies for traditional forms of discrimination, particularly in patriarchal societies. The arguments of both these philosophers lead Brazal to call for "participative community mediation" in any approach to justice. This entails a democratic deliberation that should move the church itself toward just participative decision-making, including women in roles of true authority in the church.

Part I concludes with chapter 9, an examination of justice as a characteristic of social structures, written by Daniel Finn. The chapter presents the analysis of social structures arising from the "critical realist" school of sociology. Rooted in the philosophy of science of Roy Bashkar, critical realism understands social structures as constituted by the relations among social positions that persons take on in their daily lives. Social structures, then, are ontologically real and generate incentives (restrictions and opportunities) that tend to influence the free choices that persons within those structures make. An unjust social structure encourages persons to make unjust choices. The chapter then applies these insights to the three dimensions of justice—commutative, distributive, and general—that the modern tradition of Catholic social thought inherited from Aquinas.

There is a significant diversity of approaches in the chapters of part I. The reader will encounter different types of evidence and modes of argumentation employed by different authors. This might seem frustrating, but in the language of contemporary software design, this is a feature, not a bug. This project has challenged the authors of part I to employ their professional judgment to report on what they consider to be the most important insights from nine quite different "sources"—the insights they judge will be most helpful for the deliberations in parts II and III, where re-thinking justice occurs. This method employed for the project and the book inherently bends toward the individual differences among the scholars. Their judgments concern not only what "content" elements are stressed but also what sorts of evidence and modes of argument in the sources are most helpful. Conversations at both conferences were enriched by the interplay of the differences. We believe these differences reflect differences existing today in our church and world.

Part II of this volume comprises three constructive statements, each proposing an understanding and definition of justice for Catholic social thought. These were created by three scholars involved in this project's deliberation over the source papers at the first conference. These statements formed the basis for a lively discussion as to whether there may be an optimal way to describe justice in Catholic social thought today, or at least whether this group of scholars might come to a consensus about the issue. Each ends with the author's proposal for a definition of justice.

In chapter 10, Agbonkhianmeghe Orobator, SJ, calls for an approach to justice that resists "hegemonic cultural tendencies" of colonialization and is attentive to the cultural assets of diverse peoples. Justice is more communal than traditional Catholic views indicate. It must be understood to be "global (spatial), integrative (open-ended), or multivalent (extensive), depending on the context, the issue, and the objective." Orobator highlights issues of gender, environment, and the continuing impact of slavery. Any re-thinking of justice in Catholic social thought must be enculturated, dialogical, inclusive of the natural world, and "a practice to be lived."

Chapter 11 is a statement by David Cloutier that understands an appropriate Catholic account of justice as three-dimensional. The first dimension is "subjective justice." Justice is a virtue, an ongoing personal disposition relating to desert and equality. The second dimension is "objective justice," commitments concerning rights, dignity, and the common good. A "pluralist social ontology" helps to avoid the mistake of resisting appropriate change in church teaching on justice. Yet it insists on an objective core to such teaching to resist the dominant individualistic urge that bases notions of justice on nothing more substantive than subjective rights. The third dimension is "eschatological justice," entailing insights into sin, mercy, and the preferential option for the poor.

Chapter 12 presents Lisa Sowle Cahill's view on what a re-thinking of justice in Catholic social thought would entail. She argues that the fundamental traditional insight of justice as a virtue can be expanded—following a suggestion from John Rawls—so that it is understood as a virtue of social institutions as well as of persons. Arguing carefully from official Catholic teaching, she cites various dimensions of what justice requires, including the common good, the dignity of persons, the preferential option for the poor, participation, and solidarity. If these are properly structured within institutions and culture in society, they play a role parallel to the role of good character in the decisions of individuals: they make just outcomes more likely.

Part III of the volume includes a single brief chapter by Daniel Finn. It summarizes the group's efforts to move toward a consensus statement on justice. Listening to the insistence of voices from the Global South on the centrality of experience, the ultimate definition begins with justice as a lived experience of communal life, and only secondarily as a virtue, a norm, or a goal to be achieved. This reverses the classical theological and philosophical order that identifies justice as a norm or goal to be then lived out by virtuous people. As the definition makes clear, that lived experience is animated by both personal virtue and social structures and culture—and its fundamental characteristics can be described.

We are past the age of monocultural overconfidence. Catholicism is a global reality, not simply a European or North Atlantic one. A comment by Agbonkhianmeghe Orobator in chapter 1 captures an essential caution about the necessary intercultural conversation. "No matter how hard I try, I cannot articulate in my mother tongue the classic Western European categorization and corresponding definitions of justice." Conversation that extends from one culture to another, or from one century to another, or from one philosophical perspective to another is never precise in translation. Yet this is what is entailed when we say that Christianity is a living tradition. At each stage in its history, leaders in this religious tradition address problems in their own age by applying insights inherited from the tradition to new situations—with their own insights becoming part of that tradition for those who came after. This volume aims to do the same today.

Simple summaries such as Josef Pieper's three-part typology of justice must give way to a more subtle discernment of today's diversity of contexts and perspectives. The ongoing relevance of the Catholic tradition to the many struggles for justice around the world requires it.

Daniel K. Finn
April 22, 2024

PART I

Sources for Re-thinking Justice

CHAPTER 1

African Understandings of Justice

Agbonkhianmeghe E. Orobator, SJ

Christianity arose in the Middle East and grew into the Greek and Roman worlds. For centuries, Roman Catholic theology developed almost exclusively in a European context. Yet with the expansion of Christian faith to all the ends of the Earth, Catholic theology has come to recognize that some of its assumptions that seemed "natural" turn out to be rooted in cultural features "of the West." They appear quite unnatural to Christians in places like Africa and Asia.

Consider an example. Although in the more individualistic West, marriage is thought to occur at the moment two people each say "I do," in traditional Africa, the marriage of two people is a communal process that occurs in stages over several days.[1] Similarly, regarding the re-thinking of justice explored in this volume, African understandings of what Catholic moral theology has called commutative justice require far more than a one-to-one rectification of injustice that Thomas Aquinas envisioned. Only a social, restorative process that heals the wounds of the community will be adequate.

This chapter explores three culturally rooted realities that shape African understandings of justice: Ubuntu, palaver, and ritual. *Ubuntu* is an idea that generates the philosophical and cultural basis of an African conception of justice. *Palaver* is a social encounter emphasizing conversation and location in the practice of justice. *Ritual* is a communal experience that acknowledges the religious guarantors of justice in social contracts or covenants. The concluding comments and a critique of the key aspects of African understandings of justice provide instructive lessons in advancing the project to develop a new typology of justice for Catholic social thought.

At the onset, a caveat is in order. No matter how hard I try, I cannot articulate in my mother tongue the classic Western European categorization and corresponding definitions of justice. This does not mean that the Edo-speaking people of Midwestern Nigeria—or by extension, other African linguistic groups—do not possess a conception of justice worth analyzing. Words do not create reality. As the Edo say, a cloudy sky at midday offers no proof that the sun has ceased to shine. This chapter is positioned halfway between the different lived embodiments of justice in African settings and the task of this volume to re-think justice in Catholic social thought. The claim here is that the unique insight and wisdom of Africa can provide assistance in this process.

A BLENDED CONTEXT: AFRICAN, CHRISTIAN, MUSLIM

The last one hundred years have seen a historic southward shift of Christianity's centre of gravity to Africa, largely due to an impressive expansion of Christianity in sub-Saharan Africa.[2] Consequently, "Africa is now, in one sense, the centre of the Christian world. . . . Africa has been very receptive to Christianity, but it has made Christianity decidedly its own."[3] Yet this "centre" is a crowded space of religious traditions with an ample reservoir of claims and contestations, originating in a layering of religious identities, aspects of which influence, if not determine, the conception and practice of justice.

The religious African bears multiple identities shaped by African religion, Christianity, and Islam, even though the latter two arrived from abroad. The relationship of these three in Africa shows some similarity to the interaction of Hinduism and Buddhism in India, as described in the chapter in this volume by George Kodithottam, but in several ways it is even more complex. Although foreign, Islam and Christianity have become indelible patterns woven into Africa's religious tapestry: "Christianity and Islam are now the two largest religions in Africa."[4] Nonetheless, "Underpinning these faiths, both of which come from outside Africa, is a substratum of traditional African religion that often influences individual behavior."[5] Seen as a "substratum," African religion shapes and influences some fundamental value systems of these major world religions, including the understanding of justice.[6]

Africa's layered and multiple religious identities create competition among dominant traditions to impose core beliefs, values, and principles in private and public spheres of life. Such intense competition makes defining justice a complicated process. In several African countries, like Nigeria,

Tanzania, and Kenya, agreeing to a justice system and an underlying set of definitions, principles, and criteria for its application can result in intense political debates and degenerate into physical conflict.

Many Muslims in these countries advocate Sharia, an all-encompassing Islamic legal code, as the basis of the justice system. Sharia draws explicitly on a complex collection of written and oral sources of Islam. In predominantly Islamic African areas, with firm conviction that divine revelation is the source of the law, little if any account is taken of the existing religious diversity in such societies. God is synonymous with the law in a way that negates any Christian arguments that God is beyond legal systems. Thus, in a conflict between common law and Sharia, priority is accorded to the latter. Christians uphold a common-law framework and constitutional jurisprudence handed down by the colonial West, appealing to Judeo-Christian traditions and propositions with significant implications for how such systems should function.[7] Between these two religious systems lies so-called customary law derived from principles of justice in traditional African religion and cultures.

Clearly, the convergence at national and local levels of these religious traditions, each with its own legal system, generates controversy and conflict. Given Africa's controversial colonial history, the continent lies at the crossroads of the ancient and modern—neither fully integrated into the stream of modernization nor wholly detached from its traditional religious foundations. The resulting tension and contradiction render neat conceptualizations of notions like justice almost impossible.[8]

AN INCARNATED UNDERSTANDING

African philosophical perspectives are incarnational. Ideas are seldom approached from an exclusively theoretical perspective. There is no universal notion of justice deducible from natural law and applicable generally, without regard for local laws, cultural preferences, and religious prescriptions. Practice is held in higher esteem than theory. In terms proposed in the chapter by George Kodithottam in this volume, traditional African culture takes a "realization-focused" understanding of justice, which he calls *nyāya*, rather than a more conceptualized approach (*nīti*). Only rarely are descriptions of justice in African languages developed to a high level of abstraction. Yet this semantic economy does not imply a conceptual deficiency. Justice can only be articulated in embodied terms.

Rather than defining justice abstractly, the preference is to observe its qualities in concrete situations in life and to apply them there. Thus, while the judgment that a person is "just" includes the qualities and values of that person, such a judgment takes into account a whole range of circumstances, principles, and practices that shape the moral universe of their community. Consider, for example, the notion of life as a moral principle for evaluating right and wrong. According to Laurenti Magesa, "Everything is perceived with reference to this [life]. It is no wonder, then, that Africans quickly draw ethical conclusions about words and actions of human beings, or even of 'natural' cosmological events, by asking questions such as: Does the particular happening promote life? If so, it is good, just, ethical, desirable, divine. Or, does it diminish life in any way? Then it is wrong, bad, unethical, unjust, detestable."[9]

Accordingly, in the context of African religion and cultures, ethical principles derive their validity not from abstract metaphysical sources but from the objective of "preserving human life and its 'power' or 'force.'"[10] In other words, the "morality of an act is determined by its life-giving potential."[11] Analogously, the criteria for justice in the African context are embodied in diverse contexts of human life in interpersonal and societal relationships.

THE SOCIAL DIMENSION OF JUSTICE

African philosophical and cultural worldviews contain an understanding of justice that prioritizes the relationships of people in community. The intensity may vary, but the essence is consistent. There is a strong consensus among scholars that traditional African morality is "quintessentially social." The identity and the norms by which a person's actions are evaluated are linked to the identity of the whole, whether family, clan, community, or the larger society.[12] Stated differently, norms of behavior are determined and evaluated by their impact on the well-being of communal structures and relationships.[13] This aligns well with Maria Inês de Castro Millen's insight that in Latin America, people must be at the center of the discernment of justice and that traditional knowledge has much to teach us today.

The prioritization of the social context (family, clan, or community) creates a tightly knit system of mutually beneficial rights, privileges, expectations, and obligations. But because the extent of "the community" is limited, the rights of nonmembers are too often violated. Paul Kollman formulates this problem: "The clan or tribe . . . is in traditional Africa the only locus for justice . . . outside of which all others are strangers and inferiors, if not enemies."[14] This inward-looking, exclusive understanding of justice is inadequate precisely because "there is no need for universal social concern.

The neighbour is narrowly defined as the in-group, while all others may be deceived and exploited as fair game. Justice applies only to the in-group."[15] This ancient coexistence of just and unjust practice finds resonance in Hinduism, described in George Kodithottam's chapter, where admirable moral commitments perdure in an unjust caste system.

This pervasive constriction of justice in the African context is a serious problem, but the idea that justice is essentially communal is important for re-thinking justice. Justice is hardly meaningful without consideration for the beneficiaries, as individuals, communities, and institutions. This idea introduces a quality of contingency into the conception of justice on three counts. First, justice does not exist in a distant space of abstraction but always relates to concrete needs of persons, their community, society, and social structures. Second, without subjecting the well-being of the individual to the predominant control of the whole, each person discovers their responsibility largely in relation to the whole. Third, because of this diversity in context, there is diversity in the understandings of justice.[16]

GENERATIVE SITES FOR RE-THINKING JUSTICE IN CATHOLIC SOCIAL THOUGHT

Given the considerations outlined in the preceding sections, the following elements from African nations of justice provide promising resources for re-thinking the notion of justice.

Ubuntu

The notion of Ubuntu is a clear manifestation of an understanding of justice in Africa based on the idea of relationships among members of a given community. This concept is open to multiple interpretations and has been applied to various issues by philosophers, lawyers, politicians, clerics, and theologians. It originates from two expressions in Bantu cultural groups of southern and eastern Africa and beyond: "*Umuntu ngumuntu ngabantu*" or "*Motho ke motho ka batho*." Both translate loosely as "A person is a person because of/through other persons" or "I am, because we are."

First, Ubuntu affirms the primacy of human relationship in social, communal, and corporate activities. South African political theorist Charles Villa-Vicencio points out that "the underlying principle of ubuntu is that human existence is interconnected and communal. . . . Ubuntu suggests that the realization of one's human potential can only be achieved through interaction with other people."[17] Humanity thrives on interdependence and relationality. Second, Ubuntu affirms a quality of being that is anchored in integrity.

Taken together, the two aspects yield a unique anthropological conception. The human person, far from being isolated and self-sufficient, depends vitally on other people to fulfill the deepest meaning of existence. To be human is to be open, to reach out to others, and to engage them in their irreplaceable uniqueness and difference. The human person is not reducible to a closed entity. Humanity is reflected through the mirror of the other's existence: the other's humanity illuminates my humanity and vice versa. The concept of Ubuntu is "a living tradition that is constantly reinvented owing to cultural dynamism" and when "infused with Christian and human rights discourses . . . it is an ontological and hermeneutical African reality."[18]

Ubuntu weaves the diverse strands of human existence into a social fabric through cooperation, collaboration, and even communion. Its central theme of interdependence underscores the centrality of mutuality in human relationship. To say "I am, because you are" is to embrace the possibility of infinitely open and mutually enriching relationships for person, community, and the wider environment. Yet the mutuality and relationality of humanity are not simply facts to be observed; instead, they provide vital criteria for ethical action. Thus, for example, the acknowledgment of the humanity of the other entails a moral imperative to defend it. "Disregard for the duty to cultivate and maintain a proper relationship with my neighbour, for whose care and custody I am responsible, ruins my relationship with my own self, with others, with God and with the earth."[19] As an all-embracing principle, Ubuntu even "implies a relationship of mutual responsibility between human beings and nature."[20] Christians, of course, can see commitments in Ubuntu parallel to the common good, as described in Lisa Cahill's chapter.

From the uniquely African perspective of Ubuntu, part of the vocation of individuals and communities is to strive to overcome tensions and divisions that hinder relationships—to sow seeds of peace, harmony, and hospitality. As such, Ubuntu prioritizes inclusivity over exclusivity, community over competition, hospitality over hostility, dialogue over confrontation, and respect over domination.[21]

According to Villa-Vicencio, Ubuntu "can be developed and expanded in relation to a range of contemporary challenges facing the modern state."[22] He and other scholars have presented evidence to demonstrate that the constitutional order and jurisprudence of post-apartheid South Africa, including the Truth and Reconciliation Commission (TRC), draw on the values of Ubuntu.[23] They represent inherent values of Africa's vibrant religious and cultural traditions that engender a richer understanding of justice.[24] The vision and the effect of the TRC are clear indications of a renewed understanding of justice, peace, and reconciliation.[25] And in this volume, themes of Ubuntu serve as important resources for reimagining justice.

Some have compared Ubuntu, as an African communitarian principle of justice, to John Rawls's theory of justice as fairness. But this effort seems far-fetched or contrived, even though there is a family resemblance between these two approaches. Ubuntu does not need to qualify as a communitarian principle of justice in Rawlsian terms for it to acquire conceptual respectability.[26] Ubuntu is not a semantic equivalence of fairness. It denotes a rich field of meaning encompassing a moral theory, a philosophical worldview, and an epistemological category.

Essentially, Ubuntu teaches that justice is measured relative to an integral human development and communal well-being, especially where and when inequities threaten these.[27] In light of this understanding, justice is a living and thriving reality. In concrete circumstances, this approach "takes the quest for justice beyond the level of abstract rules and rigid legal formulations to a richer understanding of truth discernment and justice. It opens a space for the pursuit of a better and more just future by enabling victims, perpetrators, and the broader community to address the underlying causes that gave rise to past conflicts."[28]

At the core of the understanding of justice in light of Ubuntu is the priority of relationality, balance, and harmony, also basic to the Buddhist view of human life described in the chapter by George Kodithottam. When these are threatened or violated by individual or collective wrongdoing, justice assumes a restorative quality. In the view advanced here, "Most African justice systems incorporate restorative and transformative systems of justice."[29] Yet what is restored transcends an individualistic vision of social equilibrium or cohesion. More importantly, justice aims to restore humanity to its ideal state in keeping with the idea of integrity and wholeness central to Ubuntu. Veteran anti-apartheid campaigner Desmond Tutu once queried, regarding the Truth and Reconciliation Commission, "What is it that constrained so many to choose to forgive rather than demand retribution, to be so magnanimous and ready to forgive rather than wreak revenge?"[30] His answer unequivocally credits Ubuntu as a principle of justice suited for affirming our shared humanity. It engages even perpetrators, not through humiliation but in a restoration that redounds to the well-being of society. He adds: "Social harmony is for us the *summum bonum*—the greatest good. . . . Anger, resentment, lust for revenge, even success through aggressive competitiveness are corrosive of this good. To forgive is not just to be altruistic. It is the best form of self-interest. What dehumanizes you inexorably dehumanizes me."[31]

Tutu introduces the notion of forgiveness as a common theme of African restorative justice, to which I will return later. Yet the value of forgiveness has limits. There is no exemption from punishment, no silent signaling of impunity, and no undue psychological burden of expectation on victims to simply forgive.[32] Also, there is an unresolved tension between restitution and retribution in how Ubuntu is applied as a principle of justice, although little doubt exists about the primacy of the former. "Retributive justice is largely Western. The African understanding is far more restorative—not so much to punish as to redress or restore a balance that has been knocked askew. The justice we hope for is restorative of the dignity of the people."[33]

Although some African scholars would question Tutu's somewhat romanticized formulation,[34] there exists a broad consensus to affirm the validity of his claim regarding the understanding of justice in the context of Africa. The transcultural profile of Ubuntu renders it immediately recognizable across Africa as a vital element of both a process and an outcome of the conception of justice.

African Palaver: Public Pursuit of Justice

Orality takes precedence over literacy in Africa, particularly in sub-Saharan Africa. The second element for re-thinking justice from an African perspective draws on the practice of speaking as an essential indicator of communal life in Africa. The notion that best exemplifies this insight is "palaver." As a concept and a practice, palaver is rooted in the African ethics of communication based on extensive consultation and sustained participation. It aims for a consensus regarding ethical imperatives and principles that guide individual and communal actions. Ethicists and theologians agree that palaver provides a process that can enhance reconciliation, justice, and peace. Synonyms of palaver include dialogue, open conversation, participatory discourse, and consensus building.

In its various manifestations, the practice of palaver translates as "conversation" among stakeholders in any given situation in life.[35] Palaver "emphasizes open conversation in community and prioritizes consensus over confrontation."[36] Yet, despite the importance of palaver in African communicative ethics, some have naively derided it as a "pointless banter presided over by an African chief."[37]

Palaver connects the idea of justice to space, locus, and geography. *Where* justice is discoursed, practiced, and dispensed carries importance and opens a window on *how* it is understood. We see here parallels with participative community mediation in Agnes Brazal's chapter and with the practice of justice endorsed in the chapter by Maria Inês de Castro Millen. Across Africa, European colonial jurisprudence consolidated the institution of the courthouse or *palais de justice* as the fixed location for dispensing justice, accessible to and controlled by wigged and gowned experts. However, in several parts of precolonial Africa, the locus of justice was anything but a restricted space. The precolonial locus of justice was not detached from the existential space of the community's concerns. This space is variously named across the continent as *Baraza* (Eastern Africa), *Ingando* (Rwanda), *Indaba, Insaka, Lekgotla,* or *Pitso* (Southern Africa).[38] Each term denotes both the place and the process of gathering for debating, deliberating, and adjudicating consequential matters. Each names an open space where not only litigants but the entire community participates.

This idea of space depicts and reinforces three constitutive dimensions of the conception of justice, as illustrated in the Igbo justice system of Eastern Nigeria. First, it is a participatory process where "decisions are reached through consensus. Everybody has equal access to and participation in the justice system." Second, "the goal of justice is the restoration of relationships and social harmony disrupted by the conflict." Third, the violation of relationships and disruption of social order take precedence over the infringement of legal codes.[39] In the palaver space, norms and values would not be the object of categorical assertion and impositions forced on the community by a sole authority, even though the influence of older men tends to be more pronounced compared to other segments of the community. African palaver accords everyone, including "the invisible community of the ancestors," their due and a voice in the formulation of norms and judgments.[40] There are echoes here of Agnes Brazal's notion of discernment as an integral component in how a community discovers the meaning and implications of justice.

This understanding of palaver meshes well with the principle of Ubuntu[41] and echoes Amartya Sen's assertion that "open-minded engagement in public reasoning is quite central to the pursuit of justice."[42]

Even some Western scholars adopt a spatial model to explain the process of transformation of conflict through reconciliation as a constitutive element of justice. John Paul Lederach has argued that reconciliation is rooted in a relational space that elicits and engages all the energies, personalities, and activities implicated in a conflict: "Reconciliation, in essence, represents a place, the point of encounter where concerns about both the past and the future can meet. Reconciliation-as-encounter suggests that space for acknowledging the past and envisioning of the future is the necessary ingredient for reframing the present. For this to happen, people must find ways to encounter themselves and their enemies, their hopes and their fears."[43] Further, according to Lederach, the essential constituents of this space are truth, mercy, justice, and peace. Thus, the praxis of reconciliation articulates these constitutive elements, as several examples in this chapter show.[44] Reconciliation offers a fitting transition to the third and final element considered essential to African understandings of justice.

Rituals of Justice: Forgiveness and Reconciliation

To recall a personal experience, forgiveness among the Edo people is a commonly ritualized experience, which suggests that forgiveness is both an event and a process, underpinned by ancestral spirits and communal deities, not unlike in other world religions.[45]

In a ritualized process of reconciliation, justice is served when the wrongdoing that destabilized social equilibrium is addressed and relationships are restored. Daniel Philpott corroborates this understanding that "reconciliation is a concept of justice. . . . The central meaning of reconciliation is the restoration of right relationship."[46] Also, Philpott is quite explicit in acknowledging the religious foundations of this conception of reconciliation as a concept of justice. Although he limits his study to Judaism, Christianity, and Islam, there is ample evidence in African religion to justify its inclusion. Desmond Tutu formulates the argument for this inclusion:

> We contend that there is another kind of justice, restorative justice, which was characteristic of African jurisprudence. Here the central concern is not retribution or punishment. In the spirit of *ubuntu*, the central concern is the healing of breaches, the redressing of imbalances, the restoration of broken relationships, a seeking to rehabilitate both the victim and the perpetrator, who should be given the opportunity to be reintegrated into the community he has injured by his offense. . . . Thus we would claim that justice, restorative justice, is being served when efforts are being made to work for healing, for forgiving, and for reconciliation.[47]

The ritualization of forgiveness, reconciliation, and dispute resolution concretely manifest elements of traditional practice of justice. Rituals and symbols are crucial to healing and changing attitudes in Africa and a resource for re-thinking justice.[48] This approach to justice does not contradict Western notions of justice. It is complementary and can expand those notions. These examples illustrate the significance of rituals and practices.

Mato Oput (Northern Uganda)

Mato Oput is "a reconciliation process conducted under the auspices of traditional Acholi chiefs, in which offenders acknowledge their crimes, offer reparations to their victims, and finally participate in a cleansing ceremony in which they are received back into the community."[49] This process takes the form of a religious ritual involving all those affected by a conflict, including perpetrators, enablers, victims, and community. Kenyan peace expert Elias Omondi Opongo identifies three critical elements of this process. First, it is a communal experience because responsibility entails accountability, and both are assessed within a social framework. Second, the process is conducted under the effective oversight of the spirits of the community's departed ancestors or the "living dead." Third, the ritual is inherently restorative, aiming to reconstruct relationships upended by wrongdoing or criminal conflict.[50] In essence, this practice creates a space and a framework for attaining justice as a shared value for individuals and communities.

Gacaca (Rwanda)

Gacaca (pronounced ga-CHA-cha) is Kinyarwanda for "grass" and refers to a traditional assembly of people seated on the grass in a designated neighborhood to hear, assess, adjudicate, and resolve a dispute, litigation, or conflict among members of the community.[51] The idea of locus or space surfaces again. This traditional African justice system regained prominence in response to the crimes of the 1994 genocide against Tutsis and moderate Hutus in Rwanda. Conscious of the burden of time involved in bringing all the accused to trial in conventional courts, the government created community-based tribunals modeled on the Gacaca traditional justice system. The community elected members deemed to be "people of integrity" who facilitated the processes and participated actively in deciding the appropriate penalties or decisions. Although Gacaca recognizes the role of witness, testimony, and accountability, the primary objective is neither punitive nor retributive. It focuses on healing traumatized memories and restoring broken relationships through a process of encounter, repair, and transformation that involves the community. Like Mato Oput, the Gacaca process underlines the significance of space and communal participation in both the understanding and practice of justice.

Ubushingantahe or Bashingantahe (Burundi)

Neighboring Burundi, which shares in part Rwanda's history of genocide, provides the third and final example, *Ubushingantahe*. In this model, the family, clan, or community has recourse to its respected and trusted members to resolve disputes at interpersonal and communal levels. In precolonial times, this mechanism was effective for conflict resolution between litigants and was a guarantee of contract between parties or disputants. More importantly, it served as a means for preventing conflicts and preserving social cohesion. Like *Gacaca,* this mechanism values accurate testimony, mediation, and arbitration in view of establishing truth and attaining justice.[52] According to Agnes Nindorera, *bashingantahe* rests on three fundamental principles: "*Ibanga* or the sense of confidentiality/secret and responsibility, *Ubupfasoni* or dignity and respect, and *Ubuntu* or humanity and sense of personality."[53] Ubuntu is considered "the heart of *ubushingantahe,*" as a quality of being that "describes a set of personal virtues, including a sense of equity and justice, a concern for truth, a righteous self-esteem, a hard-working character—all of which could perhaps be summed up in the word 'integrity.'"[54] The possession of this integrity represents a necessary condition for membership in any grassroots *bashingantahe* council, whose primary purpose is restoring and preserving human dignity through a process of justice.[55] Justice in this sense has a humanizing function. Furthermore, *Ubushingantahe* and Ubuntu constitute "the missing links capable of 'harmonizing and integrating traditional/non-formal systems of justice with the formal/modern judicial process.'"[56] Thus, "As Ubuntu has inspired the Truth and Reconciliation Commission in South Africa, so the tradition of *Ubushingantahe* in Burundi has inspired a perceived obligation to manage conflict by hearing the disputants and finding out the truth before making any decision. Following the inspiration of *Ubushingantahe*, a decision would be made in the spirit of arbitration and reconciliation instead of repression."[57]

The preceding examples illustrate "community-informed forms of justice where communities take charge of the issues affecting them and where restorative forms of justice take precedence over a system that emphasizes retribution."[58] The African traditional justice system translates into real "law and practice" in concrete circumstances that integrate communal rituals.[59] Justice is served through processes of reconciliation, reparation, and restoration that prioritize the needs of the larger community. Consequently, "restitution to the victim is integral to the settlement of the disputes because of the understanding in the community that a victim whose needs are not addressed is a potential offender."[60] Quite clearly, elements of this approach resonate with the approach of restorative justice movements across the globe, particularly the aspects of encounter, reparation, and transformation.[61]

ASSESSING THE AFRICAN CONTRIBUTION

As we have seen, African understandings frame justice in restorative terms. And yet they also include truth-telling and individual accountability for injustice. They do not belittle the gravity of an injustice or the consequences for its victims. Thus, penalties and punishments serve a broader restorative purpose: community reconciliation, reestablishment of relationships, and peaceful cohabitation. This vision is complementary to the principles and practices of modern criminal justice systems.[62] More importantly, in the understanding of some African societies, this approach implements justice. Restoration recalls the idea of Ubuntu as an essential aspect of the conception and practice of justice. As one participant in the truth and reconciliation process in Sierra Leon put it, "[European philosophy] says, 'I think, therefore I am.' Here, it's 'I'm related, therefore, I am. . . .' You don't exist if you don't belong, if you are not related to somebody. This is the centripetal force in the culture that brings people into unity. They find strength in being together. They also find the courage to open up in the group, because somehow they know the group is there for healing."[63]

Yet restorative justice generates controversy. The prioritization of forgiveness, healing, and restoration generates resistance and suspicion from people for whom it seems an inadequate response to the magnitude of an atrocity or, worse, seems to be a clandestine option for community health instead of justice. This concern is legitimate, but in African settings, a holistic vision of well-being strives for both.

Nonetheless, it is essential to recognize that the pursuit of justice via healing, restoration, and reconciliation appears as a second-best option from the point of view of advocates of a prosecutorial approach. As Martha Minow has observed, "The very vocabularies of healing and restoration are foreign to the legal language underpinning prosecutions."[64] Such concerns remind us that although the preeminence of healing and restoration in African understandings of justice is critical for re-thinking justice today, it cannot alone constitute a complete view of justice in Catholic social thought.

There is another important limitation in the understandings of justice from the African perspective discussed in this essay. An appreciative view of African understandings of justice, particularly the cultural tradition and humanist philosophy of Ubuntu, needs to be tempered by a critical scrutiny. The African conception of justice remains patriarchal and androcentric. In general, similar to the typically male-dominated biblical context that Anathea Portier-Young analyzes in her chapter—and Agnes Brazal's critique of gender-based exclusion of women in hers—African cultures constitute a stronghold of patriarchy. Power is concentrated massively and inordinately in the hands of men. This reality challenges the conventional certainty of Ubuntu as inspiration for a vision of justice that humanizes individuals and harmonizes communities.

There is a pervasive tension between endorsing Ubuntu as a humanizing vision capable of generating a holistic approach to justice and the unquestionable evidence of the exclusion of women from forums designed to implement justice, like Indaba, Baraza, and Ingando. In specific instances, such processes are applied with gender-based biases that diminish, marginalize, or exclude the active participation of women. The systemic nature of these biases—often embedded in religious beliefs, cultural practices, and social structures—further proves the urgency of a sustained inquiry into gender justice in Africa.

For Ubuntu to fulfill its promise of inclusivity, holistic humanization of society, and integral human development, proponents must account for this *omission* and confront the multiple determinants of gender inequity and inequality. Stated differently, gender justice remains a vital need, not merely as a subset of concerns but as a constitutive and crosscutting structural component of justice in light of Ubuntu. We can only align Ubuntu with contemporary insights of gender equity as an undeniable condition for justice in society by eliminating the shadow of gender-based inequities. This opens a rich domain of inquiry into the restorative, reconciliative, and transformative dimensions of justice, not as an achieved state but as a compelling call for further development.

CONCLUSION

The evidence suggests that the dominant Christian conceptions of justice, typically assuming a universal applicability, are conceived largely in terms of the principles, criteria, and values prevalent in the discourses of Western Europe and North America. This essay has presented a brief outline of principles and practices, dynamics and processes, and conceptions and themes of justice in Africa that can be helpful in re-thinking justice in Catholic social thought.

From an African perspective, justice as the ultimate end favors its reconciliative, restorative, restitutive, reintegrative, and transformative dimensions. This approach accords a crucial role to the community and anchors the ideas and practices in the lived reality of its members. If the responsibility of tending justice rests on community, no matter how it is composed, the exercise of that function is not reserved to an elite group. A broader participation is possible in the meaning-laden processes that envisage the community's well-being. Villa-Vicencio summarizes this fundamental insight incisively: "The strength of African justice and reconciliation mechanisms is that they are grounded in the social fabric of the communities they represent. They seek to overcome social polarization, and where appropriate they explore ways of reintegrating perpetrators into society. They regard community reconciliation as an ultimate goal against which censure, retribution, and restoration need to be measured."[65]

Justice relates directly to human development. African religion plays a vital role in this process. While this role is intended to be constructive, the risk exists of generating a narrowly theistic reading that lends itself to legal rigidity and literalism while overlooking the original intention of justice as a path toward charity and compassion for the neighbor.[66]

In the final analysis, an African communal notion of justice contains well-established elements. The focus, with negligible exceptions, is consistently communal, holistic, and person-centered. The processes are varied, broadly inclusive, and do not rely solely on abstract discourses accessible exclusively to legal experts. Although shaped by historical, religious, and cultural influences that may seem obscure to some, the often-ritualized mechanisms are easily understood by those for whom forgiveness, reconciliation, and restitution play a significantly greater role in justice than retribution. It is possible to harness the conception of an African communal justice to make a completely new and different contribution to re-thinking justice in Catholic social thought.

BIBLIOGRAPHY

Allen, John L., Jr. *The Future Church: How Ten Trends Are Revolutionizing the Catholic Church*. Random House, 2009.

Bediako, Kwame. *Christianity in Africa: The Renewal of a Non-Western Religion*. Edinburgh University Press, 1995.

Bujo, Bénézet. *African Theology in Its Social Context*. Paulines, 1992.

Bujo, Bénézet. *Foundations of an African Ethic: Beyond the Universal Claims of Western Morality*. Translated by Brian McNeil. Crossroad Publishing, 2001.

Bujo, Bénézet. *Plea for Change of Models for Marriage*. Paulines, 2009.

Campbell, John, and Matthew T. Page. *Nigeria: What Everyone Needs to Know*. Oxford University Press, 2018.

De Coninck, John. "Furthering an African Perspective on Social Justice: East Africa Social Justice Group." In *African Perspectives on Social Justice*, edited by John de Coninck, Julian Culp, and Viviene Taylor, 3–11. Friedrich-Ebert-Stiftung, 2013.

Doe, Norman. *Comparative Religious Law: Judaism, Christianity, Islam*. Cambridge University Press, 2018.

Domingo, Rafael. *God and the Secular Legal System*. Cambridge University Press, 2016.

Francis. *Laudato Si' ("Praise Be to You")*. *Encyclical on Care for Our Common Home*, May 24, 2015. https://www.vatican.va/content/francesco/en/encyclicals/documents/papa-francesco _20150524_enciclica-laudato-si.html

Hinchliff, Peter. "Africa." In *The Oxford Illustrated History of Christianity*, edited by John McManners, 455–87. Oxford University Press, 1990.

Ingelaere, Bert. *Inside Rwanda's Gacaca Courts: Seeking Justice after Genocide*. University of Wisconsin Press, 2016.

Jenkins, Philip. *The Next Christendom: The Coming of Global Christianity*. Oxford University Press, 2002.

Johnstone, Gerry, and Daniel W. Van Ness. "The Meaning of Restorative Justice." In *Handbook of Restorative Justice*, edited by Gerry Johnstone and Daniel W. Van Ness, 5–23. Willan Publishing, 2007.

Kollman, Paul. "Tribalism and Justice." *African Christian Studies* 4, no. 2 (June 1988): 49–70.

Lederach, John Paul. *Building Peace: Sustainable Reconciliation in Divided Societies*. United States Institute of Peace Press, 2002.

Letseka, Moeketsi. "Ubuntu and Justice as Fairness." *Mediterranean Journal of Social Sciences* 5, no. 9 (May 2014): 544–51.

Magesa, Laurenti. *African Religion: The Moral Traditions of Abundant Life*. Orbis Books, 1997.

Majinge, Charles. "The International Criminal Court and the Question of Alternative Justice System in Africa: A Case of Be Careful What You Wish For?" *Verfassung und Recht in Übersee/Law and Politics in Africa, Asia and Latin America* 42, no. 2 (2009): 151–72.

Mamdani, Mahmood. *Citizen and Subject: Contemporary Africa and the Legacy of Late Colonialism*. Princeton University Press, 1996.

Manirakiza, Zenon. *La justice transitionnelle pour la paix sociale: Le système bashingantahe au Burundi*. Bujumbura, Burundi. September 21, 2007. https://medialibrary.uantwerpen .be/oldcontent/container2143/files/DPP%20Burundi/Pouvoir%20judiciaire /Bashingantahe/ZenonManirakiza_TJ_et_Bash_210907.pdf

Manirakiza, Zenon. *Modes traditionnels de règlement des conflits: l'institution d'Ubushingantahe*. https://medialibrary.uantwerpen.be/oldcontent/container2143/files/DPP%20 Burundi/Pouvoir%20judiciaire/Bashingantahe/ZenonManirakiza_ACA_2002.pdf

Minow, Martha. *Between Vengeance and Forgiveness: Facing History after Genocide and Mass Violence*. Beacon Press, 1998.

Moore, Jennifer. *Humanitarian Law in Action within Africa*. Oxford University Press, 2012.

Nindorera, Agnes. "Ubushingantahe as a Base for Political Transformation in Burundi." Boston Consortium on Gender, Security, and Human Rights, Working Paper No. 102, 2003.

Oba, Abdulmumini Adebayo. "Between Willingness and Unwillingness: Christians as Litigants and Accused Persons in Islamic Courts in Northern Nigeria." In *Religious Freedom and Religious Pluralism in Africa: Prospects and Limitations,* edited by Pieter Coertzen, M. Christian Green, and Len Hansen, 177–92. SUN MeDIA, 2016.

Oko, O. Elechi. "The Igbo Indigenous Justice System." In *Colonial Systems of Control: Criminal Justice in Nigeria,* edited by Viviane Saleh-Hanna, 395–416. University of Ottawa Press, 2008.

Oladiti, Abiodun Akeem. "Justice in the Threshold of Culture: A Comparative Study of Yoruba and Islamic Legal Systems." In *Law and Religion in Africa: The Quest for the Common Good in Pluralistic Societies,* edited by Pieter Coertzen, M. Christian Green, and Len Hansen, 119–128. SUN MeDIA, 2015.

O'Neill, William. "No Amnesty for Sorrow: The Privilege of the Poor in Christian Social Ethics." *Theological Studies* 55, no. 4 (1994): 638–55.

Opongo, Elias O. "Between Violence, Reconciliation Rituals, and Justice in Northern Uganda: The Church in Africa and the Challenge of Post-Conflict Reconstruction." In *Practising Reconciliation, Doing Justice, Building Peace: Conversations on Catholic Theological Ethics in Africa,* edited by Agbonkhianmeghe E. Orobator, 23–29. Paulines, 2013.

Orobator, Agbonkhianmeghe E. "Introduction: Doing Theology as a Collaborative Effort." In *Theological Reimagination: Conversations on Church, Religion, and Society in Africa,* edited by Agbonkhianmeghe E. Orobator, 9–25. Paulines, 2014.

Orobator, Agbonkhianmeghe E. *Reconciliation, Justice, and Peace.* Orbis Books, 2011.

Orobator, Agbonkhianmeghe E. *Religion and Faith in Africa: Confessions of an Animist.* Orbis Books, 2018.

Orobator, Agbonkhianmeghe E. "Synod as Ecclesial Conversation." In *Reconciliation, Justice, and Peace: The Second African Synod,* edited by Agbonkhianmeghe E. Orobator, 1–10. Orbis Books, 2011.

Penal Reform International. *Access to Justice in Sub-Saharan Africa.* Penal Reform International, 2001.

The Pew Forum on Religion & Public Life. *Tolerance and Tension: Islam and Christianity in Sub-Saharan Africa.* April 15, 2010. https://www.pewresearch.org/religion/dataset/tolerance-and-tension-islam-and-christianity-in-sub-saharan-africa/

Philpott, Daniel. *Just and Unjust Peace: An Ethic of Political Reconciliation.* Oxford University Press, 2012.

Plaatjies van Huffel, Mary-Anne. "From Conciliar Ecumenism to Transformative Receptive Ecumenism." *HTS Teologiese Studies/Theological Studies* 73, no. 3: a4353. https://doi.org/10.4102/hts.v73i3.4353.

Sakupapa, Teddy C. "Ecumenical Ecclesiology in the African Context: Towards a View of the Church as Ubuntu." *Scriptura* 117 (2018) : 1–15.http://dx.doi.org/10.7833/117-1-1384.

Sen, Amartya. *The Idea of Justice.* Belknap Press of Harvard University Press, 2008.

Skelton, Ann. "Section A: Africa." In *Handbook of Restorative Justice,* edited by Gerry Johnstone and Daniel W. Van Ness, 468–76. Willan Publishing, 2007.

Stinton, Diane, "Introduction." In *African Theology on the Way: Current Conversations,* edited by Diane Stinton. SPCK, 2010.

Tassi, Yves. "The 'Crisis' of Ubuntu: Understanding African Identity in an Ever-Fragmented World." *Chiedza* 21, no. 2 (December 2019): 138–66.

Taylor, Viviene. "Social Justice: Reframing the 'Social' in Critical Discourses in Africa." In *African Perspectives on Social Justice,* edited by John de Coninck, Julian Culp, and Viviene Taylor, 16–29. Friedrich-Ebert-Stiftung, 2013.

Tutu, Desmond. *No Future Without Forgiveness.* Doubleday, 1999.

Van der Walt, B.J. "Morality in Africa: Yesterday and Today. The Reasons for the Contemporary Crisis." *Die Skriflig* 37, no.1 (2003): 55–56.

Villa-Vicencio, Charles. *Walk with Us and Listen: Political Reconciliation in Africa.* Georgetown University Press, 2009.

NOTES

1. Bujo, *Plea for Change of Models for Marriage* (Paulines, 2009).
2. Bediako, *Christianity in Africa,* 152–57; see also Jenkins, *The Next Christendom*; Allen, *The Future Church.*
3. Hinchliff, "Africa," 506.
4. The Pew Forum on Religion & Public Life, *Tolerance and Tension.*
5. Campbell and Page, *Nigeria,* 72.
6. This is the central thesis that I advance and develop in my book *Religion and Faith in Africa.*
7. See Domingo, *God and the Secular Legal System,* 23–72. The majority of Muslims in sub-Saharan Africa favor the imposition of Sharia as the official law of the land. Campbell and Page, *Nigeria,* 77. For example, presently, twelve out of thirty-six states in Nigeria have adopted the Sharia system of justice on account of the Muslim majority of their populations. These states allow only Muslims to be tried under Sharia law, but Christians can also elect via written consent to litigate a case in a Sharia court. The Sharia system of justice operates a two-tier format of lower and appellate courts in matters relating to criminal prosecution and civil dispute. They are presided over by government-appointed judges. Litigants have the option of challenging the rulings of Sharia courts in Nigeria's secular courts of appeal and the supreme court. One highly contentious aspect of the Sharia justice system relates to sentences, which include public floggings, amputation of limbs, and capital punishment.
8. This is a key thesis of Mamdani's *Citizen and Subject.*
9. Magesa, *African Religion,* 77.
10. Magesa, 77.
11. Bujo, *African Theology in Its Social Context,* 22.
12. Viviene Taylor presents a compelling narrative to substantiate this observation in "Social Justice," 16–29.
13. Van der Walt, "Morality in Africa," 55–56.
14. Kollman, "Tribalism and Justice," 59.
15. Van der Walt, "Morality in Africa," 61.
16. Taylor, "Social Justice," 17, 22.
17. Villa-Vicencio, *Walk with Us and Listen,* 114.
18. Sakupapa, "Ecumenical Ecclesiology in the African Context," 1–15.
19. Francis, *Laudato Si',* no. 70.

20. *Laudato Si'*, no. 67.

21. Villa-Vicencio, *Walk with Us and Listen*, 113.

22. Villa-Vicencio, 117.

23. Villa-Vicencio, 117–19; see Skelton, "Section A: Africa," 470.

24. Van Huffel, "From Conciliar Ecumenism to Transformative Receptive Ecumenism."

25. Similar examples of truth and reconciliation commissions exist in Sierra Leone and Rwanda.

26. See Letseka, "Ubuntu and Justice as Fairness," 547–48.

27. De Coninck, "Furthering an African Perspective on Social Justice," 4–5.

28. Villa-Vicencio, *Walk with Us and Listen*, 122.

29. Elechi, "The Igbo Indigenous Justice System," 401; Villa-Vicencio, *Walk with Us and Listen*, 126.

30. Tutu, *No Future Without Forgiveness*, 31.

31. Tutu, 31.

32. Minow, *Between Vengeance and Forgiveness*, 9–24.

33. Minow, 81.

34. See Tassi, "The 'Crisis' of Ubuntu," 138–66.

35. Stinton, "Introduction," xv–xx. Increasingly, theological scholarship recognizes the potential of "conversation" as an important theological methodology. See Orobator, "Synod as Ecclesial Conversation," 1–10, in Orobator (ed.), *Reconciliation, Justice, and Peace*.

36. Orobator, "Synod as Ecclesial Conversation," 3.

37. Orobator, "Introduction: Doing Theology as a Collaborative Effort," 9.

38. See Letseka, "Ubuntu and Justice as Fairness," 547–48.

39. Elechi, "The Igbo Indigenous Justice System," 398–99. See Bujo, *Foundations of an African Ethic*, 73–74.

40. Bujo, *Foundations of an African Ethic*, 79.

41. See Letseka, "Ubuntu and Justice as Fairness," 549.

42. Sen, *The Idea of Justice*, 390.

43. Lederach, *Building Peace*, 27; Villa-Vicencio also highlights the significance of healing and reconciliation practices that provide a "sacred space" and "a quiet and secure place" for transformation of individuals, communities, and social structures in *Walk with Us and Listen*, 143–44, 149.

44. Lederach, *Building Peace*, 30–35.

45. Lederach, 276.

46. Lederach, 5.

47. Tutu, *No Future Without Forgiveness*, 54–55.

48. See Villa-Vicencio's incisive analysis of traditional African reconciliation rituals and practices in *Walk with Us and Listen*, 129–50.

49. Moore, *Humanitarian Law in Action within Africa*, 216.

50. Opongo, "Between Violence, Reconciliation Rituals, and Justice in Northern Uganda," 25–26.

51. For a detailed description and discussion, see Ingelaere, *Inside Rwanda's Gacaca Courts*; Skelton, "Section A: Africa," 470; Penal Reform International, *Access to Justice in Sub-Saharan Africa*, 73.

52. Manirakiza, "*La justice transitionnelle pour la paix sociale: le système bashingantahe au Burundi*"; Manirakiza, "*Modes traditionnels de règlement des conflits: l'institution d'Ubushingantahe.*"

53. Nindorera, "*Ubushingantahe* as a Base for Political Transformation in Burundi," 18; Moore, *Humanitarian Law in Action*, 305–6.
54. Nindorera, "*Ubushingantahe*," 1.
55. Moore, *Humanitarian Law in Action*, 306; Nindorera, "*Ubushingantahe*," 15.
56. Moore, *Humanitarian Law in Action*, 306.
57. Nindorera, "*Ubushingantahe*," 16.
58. De Coninck, "Furthering an African Perspective on Social Justice," 8.
59. Ann Skelton has identified and explored the application of African traditional justice notions to the reform of juvenile and penal justice systems, programs, and processes in several countries in sub-Saharan Africa: "Section A: Africa," 471–75.
60. Elechi, "The Igbo Indigenous Justice System," 405.
61. These conceptions of restorative justice are discussed extensively in Johnstone and Van Ness, "The Meaning of Restorative Justice," 5–23. See Skelton, "Section A: Africa," 469–70.
62. It should be noted that complementarity is not a given. Real tension exists between the international criminal justice system and national and domestic systems, as the situation of the beleaguered International Criminal Court (ICC) has shown since the adoption of the Rome Statute in 1998. See Majinge, "The International Criminal Court and the Question of Alternative Justice System in Africa," 151–72.
63. Moore, *Humanitarian Law in Action*, 260.
64. Minow, *Between Vengeance and Forgiveness*, 63.
65. Villa-Vicencio, *Walk with Us and Listen*, 149.
66. See O'Neill, "No Amnesty for Sorrow," 651–55.

CHAPTER 2

Hindu and Buddhist Understandings of Justice

George Kodithottam, SJ

Hinduism and Buddhism are two of the world's great religions, with nearly 2 billion followers worldwide, an overwhelming majority of them in Asia. Their traditions are intertwined. Although there are fundamental differences in their perceptions of reality, there are convergences in their prescription for achieving liberation (*mokṣa, nirvāṇa*) and in their religious guidelines for practical living. In particular, their understanding of and teachings on justice are similar and have influence beyond their adherents. In the Indian subcontinent, the Hindu and Buddhist thought and traditions have a decisive influence in the practical living not only of Hindus and Buddhists but of people of other faiths as well, including ordinary Muslims and Christians.

Today, about two-thirds of all Catholics live outside Europe and North America. Thus, because the Catholic Church is no longer a Eurocentric church but a truly "world church," it is appropriate that Catholic theology should attend to religious insights available in Africa, Latin America, and Asia. This chapter does not aim to summarize the teachings on justice in Hinduism and Buddhism, an impossible task in so limited a frame. Instead, it provides a view of some of the most important insights of those religious traditions for this volume's effort to re-think justice in Catholic social thought.

TWO PERSPECTIVES ON JUSTICE

Nobel laureate Amartya Sen discusses two different perspectives on justice. He distinguishes between an "arrangement-focused" understanding of justice that he calls *nīti* and a "realization-focused" understanding of justice that he calls *nyāya* (both Sanskrit words). *Nīti* is justice conceptualized abstractly in terms of just rules and institutions, the active presence of which is taken as justice being done. *Nyāya* focuses on the realization of justice in the actual life of people; assessing the actual world that emerges, which includes the institutions and arrangements that are present; and also, most importantly, the lives that the people are able to lead.

Nīti follows a definitive and consequence-independent reasoning, a transcendental view of justice,[1] and focuses on organizational propriety and behavioural norms. *Nyāya* is more argumentative, takes up a comparative weighing of the positions, and looks for better and more acceptable consequences or realizations in personal and social life. *Nyāya* goes beyond organizations and rules to focus on actual social realizations. Realizations of justice in the sense of *nyāya* are not simply a matter of having institutions and rules for justice and judging their performances, but of judging the societies themselves. Sen favours *nyāya*, as it concentrates on the actual behaviour of people rather than presuming compliance by all with ideal behaviour.[2]

Sen argues that the role of ethics is to ensure that its theoretical acumen must have a bearing on the actual problems that human beings face in their existential contexts.[3] He advocates ethical decision-making on the basis of "a comprehensive outcome."[4] "The subject of justice is not merely about trying to achieve some perfectly just society or social arrangements, but about preventing manifestly severe injustice."[5] The outcome-focused perspective of *nyāya* makes it easy to see the importance of preventing obvious injustices in the world.

Sen also observes that the *nīti*-oriented approach to justice makes the practice of justice more institutional, absolutist, and authoritarian in character, an approach summarized by Roman Emperor Ferdinand I: "Let justice be done, though the world perishes."[6]

Justice in Catholic social thought has traditionally focused on the *nīti* (principle-focused) perspective of justice. The Hindu and Buddhist understandings of justice focus more on *nyāya* (outcome-focused)—and so do the traditional African insights into justice described in Agbonkhianmeghe Orobator's chapter in this volume. In re-thinking a Catholic understanding of justice in today's pluralist and secular world with a prevalence of functioning democracies and new economic systems, more importance needs to be given to the *nyāya* perspective of justice. The caste system—obdurate and totally unjust as it is practised—failed to implement *nyāya*. Nonetheless, insights from the Hindu and Buddhist traditions can be helpful in the effort to re-think justice in Catholic social thought.

THE UNDERSTANDING AND PRACTICE OF JUSTICE IN HINDUISM

In Hindu thought for more than 3,000 years, from the Vedic period[7] onward, justice and righteousness are conceived as microcosmic reflections of the natural order and harmony of the macrocosmic universe. While not the same, this conviction resonates with the Hebrew insight that humans participate in divine creative work (discussed in Anathea Portier-Young's chapter), with the Thomistic understanding of creation (discussed in Jean Porter's chapter), and with the moral realism advocated by Agnes Brazal in her chapter. For Hindus, the cosmos has an inherent structure and functional pattern called *rita*,[8] in which humans participate. This principle, which guides the universe, embodied in ethical terms in the individual and social lives of people. By the end of the Vedic period (sixth century BCE), justice was equated with *rita*, the cosmological principle that governs nature as well as human ethical conduct. To follow *rita* is to act in accordance with justice, or natural law, and it is the dharma.

Dharma

Dharma is one of the key concepts in Indian thought, and it is central to classical Hinduism's understanding of justice. The concept of dharma originated in the *Vedas*,[9] which in Hinduism are the supreme source of knowledge for humans. In the long history of India's cultural and spiritual evolution, the concept of dharma acquired various senses. One must examine the context carefully before determining the sense in which the word is used. Primarily, dharma is the obligation to follow the *rita*, the cosmic–moral principle of order that establishes regularity and righteousness in the world.

The word *dharma* has as its root *dhr*,[10] meaning to uphold, to support, and to sustain. Dharma upholds and sustains the created universe. Without it, the universe falls apart. Dharma in its primary sense refers to the essential nature of a thing, without which it cannot exist. The dharma of a thing is that because of which a thing continues to be the thing itself, without which the thing cannot continue to be that thing. For example, fluidity is the dharma of water, and if water loses fluidity, it will become either vapour or ice; then we cannot call it water. Dharma is the basis for the existence of a thing as that thing.

Dharma also sustains and maintains the social, moral, political, and economic order. There is an elaborate discussion of the concept in the *Mahābhārata*.[11] This great epic has had a very significant influence on the ethical consciousness and practical living of ordinary people in the Indian subcontinent. On being asked by Yudhiṣṭhira[12] to explain the meaning and scope of dharma, *Bhīṣma*,[13] who has mastered the knowledge of the concept, explains it as that which helps the upliftment of living beings. Dharma ensures their welfare; it sustains the universe.[14]

The meaning, nature, and field of dharma qualitatively changed in *Manusmṛti*.[15] In the Vedic *Saṃhitās*, dharma referred to forces that supported and sustained the cosmic order. In *Manusmṛti*,[16] it came also to refer to the rights and duties of individuals and various groups in society to support the social order. According to *Manusmṛti*, dharma sustains and maintains the social, moral, political, and economic order. Manu described in minute detail the dharma of each person on the basis of the institutional units in the society, *varṇas*.[17] Each varṇa encompasses numerous *jātis* (castes).[18] The dharma is the practical law of conduct for every person individually, based on their varṇa, and for every varṇa collectively.

Dharma has great moral significance because of the essential nature of humans. What is morally good for humans depends on what humans essentially are, an insight parallel to the natural law ethics of Aquinas described in Jean Porter's chapter. All Indian systems of philosophy build their understanding of morality on the notion of the essential nature of humans. The *Upaniṣads* teach that a human's true nature is divine. The supreme reality behind this universe is *Ātman*[19] or *Brahman*. Ātman is the very essence of one's being. Realizing *Ātman* is the ultimate liberation and goal of human life, and adhering to one's dharma is the only way to that realization. In sum, dharma not only keeps everything and everybody in existence but also indicates everyone's obligations to society based on one's stage of life and status in society. Dharma also prescribes religious rites, ceremonies, and even rules, laws, customs, and manners of society. A just life is rooted in dharma.

Karmic Retribution

Karma signifies a kind of impersonal moral causation. The consequences of a person's actions live on to determine their current and future well-being or lack of it, including in the next life in the cycle of rebirth. Good actions are rewarded and bad actions punished, if not in this life, then in the next. As a result of this karmic retribution, a person may be reborn at several different levels within the order of nature as they progress (or retrogress) on the evolutionary scale. The ultimate perfection of life, mokṣa (spiritual emancipation), is usually achieved only after the individual passes through several animal and human rebirths. Because only humans have an opportunity to attain spiritual liberation, humanity is at the peak of the chain of existences.

The karmic retribution may take place during one's current life as misfortune or honour, or in the subsequent life by being born in a lower or higher station. The condition of an individual in any birth is understood as the totally inevitable and impersonally just result of one's own behaviour in the earlier birth. This notion is reinforced through its association with the varṇa stratification of society. A *brāhmaṇa* at the apex of the four varṇas reaps the reward of one's own actions in the previous life. A *śūdra*, member of the lowest varṇa, is presumed morally and socially inferior to the brāhmaṇa due to their own actions in the previous life. But looking forward to future lives, a śūdra could hope to improve their position through righteous conduct according to the dictates of their present station. Here the doctrine of karma upholds the moral equity of varṇa stratification and provides an incentive for ethical behaviour in hopes of self-advancement.

Understanding Justice

In the Hindu conception, justice is a human expression of a wider universal principle of nature. If humans were entirely true to nature, their actions would be spontaneously just. Nature itself is the ultimate and final arbiter of justice because justice is cosmic. The different forms of justice—moral, social, and legal—are viewed as particularizations of the general principle of the universe to achieve distributive equity in society.

The cosmic order, centrally governed by the Ātman, is the locus of all ethical operations of humans. Only within humans can this principle come to full consciousness and realization. Therefore, human life is conceived of as an opportunity to work toward the ultimate goal of achieving spiritual emancipation. This understanding informs a broad range of Indian institutions, religious and secular, and it influences the regulation of social life both in religious and secular spheres. The individual—not the community—is regarded as the locus of the highest spiritual value. This stress on the individual is not nearly so strong as in the liberalism outlined in Francis Fiorenza's chapter, but is important for Hindus, nonetheless. Every individual, consciously or not, is on the path to the highest goal and is, therefore, an inviolable centre of potential spiritual realization. This fundamental notion, articulated in various expressions, becomes the matrix of the Hindu sense of justice and just institutions.[20]

Natural balance and normative harmony apply descriptively to all functions of the universe. They also apply to humans' moral behaviour because each person is part of nature. The human person ideally has perfect equity, interacting with the cosmic environment. However, the destiny of the individual over a series of lifetimes is determined by the quality of one's actions. One's embodiment and one's station in social life according to the varṇa classification are self-determined in the sense that they are the just results of one's past actions (karmic retribution). Each individual today is the result of past deeds over which they no longer have any control. Yet one's progress on the ladder of evolution is subject to conscious control in the present life, which the individual exercises through following the *varṇāśrama*[21] system. This system is designed around the possibility of consciously taking the harmonious development of one's nature into one's own hands, echoing liberationist commitments in the chapters by Maria Inês de Castro Millen and Agnes Brazal. In Hinduism, individual harmony, interpersonal justice, and social ethics revolve around the right of individuals and groups to advance within the teleological structure of cosmic order.

This responsibility for one's own position in society means that the hierarchy of varṇas and castes is itself regarded as a reflection of karmic justice. Unlike in liberation theology, social inequality is seen as equitable in the Hindu worldview because the privileges and responsibilities of each particular varṇa are understood as proportionate to the levels of spiritual and moral development of its individual members. Any system of rights and duties that did not consider the actual differences between these individual levels of advancement on the path of evolution and advocated indiscriminate equality is seen as unjust. The salvation of the individual on any level lies in the quality of personal performance.[22] Therefore, to expect all humans to adhere to the same standard or to act in a manner beyond the capacities of their present stage of spiritual, moral, and intellectual unfolding would be neither just nor natural.

Administration of Justice

In the Hindu myths of origin, both society and the state are seen as natural and necessary developments informed by an underlying idea of justice, personal and social. This is already indicated in the *Ṛig Veda,* and more formal elaborations are found later in other *Vedas.*[23] In *Śānti Parva,*[24] *Bhīṣhma* explains the origin of kingship to King Yudhiṣṭira.

The original condition of humans in the Golden Age (*Kṛita-yuga*) was a stateless and spontaneously just society. (Here we see parallels in both the creation stories of Genesis and the original ideal state in traditional African insight, as described in chapter 1 by Agbonkhianmeghe Orobator.) People protected one another by means of righteous conduct (dharma). However, people eventually fell into a state of spiritual stupor, and delusion overcame them. They were overpowered by infatuation because of the delusion of understanding; their sense of righteous conduct was lost. This degeneration in human affairs led to the falling away from the Golden Age and necessitated some sort of administration of justice in society. Then Viṣṇu, the lord of creatures, gave Virajas as the first king.[25] The king's duty was to protect society, and the state was the extension of the king for this purpose.[26] The administration of justice is thus an expediency necessitated by a falling away from the Golden Age.

The state performed the duty of protecting both the individual and society through coercive enforcement of the standards of justice, which were reduced for practical purposes to the details of positive law (*vyavahāra*). Early codes of law, covering every aspect of life, are preserved in the voluminous *Dharmasūtra* and *Dharmaśāstra* literature, of which perhaps the *Laws of Manu*[27] is best known. The codes of law are fully attuned to the reality of the individual's frequent failure to act from a sense of one's own best interest and disregard for the karmic repercussions of one's deeds. Particularistic legal codes are considered concrete and detailed embodiments of the more abstract, exalted, cosmic principles of justice.

The state has a duty to use coercion to compel adherence to legal statutes directed to both the maintenance of justice in society and the moral welfare of the individual. Therefore, the king is invested with *daṇḍa* (scepter). The practical necessity of daṇḍa in the administration of justice is considered a further outgrowth of the ongoing degeneration in the *Kali Yuga*.[28] Manu, as a realist, insists on the role of punishment in ensuring justice for the weak.[29] The exercise of the coercive power of daṇḍa for law enforcement is considered just in the highest sense.

Inflicting punishment and administrating the other aspects of legal justice are not to be performed mechanically or indiscriminately without respect for persons. Justice must not be blind. The judicial authorities should adjudicate wrongdoings (crimes) and administer punishments on a sliding scale, based on both the seriousness of the offense[30] and the varṇa of the offender. Manu says, "Having fully considered the time and the place (of the offense), the strength and knowledge (of the offender), let him justly inflict that punishment on men who act unjustly."[31]

Because the varṇa hierarchy indicates karmic retribution or reward for previous lifetimes, it is only natural to consider varṇa when administering legal justice. The administrator should consider "the strength and knowledge" of the offender, which are estimated as functions their varṇa. The more elevated one's varṇa is, the more responsibility one should bear for one's misdeeds. Therefore, a greater penalty is to be prescribed for those of higher station and a milder one for the more lowly.[32] In this view, humans did not stand as equals before the law; that would be considered unjust, quite different from the liberal view of a just legal system outlined in Francis Fiorenza's chapter. The Hindu system seeks to achieve justice and equity in a universe with a natural hierarchy rather than equality, where the individuals are called to self-realization, each in their own way. Justice does not aim for equal treatment. It is concerned with equity, not equality.

INSIGHTS FROM HINDUISM FOR RE-THINKING JUSTICE

There are immense differences in the cultures out of which Hinduism and Catholicism have arisen. Yet both Hinduism and Roman Catholicism understand morality—and, therefore, justice—as rooted in a divinely founded, objective order in the world. The dharma for a Hindu calls each person to an obligation to follow the *rita*, the cosmic principle of regularity in the world and righteousness in moral life. The Catholic tradition since Aquinas has joined the Aristotelian conception of natural regularity with the Christian understanding of God's creation of the world. As Jean Porter explains in detail in her chapter, the obligations individuals face in natural law are founded on the creator's intention for human flourishing. In both religions, the fulfilment of the individual comes from aligning one's choices with an order that encompasses all things. Human morality is teleological; aligning daily choices with higher goals is not only the morally right thing to do; it is the key to personal happiness.

Christians, like Hindus, acknowledge that the universe is not egalitarian. Humans, and all other groups of creatures, differ in size, strength, and a range of other characteristics. Yet Christians today cannot adopt the traditional Hindu implication that this natural inequality justifies a system that renders some humans inferior to other humans.

Nonetheless, the Hindu resistance to the idea of equal individual rights has something to contribute to Catholic social thought on justice. The Hindu view of justice is rooted in the obligation to follow the rita rather than in rights of the individual. This obligation places more rigorous demands on persons in a more elevated varṇa than on those less privileged, and the privileged face stiffer penalties for misdeeds.

Rights in the Catholic tradition always have duties correlated with them. Yet when rights are insisted on—whether the right to life or employment—such claims are heard, even by most Catholics in a secular world, simply as claims, without perception of the necessarily attendant duties. Hindu conceptions of justice as founded in obligation rather than rights can provide a helpful corrective to offset an overemphasis on rights in Western views of justice, especially when fulfilling those obligations is the path to personal fulfilment.

THE UNDERSTANDING AND PRACTICE OF JUSTICE IN BUDDHISM

In the Buddhist understanding, goodness (or "moral living") means being actively good to (or at least not harming) all beings, including one's own self. The only reward for moral living now or in the long run is the pleasure resulting from good actions, and the only penalty is the pain resulting from evil actions. Unlike the Hebrew view outlined in Anathea Portier-Young's chapter, there is no sanction from an external divine will. In addition, the Buddha rejected deontology, the ethics of duty, because it can call for self-mortification to the extent of self-sacrifice. He advocated a middle path between the two extremes of self-indulgence and self-mortification.[33] According to Buddha, self-restraint and benefiting others—not self-mortification—is the foundation of moral life. His exhortation to his disciples was to adopt a way of life that leads to the welfare, happiness, and freedom of both oneself and others.

At a great distance from the liberalism described in Francis Fiorenza's chapter, in Buddhism, there is no metaphysical self; the idea of an "individual self" is an illusion. Yet one has to cultivate compassion for one's own person, which should be extended to others as well. "Be a friend to yourself and be a friend to others." Buddhism rejects complete and unqualified self-sacrifice. The noble person is the one who avoids suffering for themselves as well as others, one who contributes to their own happiness as well as the happiness of others by choosing the Middle Way.[34]

Buddhist ethics does not have a set of universal obligations but only levels of practice suiting different levels of commitment.[35] The critical conviction behind ethical action is that it is inappropriate to inflict on other beings what one finds unpleasant for oneself. The benefits for oneself and others are intertwined, so that concern to lessen one's own suffering goes hand in hand with easing that of others. One's suffering and others' suffering are not inherently different; they are simply suffering.

The barriers that keep us within our own self-interest should be dissolved to embrace the interests of all beings. Helping others helps oneself (through karmic results and developing good qualities of mind), and helping oneself (by purifying one's character) enables one to help others. Therefore, the primary ethical activity for a Buddhist is *dāna* (giving), which forms the basis for further moral and spiritual development. To grow in *dāna*, the Buddhist cultivates *śīlas* (virtues),[36] by observing the five basic ethical precepts, *panca-śīlāni*.[37]

Dhamma

Dhamma is the ultimate basis for Buddhist morality. Like the Hindu dharma, *dhamma* refers to cosmic order underlying both the laws of nature (such as gravity and causation) and the moral laws that regulate human conduct (such as *kamma*). Still, the two concepts differ in their sources. For a Buddhist, only by following *dhamma* can suffering be avoided and happiness achieved. Morality is embedded in the nature of things, and someone who leads a life in harmony with the cosmic order is living a moral life and, as a result, can reach happiness. To live such a life, Buddhism places great emphasis on cultivating virtues (*śīlas*). (Here we see a strong resemblance to the virtue ethics of Aquinas, described in Jean Porter's chapter.) The three most basic Buddhist virtues are non-greed, non-hatred, and non-delusion, opposites of the three roots of evil, namely greed, hatred, and delusion, which are the ultimate cause of suffering.

The virtues and morals that constituted Buddha's "noble life" are not presented as laws or even commands but as things to be cultivated. He expected rulers to follow these principles in formulating specific laws needed to govern a particular society. Morals and laws differ in how the consequences of actions are experienced. In the sphere of morality, the consequences are decided by a natural process of causation (*kamma*). In the case of laws, the community prescribes the consequences (punishments).[38]

The truth value and usefulness of an action are key to determining whether the action is right or wrong. Yet a third factor is also essential because of the importance of compassion for all beings: the effect of the action on others at any specific time. This great compassion includes all virtues and is manifested in unfailing, indefatigable fortitude for the sake of all beings.[39]

The Doctrine of Dependent Origination

As in Hinduism, Buddhist understandings of justice are rooted in descriptions of the nature of things. The Buddhist doctrine of "dependent origination" asserts that all phenomena are caused; they are dependent on causes and on the conditions in which those causes operate. This is true of daily life as well as the cosmic order. The simplest expression of this doctrine is *idam sati ayambhavati*, "when this exists, that arises." Prebish and Keown[40] explain this proposition in the logical form: A→B (when condition A exists, effect B arises) or as its negation -A→ -B (where condition A does not exist, effect B does not arise). Nothing comes into being through its own power or volition; nothing has intrinsic being of its own.

The cosmic order itself arises from the interdependence of matter with flows of consciousness, both having coexisted for all time. A critical result of this view is that there are no metaphysical realities, such as a God who created the cosmos. Nor is there a personal soul. This understanding of the cosmic order as "dependently originated" enabled the Buddha to explain the morality of human behaviour without resorting to any form of moral absolute. Unlike in Christianity, there is no divine source of morality.

Instead, the Buddha attributed his compassion to this understanding of the nature of the causal process, dependent origination, which leads him to treat each situation carefully, evaluating the conditions involved. The practices of compassion and nonviolence come naturally from this understanding of causality in the world. Dependent origination means that humanity is essentially interdependent. This realization promotes harmony and underlines the importance of dialectical deliberation on how to promote the welfare of both individuals and society, even on a global scale.[41] Here Buddhism is close to the notion of the common good in Catholic social thought, as discussed in Lisa Cahill's chapter.

Understanding Justice

Because the Buddha's philosophy does not recognize a celestial–terrestrial distinction, justice cannot be a matter of conforming human actions to "the immutable and unwritten laws of Heaven." The Buddha's conception of justice emerged from his understanding of the nature and status of both the individual and society. According to Buddha, the individual is a person with self-interest, and the society represents "mutual self-interest." Therefore, justice is that which promotes mutual self-interest. As a rational person, one cannot expect others in the community to respect one's interests unless one is prepared to respect the interest of others. In Buddhist rationality, the just act leads to the welfare of both self and others.

In addition to rationality, another critical reason for the importance of justice in Buddhism is the concept of purity (*visuddhi*).[42] Justice as fairness is not for its own sake but for the purity of oneself and for ultimate freedom.

Rationality and purity, and Buddha's great compassion for all sentient beings, are fundamental to the Buddhist conception of justice. This identification of the obligations of justice with personal spiritual fulfillment echoes a similar relation outlined in the chapters by Jean Porter and Lisa Cahill.

The *Pāli* scriptures of early Buddhism,[43] dating from about 300 BCE, give a clear view of the role of practical justice in the formation of the principal institutions of society and the state. In the original condition of things when all humans dwelt in the "Shining World," there were no distinctions that apply today. People were simple food gatherers, without even the basic institutions of marriage and the family or any sense of personal property. However, the emergence of social institutions due to social and economic developments created the need to regulate the social sense of equity and justice within those institutions. This gradually produced a collective appeal for the administration of justice.

Social and economic developments further produced distinctions and classifications in the community (the four varṇas) and led to the destruction of the Shining World. Although the texts indicate that the social classes arose based on inter-cooperative function, presumably for the benefit of all, they also view social status, whatever its origins in terms of practical social justice, as a reflection of individual karmic justice manifested in rebirths.[44] Ultimate justice, therefore, is moral and based on natural law; it is not merely an economic convenience.

The Basis for Justice: Responsibility Toward Others, Not Individual Rights

For Buddhists, the fundamental reality of life is our mutual interdependence, our pervasive interconnectedness. As a result, everyone has responsibility for the well-being of others, making this notion the basis of justice but, in contrast to both liberalism and Catholic social teaching, without individual rights. To a Buddhist, the emphasis on the individual in the West focuses on something that does not and cannot ever exist. Such a focus only aggravates self-centredness and a tendency toward egomania. The Buddha spoke of the "non-self," not their-self. There are no autonomous individuals and no individual rights.

In addition, the Western notion of rights carries the connotation of an adversarial stance: me vs. the other, deepening the problem of self-centeredness.[45] With its emphasis on compassion and responsibility toward others, Buddhism engenders compassionate action to protect the poor and weak—both individuals and groups—from the powerful, what we might call a Buddhist version of the preferential option for the poor addressed in the chapters by Maria Inês de Castro Millen and Agnes Brazal. Buddhist precepts provide a list of the responsibilities: not to harm living beings, not to steal, not to lie, and so on. Stressing collective responsibility, this view of justice avoids the adversarial stance of individual rights.

Economic Justice

Spiritual liberation—enlightenment—remains the most crucial goal for the Buddhist. However, spiritual liberation rests on an essential base of psychological, social, economic, and cultural prerequisites. These aspects of human life directly influence the fortunes of an individual's spiritual aspirations and efforts. Therefore, the concept of interconnectedness means that the spiritual aspect of life cannot be separated from the economic, social, political, psychological, cultural, and other dimensions of life.

Because Buddhism has always recognised that prosperity is a significant component of a happy life, it provides insight into enhancing the prosperity of the individual while also contributing to society's overall prosperity. It calls for a particular perspective on moral reasoning, *yoniso manasikāra*[46]—an attitude that induces a personal realization of how one's highest good can be achieved while simultaneously increasing benefits to others. Buddhist economics tries to maximise human satisfaction by an optimal pattern of productive effort that creates both personal and social benefits.

Achieving individual happiness and profit without benefiting others harms the public interest and violates the fundamental Buddhist principle for action, "compassion for all sentient beings." The Noble Eightfold Path[47] is the Buddhist prescription for correcting a mindset that justifies such actions. By following the Eightfold Path, a person develops a healthy mind that conceives of good economics as an increase in personal and social benefits and gets *anavajjasukha*[48]—a state of mind that experiences economic life in a wholesome way, accompanied by an undisturbed consciousness.

The Buddhist conception of enlightenment entails both personal enlightenment and the behaviour of the enlightened in society. Enlightenment leads the individual to help enrich the quality of life of others so that enlightenment becomes a social phenomenon. With this perspective, Buddhism enriches the quality of life for a large segment of the world's people.[49] It stresses that the experience of enlightenment is both an individual pursuit and a manifestation of global justice.

Environmental Justice

The Buddha's realization that all experienced phenomena are effects of causes (dependent origination) prevented him from perceiving any sharp dichotomy between humanity and the natural world. He uses two metaphors, the flow of a stream and the lotus, to explain the relationship. The flow of a stream illustrates human life as it drifts along, conditioned by various physical, psychological, and social factors. The Buddha and others who attained enlightenment in their present life have ended the process of becoming. They are in the world like the lotus in a pond, living in the stagnant water of the world, dependent on it yet remaining uncorrupted by it.

The principle of dependent origination provides a philosophical basis for relating oneself to the natural world. Nature is not something to be renounced for the sake of some higher spirituality, and it is not something available primarily for the benefit of humans. This realization leads to developing a feeling of kinship with nature. Respect for all other sentient beings inspires the desire to live in harmony with others and with one's natural environment. While Christians have had to work in recent decades to recover theological resources in the scriptures and tradition for ecological care (as discussed in the chapters by Anathea Portier-Young and Lisa Cahill), Buddhists have endorsed this commitment from the beginning.

INSIGHTS FROM BUDDHISM FOR RE-THINKING JUSTICE

Buddhism differs from Catholicism in not attributing the cosmos to a divine creator, but, like Christian doctrine, holding that people can experience their individual highest good while increasing the well-being of others—a *yonisomanasikāra* perspective on moral reasoning. The principle of dependent origination, a characteristic of the natural world, also applies to social life. It is an empirical fact that humans are fundamentally interrelated, which has ethical implications.

This insight led the Buddha to focus on relieving suffering as the most fundamental task, and this compassion is the road to justice. (One sees strong parallels in Pope Francis's stress on compassion and mercy, as Lisa Cahill describes in her chapter.) The noble path has an economic value as it results in anavajjasukha, described above. The Buddhist approach envisions an economic system that creates individual wealth in a way that benefits public interest and communitarian values.

Rather than talk of rights and self-interest, the Buddhist view of life begins with the commonsense conviction that it is not rational to expect others to respect my interests if I don't respect theirs. Insights of interdependence rather than abstract concepts of justice are the key. Because persons are so fundamentally interrelated, justice requires regular dialectical deliberation on how to promote the welfare of individuals and society.

One strives for justice as part of striving for purity of self. Linking justice with personal fulfilment can help mitigate the tension in Western thought caused by treating justice as a set of obligations that constrain one's options.

Dependent origination also leads to respect for all other sentient beings and inspires the desire to live in harmony within one's natural environment. Nature is not something to be renounced for the sake of some higher spirituality or to be plundered for the benefit of humans. The Buddhist view of nature integrates a concern for the natural world into the same moral logic that characterizes human sociality. This insight can assist Catholic social thought in addressing environmental justice.

CONCLUSION

This chapter has summarized some of the most critical insights of the Hindu and Buddhist traditions into the character of justice. Four stand out as particularly helpful in re-thinking justice in Catholic social thought.

First, there is no justice without personal commitment. Buddhism and Hinduism are religions, and justice is elemental in religious practice. Whether understood as part of the Buddhist view of purity of self or the Hindu dharma, a commitment to justice cannot be simply institutional but must be deeply personal. In this, and in the emphasis on compassion, we hear an echo of the call for "social charity," as Lisa Cahill's chapter explains, that Pius XI pointed to in *Quadragesimo anno* as essential to accompany social justice. Definitions of justice in the Catholic tradition often speak more abstractly than either of these two great world religions would recommend.

Second, justice concerns our obligations, not our rights and interests. In the West, individual rights are understood as claims of persons that other persons must respect. In Hinduism, it is understood as the right of individuals and groups to advance within the teleological structure of cosmic order following the *varṇāśrama* system without any interference from others. The Hindu obligation to follow the rita and the right to advance within the teleological structure of cosmic order aim for natural balance and normative harmony, where the relation of conflicting rights in the West so often puts contention at the centre of social life. Buddhism's dependent origination means that all persons are fundamentally interrelated, and the Buddha's commitment to relieving suffering wherever it occurs calls everyone to move beyond the assertion of self.

Third, justice is not only for humanity. When the moral theory of justice is founded in the rights claims of individuals—or even in the human dignity of others—it is difficult to conceive of the natural world as eligible for just treatment. The Hindu awareness of humanity as part of a cosmic order and the Buddhist insight into human kinship with nature because of dependent origination both allow an understanding of justice that requires living in harmony with the natural world.

Fourth, justice realized is more important than justice conceptualized. Neither Hinduism nor Buddhism has developed a theoretical analysis of justice as has Catholicism. Yet both have deep commitments to living a life of justice. Here, Amartya Sen's argument stands as a recommendation from both traditions to Christianity. There are two "kinds" or dimensions of justice: *nīti* and *nyāya*. The former represents the best and most precise conceptual articulation of what justice is and what it requires. The latter sums up the current situation of justice and injustice in the lives that people here and now are able to lead.

Nyāya reminds us that although re-thinking justice in Catholic social thought is needed, a perfect conceptualization is not the ultimate goal for justice in this world. Like the Buddha's commitment to relieve suffering, the concrete task of justice today is not first to implement the most perfect institutions or to start with the logically most basic claims of justice. It is to insist on actions and structures that will eliminate the most severe injustices plaguing so many in our world today. Our thinking and writing about justice need to attend to humanity's greatest needs.

BIBLIOGRAPHY

Amin, Gordhandas Kahandas, trans. *Neeti Sastra Pravesh*. In Gujarati. Gurjar Grandaratna Karyalaya, 1937.

Basham, A.L. *The Wonder That Was India*. Grove Press, 1959.

Chackalackal, Saju. "In Defence of Theoretical Ethics, A Critique on Amartya Sen's *The Idea of Justice*." *Journal of Dharma* 35, no. 4 (October–December 2010): 369–92. https://philpapers.org/rec/CHAIDO-6.

Chethimattam, J.B. "Towards a World Morality." *Journal of Dharma* 16, no. 4 (October–December 1991): 317–36. https://philpapers.org/rec/CHETAW.

Davids, Caroline Rhys. *Buddhism: A Study of the Buddhist Norm*. Abhijeet Publications, 2015.

Deva, Raja Radhakant. *The Sabdakalpadruma: An Encyclopaedic Dictionary of Sanskrit Words*. 5 vols. Nag Publishers, 1987.

Hadley, Michael L., ed. *The Spiritual Roots of Restorative Justice*. In SUNY Series in Religious Studies, edited by Harold Coward. State University of New York Press, 2001.

Harvey, Peter. *An Introduction to Buddhism: Teaching, History, and Practices*. Cambridge University Press, 2005.

Humphreys, Christmas. *Studies in the Middle Way*. Luzac, 1946.

Humphreys, Christmas, ed. *The Wisdom of Buddhism*. Harper Colophon, 1960.

Jhingran, S. *Aspects of Hindu Morality*. Motilal Banarsidass, 1989.

Kalupahana, David J. *Ethics in Early Buddhism*. Motilal Banarsidass, 2008.

Kalupahana, David J. *Nagarjuna: The Philosophy of the Middle Way*. State University of New York Press, 1986.

Keown, Damien. *The Nature of Buddhist Ethics*. Palgrave, 2001.

King, Sallie B. "A Buddhist Perspective on a Global Ethic and Human Rights." *Journal of Dharma* 20, no. 2 (April–June 1995): 122–36. https://philpapers.org/rec/KINABP.

Kochumuttom, Thomas. "Ethics-Based Society of Buddhism." *Journal of Dharma* 16, no. 4 (October–December 1991): 410–20. https://philpapers.org/rec/KOCESO.

Kuppuswamy, B. "A Modern Review of Hindu Dharma. *Journal of Dharma* 1, no. 1 & 2 (July 1975): 118–36. https://philpapers.org/rec/KUPAMR.

Lele, M.P. *Humanism and Ancient Indian Dharma: A Study of Humanism in Relation to Dharma the Religion of Humanity*. Shubhi Publications, 2018.

Lindtner, Chr. *Nagarjuniana: Studies in the Writings and Philosophy of Nagarjuna*. Motilal Banarsidass, 1987.

Manickam, T.M. "Law and Morality in Hindu Dharma." *Journal of Dharma* 4, no. 4 (October–December 1979): 388–97. https://philpapers.org/rec/MANLAM-2.

Manickam, T.M. "Manu's Vision of the Hindu Dharma." *Journal of Dharma* 1, no. 1 & 2 (July 1975): 101–17. https://philpapers.org/rec/MANMVO-2

Mehta, Nimai, and Karti Snadilya. "Hinduism and Governance," *Indian Express* (Daily Newspaper). April 8, 2022. https://indianexpress.com/article/opinion/columns/hindutva-movement-bjp-india-secularism-economy-7858778/.

Miller, Leon. "A Buddhist Critique of Liberalism's Appeal to Global Justice." *Journal of Dharma* 34, no. 4 (October–December 2009): 477–93. https://www.semanticscholar.org/paper/A-BUDDHIST-CRITIQUE-OF-LIBERALISM%E2%80%99S-APPEAL-TO-Miller/f69087f0c574a7e332a3a3f9365d79001ba3c4ef.

Misra, R.S. *Studies in Philosophy and Religion*. Bharatiya Vidya Prakasana, 1971.

Murty, Satchidananda K. *Nagarjuna. National Biography Series*. National Book Trust, 1972.

Nayak, G.C. "Indian Philosophy and Its Social Concerns: With Special Reference to the Concept of Dharma." *Journal of Dharma* 26, no. 2 (April–June 2001): 252–67.

Palatty, Roy Varghese. "What Can Ethics Learn from Economics?" *Journal of Dharma* 38, no. 2 (April–June 2013): 111–130. https://philpapers.org/rec/PALWCE.

Pattery George S.J. "Justice: An Interfaith Task." *Journal of Dharma* 19, no. 3 (July–September 1994): 260–74. https://philpapers.org/rec/PATJAI.

Prebish, Charles S., and Damien Keown. *Introducing Buddhism*, 2nd ed. Routledge, 2010.

Radhakrinshnan, Vivek Kumar. "Dharma in *Manusmṛti*: Agent of Social Cohesion and Equilibrium." *Journal of Dharma* 38, no. 4 (April–June 2013): 399–418.

Ram, G.M., Dr., *The Bible of Hinduism: A Gospel of Social Reconstruction*. Allied Publishers, 1985.

Sen, Amartya. *On Ethics and Economics*. Oxford University Press, 1990.

Sen, Amartya. *The Idea of Justice*. Penguin, 2009.

Sequeira, Cinderella. "The Dilemma of Dharma in the Gītā: Religious Constraints on Moral Duty." *Journal of Dharma* 38, no. 4 (April–June 2013): 419–34. https://www.researchgate.net/publication/291965724_The_dilemma_of_dharma_in_the_gita_Religious_constraints_on_moral_duty.

Sharma, Ram Nath. *Splendour of the Hindu World*. Shubhi Publications, 2017.

Sharma, Urmila, and S.K Sharma. *Indian Political Thought*. Atlantic Publishers and Distributors, 1996.

Singh, Indra Narayan, Dr. *Fundamentals of Buddhism and Ethics*. Prashant Publishing House, 2019.

Singh, Karan, Dr. *Hinduism*. Criterion Publications, 1987.

Srampical, Thomas, and Joji Chirayil. *To Act Justly and Act Honestly*. Marymatha Publications, 2008.

Thachil, J. *An Introduction to Indian Philosophy*. Pontifical Institute Publications, 2007.

Underwood, Frederic B. "Aspects of Justice in Ancient India." *Journal of Chinese Philosophy* 5, no. 3 (1978): 271–85. https://doi.org/10.1111/j.1540-6253.1978.tb00062.x.

NOTES

1. Cf. Chackalackal, "In Defence of Theoretical Ethics," 374–75.
2. Sen, *The Idea of Justice*, 7.
3. Sen, *On Ethics and Economics*, 89.
4. Cf. Sen, *The Idea of Justice*, 326.
5. Sen, *The Idea of Justice*, 21.
6. *Holy Roman Emperor Ferdinand I*. https://www.oxfordreference.com/view/10.1093/acref/9780191826719.001.0001/q-oro-ed4-00004313.
7. The Vedic period is considered to be between 1500 BCE and 600 BCE. The *Vedas* were composed during this period, and this gives this age the name. The *Vedas* are also the chief source of information about this era.
8. Rita is the cosmic–moral principle of order that establishes regularity and righteousness in the world, and the obligation to follow the ṛita is dharma. The concepts of ṛita and dharma appeared early in the Vedic period in the *Ṛig Veda*.
9. *Vedas* are *Srutis* (Sruti meaning what is heard), the narration of everything heard from the ancient priests. Sṛuti texts consist of the four *Vedas*: *Ṛigveda, Yajurveda, Sāmveda,* and *Athrvaveda*. Each of the four *Vedas* consists of four different classes of literary works. They are: (1) *Samhitas*—the *mantrās* proper; (2) *Brahmaṇās*—the rituals and ceremonies to be performed in the sacrificial acts; (3) *Aranyakās*—supplements to *Brahmaṇās*, but go beyond mechanical performances of rites to meditation and spiritual interpretations; and (4) *Upaniṣads*—contain the knowledge and philosophy of *Vedas* relating to God, Man and the Universe. Other sources of knowledge in Hinduism are (1) *Smritīs* (what is remembered), which are the interpretation of *Vedas* by four sages, *Smritikars*—Manu, Yagnavalkaya, Brihaspati, and Nārada; and (2) *Puranās* which are eighteen in number and contain information about the creation and detailed description of *yugās* (cyclic age /epoch) in Hindu cosmology.
10. *Deva, The Sabdakalpadruma*, Vol. II, 783.
11. The *Mahābhārata*—Great Epic of the Bharata Dynasty—is one of the two Sanskrit epic poems of ancient India, the other being the *Rāmāyana*. It is an important source

of information on the development of Hinduism between 400 BCE and 200 CE and is regarded by Hindus as a text about both dharma and *itihāsa* (history). Appearing in its present form about 400 CE, the *Mahābhārata* consists of a mass of mythological and didactic material arranged around a central heroic narrative that tells of the struggle for sovereignty between two groups of cousins, the *Kauravās* and the *Pandavās*. The poem is made up of almost 100,000 couplets, about seven times the length of the *Iliad* and the *Odyssey* combined. It is divided into eighteen sections and has a supplement titled *Harivamṣa*. Its authorship is traditionally ascribed to the sage Vyasa (*Encyclopaedia Britannica*).

12. Yudhiṣṭhira was the *Dharmarāja* (righteous king) in *Mahābhārata*. He represented the perfect king for whom conforming to dharma overrode all other considerations.

13. Bhīṣma is pre-eminent among the many heroes in *Mahābhārata*. He was the greatest of the warriors of his time and was also a towering intellect and a paragon of virtues.

14. *Mahābhārata, Kamaparva*, 69, 58.

15. *Manusmṛti* (Laws of Manu or The Remembered Tradition of Manu), also called *Mānava-dharma-śastra*, is traditionally the most authoritative of the books of the Hindu code. It is attributed to the legendary first lawgiver, Manu. The *Manusmṛti* prescribes to Hindus their dharma and includes consideration of juridical matters. It makes no categorical distinction between religious law and practices and secular law. *Manusmṛti* has profound influence on all aspects of Hindu thought.

16. Radhakrinshnan, "Dharma in *Manusmṛti*," 405.

17. Varṇa system is the social stratification based on birth where four basic categories are defined—*brāhmiṇs* (priests, teachers, intellectuals), *kṣatriyas* (kings, warriors, administrators), *vaiśyas* (agriculturalists, traders, farmers), and *śūdras* (workers, labourers, artisans). The first mention of the varṇa system is found in *Puruṣa Suktam* of *Ṛig Veda* (accepted to have been compiled between the 15th and 10th century BCE).

18. The castes are the actual social groups that make up the varṇas. A caste, generally designated by the term *jāti* (birth), refers to a strictly regulated endogamous social community into which one is born. A person of one jāti is expected to interact with people of other jātīs according to the jāti's position in the social hierarchy. There are a total of about 3,000 castes and 25,000 sub-castes, generally based on specific occupations and hierarchically placed.

    There are many castes that are excluded from the four varṇas because they are considered ritually impure. They are collectively called the *Pancamās* (from Sanskrit *pānch*, "five"), "the fifth." Those castes are also hierarchically ordered, based on their traditional occupations and were formerly called *achuts*, the untouchables. Gandhiji gave them the name *Harijans*, "Children of God." In independent India today, they are officially referred to as Scheduled Castes, and they collectively account for roughly one-sixth of India's total population.

19. Ātman permeates every element and atom in the universe, and everything in it is moved from the centre and spiralled up by the stimulation of Spirit. Nothing escapes His centrifugal and centripetal operations. His presence is indiscernible and appears to our human cognition in an anomalous way as both "real and unreal." Nevertheless, He is the principle of stability as well as of continuity. His operation is like the wheel of a chariot: its fulcrum remains the centre of the wheel while the wheel revolves, and the chariot moves on. It sets everything else in motion while itself remaining stable as the principle of continuity.

20. Underwood, "Aspects of Justice in Ancient India," 272.
21. In the *varṇāśrama* system, an ideal life-program is mapped out in terms of goals to be achieved (*puruṣārtha*) and progressive stages in life (*āśramas*) in which they are to be pursued. The puruṣārtha are: (1) moral, ethical, and social rectitude (dharma); (2) aesthetic and erotic gratification (*kāma*); (3) material well-being and prosperity (*artha*); and, most important, (4) spiritual liberation and self-realization (mokṣa). In order to fulfil each of these goals in a balanced and harmonious progress, life is divided into four stages (*āśramas*): (1) student (*brahmacarya*), (2) householder (*gṛhastha*), (3) forest-dweller (*vānaprastha*), and (4) of renunciation (*sannyāsa*). This arrangement of life involves a type of personal ordering among what might otherwise be conflicting impulses and demands. The pursuit of the puruṣārtha through the *āśramas* is timed slightly differently for different varṇas.
22. Cf. *Bhagavad Gīta*, III. 35.
23. *Ṛig Veda*, X. 124 & 173, also *Yajur Veda*, IX. 22 and *Atharva Veda*, IV. 22. 1–7: III. 3.
24. *Śānti Parva*, the twelfth book of *Mahābhārata*, chapter 59.
25. *Mahābhārata*, 12.59.5., 13–30. 93–94.
26. Basham, *The Wonder That Was India*, 88.
27. The law of Manu is known as *Mānavadharmaśāstra* (Sanskrit).
28. *Yuga*, in Hindu cosmology, is an age of humankind. There are four *yugas*, namely *Krita* (1,728,000 years), *Treta* (1,296,000 years), *Dvapara* (864,000 years), and *Kali* (432,000 years). Each *yuga* is progressively shorter than the preceding one, corresponding to a decline in the moral and physical state of humanity. The four *yugas* make up the *mahayuga* ("great yuga"—4,320,000 years), and 2,000 *mahayugas* make up the basic cosmic cycle, the *kalpa*. The first *yuga* (Krita) was an age of perfection. *Kali yuga*, the fourth and most degenerate, is the present age, which began in 3102 BCE. At the close of the *Kali yuga*, the world will be destroyed, to be re-created after a period of quiescence, and the cycle resumes again. (Encyclopaedia Britannica).
29. *Manusmruti*, VII. 20.
30. In deciding the seriousness of the offence, the *varṇa* of the victim is also taken into consideration.
31. *Manusmruti*, VII. 16.
32. Manu says: "When another common man would be fined one *kārshāpana* (an ancient Indian coin current around the 6th century BCE), the king shall be fined one thousand; that is the settled rule. In (a case of) theft the guilt of a *Śūdra* shall be eightfold, that of a *Vaiśya* sixteenfold, that of a *Kṣatriya* two-and-thirtyfold, that of a *Brāhmaṇa* sixty-fourfold, or quite a hundredfold, or (even) twice four-and-sixtyfold; (each of them) knowing the nature of the offence." *Manusmruti*, VIII, 336–38.
33. *Dhammapada*, 166.
34. The Middle Way *is* the path to cessation of suffering; it is a path between the extremes of clinging and aversion, both expressions of attachment, arriving at a state of complete equanimity. It is achieved through following the Eightfold Path.
35. Harvey, *An Introduction to Buddhism*, 196.
36. *Śīla* (virtue) is a habit or pattern of behaviour that is morally exemplary.
37. The *panca-śīlāni* abstain from (1) killing any living beings, (2) taking that which is not given, (3) sexual misconduct, (4) telling lies, and (5) taking alcohol and intoxicants.
38. Cf. Kalupahana, *Ethics in Early Buddhism*, 135.
39. Humphreys, *Studies in the Middle Way*, 131.

40. Cf. Prebish and Keown, *Introducing Buddhism*, 42–45.
41. Miller, *A Buddhist Critique*, 487.
42. Purity (*Pāli: Vissudhi*) is an important concept in Buddhism. The aim is to purify the personality so that all moral and character defilements and defects (*kleśas* such as anger, ignorance, and lust) are wiped away and nirvana can be obtained. See the Buddha's exhortation to his son Rahula, *Mahā-Rāhulovāda-Sutta,* in the *Ambalatthikarahulovada Sutta* of the *Majjhimanikaya,* [M.I. 414–20].
43. In *Aggañña Suttanta,* number 27 of the *Dīghanikāya,* a Buddhist scripture, part of the *Pāli Tipitaka. Aggañña Sutta* gives the account of the evolution of human society and explains that the kingship was man-made, not created by God as indicated in Hindu tradition.
44. The early Buddhists refuted the *Brāhmaṇical* tendency to see the social order as a divine creation, and instead suggested, empirically and rationally, that it originated out of an expedient human concern for justice and protection. While upholding the original undifferentiated equality of all humans, it seems that the Buddha implicitly accepts the existence of the four *varṇas*—as in the Hindu understanding—and regards the status of rebirth in the hierarchy of *varṇas* as due to karmic fruition. However, Buddha offered the possibility for anyone to escape the conditioning effects of karma altogether by devoting full-time to the realization of the normative teleological goal of nirvāṇa, dropping all the concerns of society.
45. King, *A Buddhist Perspective*, 123.
46. *Yoniso manasikara* (in *Pāli*) is a form of "attention" purposely directed in a manner that is "wise" and at the same time "thorough" and "appropriate," in yoniso.pdf, https://www.buddhismuskunde.uni-hamburg.de, accessed on September 26, 2022.
47. The steps of the Noble Eightfold Path are: (1) Right Understanding, (2) Right Intention, (3) Right Speech, (4) Right Action, (5) Right Livelihood, (6) Right Effort, (7) Right Mindfulness, and (8) Right Concentration.
48. Anavajjasukha is the happiness derived from wealth that is earned by means of right livelihood. Suvimalee Karunaratna, *Prosperity and Happiness: The Buddhist View*, https://www.budsas.org/ebud/ebdha049.htm, accessed September 26, 2022.
49. Miller, *A Buddhist Critique*, 490.

CHAPTER 3

Justice in Latin American Theology

Maria Inês de Castro Millen

Latin America is a multifaceted, heterogeneous, and plural region. This diversity is reflected in all dimensions and realities of this continent, including its religious dimension. I highlight this diversity of Latin America at the start to avoid any misunderstanding. I will not offer an analysis that reflects the entirety of the region. A single comprehensive account—whether from theology or any other discipline—is not possible. Therefore, analyses must be developed from a concrete and well-focused perspective in order to avoid generalization and possible misinterpretations that Latin America is a homogeneous region.

Differences arising from Spanish and Portuguese colonization, distinctions in understanding and relationships with the inadequately called "minorities"—women, Indigenous people, Blacks, the LGBTQ+ population, and the poor—and disparities in the human, philosophical, and theological formation of both clergy and laity have forged a culture and a popular ethos with a great variety of conceptions about multiple existential realities, including the relationship between faith and justice. As I write from Brazil, I highlight its case.

Brazil is a continental, plural country. It is shaped by diverse peoples and cultures that blend together and create another way of being and living. There are many "Brazils" in Brazil that lead us to ask ourselves the question of anthropologist Roberto DaMatta: "What makes Brazil, Brazil?"[1] Homogenizing differences to create an analysis is a task as difficult as it is unrealistic. In contrast to most treatments of justice in the history of Catholic theology, it is necessary to be specific about the concrete object of analysis. I start with some specific elements and offer a reflection on the issue of justice and its consequences in Latin America. I will consider the reality of Brazil and the contribution for the development of justice offered by theology, in the light of Catholic social teaching, with its potential to help us to understand the present and project new alternatives for the future. I will do so with the methods offered by Francis: contemplate, discern, and propose.[2]

In this way, my movement begins by contemplating scenarios as they present themselves to us in a profusion of different colors and subtle nuances, which require careful perception. Then in the light of the word of God and Catholic social teaching, I offer a possible discernment of criteria for understanding justice. Finally, I present some propositional realities and new experiences that make sense for the lives of our peoples, experiences that can contribute to a re-thinking of justice in the Catholic Church as a global institution.

THREE CENTRAL ISSUES

Considering a historical path, I stress three aspects that I consider crucial when dealing with the issue of justice in Brazil: colonization, which is prolonged in today's historical injustice; social inequality, which generates poverty, ignorance, and exclusion; and the environmental crisis, which can lead to planetary destruction.

From a Latin American perspective, particularly considering the Brazilian experience, there is no way to think about justice—no way to advance toward a fairer society—if we do not look at history and retell it from the perspective of the oppressed. This history is not a dead thing in the past; it is still present in the experience of marginalized and exploited populations today. By attending to this experience and the struggle of these populations, with their organizational creativity, resilience, and dynamism, we can come to realize their contribution to re-thinking justice from a plural, inclusive, communitarian, and ecological perspective.

COLONIZATION

Contemplating Latin America, we face a continent that was "discovered" by the Portuguese and Spanish, as the history books tell us. But in fact, this land was reached by European expeditions that explored the seas on their way to the Indies. They settled here and imposed their ideas, culture, and beliefs.

This imposition was an invasion that did not offer any room for dialogue or mutual understanding. On the contrary, it was an invasion by force to enslave and decimate the local inhabitants, who were seen as different, uncivilized, soulless savages. Focusing on Brazil, one can say that the original peoples (named Indigenous or Indians by the invaders), even today, 500 years later, are still suffering the consequences of destructive cultural imposition and ongoing genocide.

In addition, the colonization process involved the resettlement of African people who were brought here as slave labor. Treated like beasts, compelled to work, separated from their families, and sold individually as commodities, enslaved people suffered all sorts of violence in Brazilian lands. Uprooted, they served the planters and landowners to carry out the heaviest jobs, without any reward. They were used to build a country, and still today they suffer neglect and discrimination, even after the so-called abolition of slavery in a country that has not been healed from its past.

In light of the value of justice, we can recognize the prepotency, the arrogance, the feeling of superiority, and the evangelical violations by the colonizing people. They were Christians who used their best resources, including the cross and the sword, to plunder land and goods, mistreating and killing people.

Based on Catholic social teaching, we know that the value of justice is supported by the foundation of the inalienable dignity of all people and by principles, such as solidarity, subsidiarity, and the common good. Therefore, the injustice committed here, extending so far back in history, needs to be repaired.

Some efforts have been made in this direction, but they are far from being able to overcome the wounds of such brutal historical social injustice. Indigenous nations are still fighting for the recognition of their ancestral lands and for the maintenance of their culture and beliefs. African descendants make up the majority of Brazil's impoverished population without access to education, work, and the other basic conditions required to flourish with dignity.

There is a common understanding that the Brazilian people are mixed-race, and that Indigenous and African-descendant people were and are fundamental for apprehending the character of what is called the Brazilian nation. This alleged miscegenation of races has not diminished the racism and discrimination that persist here. Portions of the population are subordinated due to racial and cultural factors. Structural racism is the legacy of the hierarchical colonial system based on race and privilege.

Laws aiming to prevent racism and protect Indigenous peoples were created in recent decades, but they are not enough. It is necessary to carry out a decolonization of the collective imagination, a key factor in re-thinking justice. In this effort, grassroots social movements have been organized to face situations of injustice and ensure that people can become agents of their own history.

Of the many Brazilian initiatives in this direction, I will point out a few that have the objective of protecting the original peoples and restoring the justice that is due to them. Learning from these efforts and hearing the demands of original peoples is essential for us to re-think justice. I stress two initiatives: CIMI and the APIB.

CIMI (the Portuguese acronym for Missionary Indigenous Council) is a Catholic organization affiliated with the National Conference of Bishops of Brazil (CNBB). It was created in 1972, during the military dictatorship in Brazil, when the State embraced policies and actions to integrate Indigenous peoples into non-Indigenous society, into "Brazilian society." In response, this council sought to facilitate conversation between villages and peoples, promoting large Indigenous assemblies, which drafted the first frameworks for a collective struggle to guarantee the right to cultural diversity. The general objective of the CIMI is to "witness and prophetically announce the Good News of the Kingdom, at the service of the life projects of Indigenous peoples, by denouncing structures of domination, violence, and injustice, by practicing intercultural, inter-religious, and ecumenical dialogue, and by supporting the alliances of these peoples with each other and with other social sectors to build a world for all—egalitarian, democratic, pluricultural, and in harmony with nature—on the way to the definitive Kingdom."[3]

This perspective understands that justice includes the recognition of what is proper of other people's worldview and traditions, in this case, what is proper of the Indigenous world. Actions for justice are oriented to promote this specificity and repair the violence that prevents them from being who they are. Some fundamental principles guiding the actions undertaken by CIMI are respect for Indigenous alterity in its ethnic–cultural and historical plurality and appreciation of the traditional knowledge of these peoples. The struggle to guarantee their historical rights and agency must reflect a commitment to the Indigenous cause within a broader perspective of a democratic, just, solidary, pluriethnic, and pluricultural society.

Over the years, CIMI has published dossiers, books, reports, and teaching materials both to develop broader awareness of the violence practiced against Indigenous peoples and to publicize the collective actions carried out by them and their partners. CIMI is an important organization that fights to repair an enduring injustice.

The second initiative is APIB (Portuguese acronym for the Union of the Peoples and Indigenous Organizations of Brazil). Created from the bottom up in 2005 at the Acampamento Terra Livre (ATL), a large assembly of Indigenous peoples and organizations, APIB aims to empower Indigenous movements in the country.

APIB facilitates the cooperation of different regions and Indigenous organizations in Brazil. It also aims to unify their struggles and demands and to mobilize Indigenous peoples and organizations against threats and attacks on their rights.[4] It is a collective effort to repair injustice and build justice from below. It is a bottom-up movement of organization and struggle, stressing that justice is not a force imposed from above, as we sometimes see in Western accounts, including Catholic theological ones, but rather a collective, communicative effort from below, from the struggle of those who have historically been victims of injustice, such as the Indigenous peoples.

The ongoing struggles led by organized grassroots efforts have produced significant achievements, such as the creation of the National Council for Indigenous Policy (CNPI), the Special Secretariat for Indigenous Health (SESAI), and the National Policy for Environmental and Territorial Management of Indigenous Lands (PNGATI). They also enable the participation of representatives of Indigenous peoples in various political and civic organizations that deal with matters of their interest, related to the promotion and enforcement of fundamental rights.[5]

Like the Indigenous population, Brazilians of African descent have also fought against historical injustices. They have always shown great creativity and resistance, from the creation of *quilombos* (communities of Black slaves who resisted slavery in colonial Brazil) to the mobilization today of Black grassroots organizations and social movements that seek to guarantee their social rights and their basic right to live. It seems strange to need to "guarantee their lives," but their lives are always under threat, and many are lost prematurely due to injustice and violence. Through collective efforts from below, aiming to confront injustice and to seek a dignified life for all, Black groups have organized themselves and created many collective structures of support and protection. I highlight two of them: the CNPD and EDUCAFRO.

CNPD (the Black Coalition for Rights) was created in 2019 at an international meeting of Black social movements in the city of São Paulo. In this context, the participants—more than one hundred entities and associated groups—published a letter with a strong purpose, which reflects the entire conflict, needs, and struggles of the Black movement in Brazil. It is worth quoting here a part of the "Proposed Letter from the Black Coalition for Rights."

> We, organizations, entities, groups, and collectives of the Brazilian black movement, reaffirm our legacy of resistance, struggle, production of knowledge, and life. Historically, we continue to face racism, which structures this society and produces inequalities that deeply affect our lives. During nearly four hundred years of enslavement and since the beginning of the Republic, we have been the target of rights violations, anti-black racism, racial discrimination, violence, and genocide. Even so, we have built, with our individual and collective trajectories, the wealth of this country. . . . History demands from the Brazilian black population and the entire African diaspora united actions to confront racism and genocide, as well as the inequalities, injustices, and violence flowing from this reality. This Coalition gathers to promote political advocacy in our own name, based on the values of collaboration, ancestry, circularity, sharing of *axé* (inherited and transmitted life force), orality, transparency, self-care, solidarity, collectivism, memory, recognition, and respect for differences, horizontality, and love. In defense of life, well-being, and rights that are hard-won, irrevocable and non-negotiable, we will continue to honor our ancestors, unifying the entire Afro-diasporic population in a struggle for a future that is free from racism and all forms of oppression.[6]

The second entity is EDUCAFRO (short for Education to Africans, in Portuguese), a civil association that promotes the inclusion of Black and poor populations in public and private universities through affirmative actions (such as the enforcement of quotas), scholarship, and research grants, with the aim of empowering and promoting social mobility for a population that has been historically excluded from these opportunities.

EDUCAFRO emerged from the ideas of David Raimundo dos Santos, a Black Franciscan friar who has been an activist in the fight for affirmative actions at universities for over twenty years. This grassroots movement is supported by Francisco de Assis: Education, Citizenship, Inclusion and Human Rights (FAECIDH), a nonprofit civil association whose mission is the inclusion of underprivileged people in higher education. EDUCAFRO presses the government to fulfill its obligations through public policies and affirmative actions in education toward the Black and the poor, the promotion of ethnic diversity in the labor market, the defense of human rights, and the fight against racism and all forms of discrimination. EDUCAFRO's work has the specific objectives of presenting public policy proposals and affirmative actions to the executive, legislative, and judiciary branches of the government, disseminating principles and values that contribute to a radical social transformation of Brazil and the Americas, based on Christian and Franciscan ideas. It is an effort to awaken in people the responsibility and autonomy in overcoming difficulties, making them agents of their own stories. This effort radically values the organization of grassroots groups as an instrument of social transformation and pressure on the State, believing that the transformation toward racial justice can only be led by the people at the bottom of society.[7]

These organizations and many others arising out of the reality of people's struggles are at the service of justice that must be done in an unequal, prejudiced, and racist country, which needs to protect its most vulnerable children. Their experiences offer precious resources to re-think justice in the Catholic social traditions, considering that there is no path to justice without historical consciousness and the collective effort and culture of those who have been kept from enjoying justice because of the actions of an elite colonizing mentality and its structures.

SOCIAL INEQUALITY

Latin America is a rich and fascinating region. It is marked by the richness of its soil, its natural beauty, and a desire for peace and harmony. This is seen in the vast potential of its multicultural peoples, great biodiversity, multifaceted languages, religiosity, music, food, dance, and stories, all thriving within a characteristic Latin American hospitality.

However, this same America also lives and survives amid wounds that endure historically and grow ever deeper. Perhaps the greatest of these are poverty, underdevelopment, and violence, bitter fruits of social inequality and the structural injustice established and perpetuated here.[8]

Revisiting history, we contemplate the Second Vatican Council, a significant ecclesial and social event that aimed to reconfigure the face of the Catholic Church, pointing to a new way of being and acting for this same church. It was in this context that we heard about a church that wanted to be poor and to be for the poor. On November 16, 1965, in the catacomb of Saint Domitila, about forty bishops, mainly from Latin America, signed the so-called Pact of the Catacombs.[9] In thirteen clauses, the signatories promised to lead a simple life without possessions. Church historian José Oscar Beozzo reports the story of the birth and consequences of this pact, so important for the following journey of the church in Latin America. "Three weeks before the end of the Second Vatican Council, in the Catacombs of Saint Domitila, on the outskirts of Rome, a group of Council Fathers discreetly celebrated the Eucharist on the tombs of the martyrs Nereus and Aquilleus and signed a commitment of life, work, and mission that became known as the Pact of the Catacombs."[10]

History tells us that the group that signed the pact, fighting for a poor church for the poor, was heard by their peers at Vatican II. This motivated an important spiritual reflection. But this group was not able to move the council in this direction. Council documents don't explicitly show this concern, except in some isolated references, such as *Lumen Gentium* no. 08.[11] The Latin American Episcopal Conference (CELAM) met after the council took up this cause, naming it as a preferential option (for the poor) in the ministry of the local churches. The CELAM conferences at Medellín, Puebla, Santo Domingo, and Aparecida all made this option a central part of the church's ministry in the region.

The text from the Medellín Conference (1968) begins by presenting the theme of justice in a non-theoretical way. Instead, it links it to facts, symptoms, and causes of the situations of injustice experienced by the Latin American people. The urgent issue is the "poverty that marginalizes large human groups. This miserable poverty, as a collective fact, is qualified as an injustice that cries out to the heaven."[12] The document stresses this situation as the tragedy of underdevelopment that impacts people's lives, preventing them from flourishing with dignity. Their marginalization points to a social order that generates exclusion. Because it affects such a large number of people, it shows the existence of structural causes responsible for this impoverishment. Poor and historically marginalized groups at the bottom of Latin American societies have no economic power. As a result, they have no access to basic goods and services needed for their flourishing.[13] In the wake of this reflection, liberation theology was born in Latin America. Its principles can be described as follows: a preferential option for the poor and solidarity with the struggle for self-liberation, a new biblical hermeneutics based on Jesus's ministry, a strong moral and social critique on the exclusionary aspects of capitalism, and the development of basic ecclesial communities among the poor as a new way of being church.

Gustavo Gutiérrez, Leonardo Boff, Juan Luis Segundo, Jon Sobrino, José Comblin, Elza Tamez, Frei Betto, Carlos Mesters, João Batista Libanio, Milton Schwantes, and Pablo Richard, among many others, were exponents of this way of doing theology that significantly fostered the new form of ecclesial organization and became their theological perspective.

I highlight the importance of these communities, which have come to be known as the CEBs in Latin America ("comunidades eclesiais de base" in Brazil). They are defined as "a people who walks."

> We walk in the light of the Project of Jesus, which he called the Kingdom of God. We walk in the light of the ecclesiology of the Church as People of God, developed in *Lumen Gentium*, a document of the Second Vatican Council. We walk in the light of the *sensus fidei*, that is, the meaning and wisdom of faith that is in the life of the people. We walk together with all those who believe that another world is possible, making our faith a fundamental reason for not disconnecting from life, from the fight for justice, from solidarity, or, in one expression: from the search for a land without evil.[14]

CEBs emerged in Brazil as a means of evangelization, aiming to respond to the challenges of liberating the poor and the oppressed. They originated in the sociopolitical context of the years of a regime of exception, under military dictatorship, and they presented themselves as a way of adapting the structures of the church to the pastoral innovations of the Second Vatican Council. CEBs are a foundation of a new model of ecclesial organization whose pastoral reference is an articulated network of small communities sharing geography and similar socioeconomic challenges. Those who are gathered in the CEBs are connected by a feeling of mutual belonging to a locality. Neighborhood relationships are privileged elements in the construction of identity. Other ties may be present but are not dominant.

CEBs are places of encounter and celebration of faith, centered on the Bible. The Word of God is read, reflected, and prayed in confrontation with the daily challenges of those who are part of the community. In other words, the reality of the community and people's experiences offer the hermeneutics to read the Bible and interpret its teaching for today's life. Another key characteristic of this ecclesial model is the relation between faith and daily life, with a central concern for aspects of social reality that disrespect human dignity, especially the dignity of the poor. For this reason, the social dimension of CEBs is usually expressed in their members' support for various forms of collective actions and sociopolitical engagement, such as public manifestations and protest, and the participation in grassroots social organizations.[15]

Bishop Aloísio Lorscheider granted ecclesial citizenship to the CEBs when he said: "In Brazil, the CEBs are a new way of being Church," which was later considered as "a new way for the whole Church to be."[16] Leonardo Boff offered an insightful perspective on this definition when he described an event during the VII Interecclesial Meeting of CEBs, in 1989.

> In front of the Cathedral of Caxias, where the VII Interecclesial Meeting of CEBs was held, the custodian (verredora) was crying while leaning on her broom. She said with emotion: "A piece of the kingdom of God has already arrived. Father, is it not a piece of the kingdom to see everyone eating, some sitting on the ground, others on the wall, others on the church stairs, others standing, bishops among the people, theologians together with peasants, pastoral agents together with some indigenous peoples, Latin Americans mixed with European guests, Andeans with Amazonians? Isn't it fraternity, union, diversity, all together, brothers and sisters, a piece of the kingdom of God?" And she wept with joy, a gift of the Holy Spirit. I, who was listening to everything, agreed with her and thought to myself: "This is a clear perception of what 'CEBs, a new way of being Church' means." And that cleaning lady also participates in this anticipated piece of the kingdom of God; because she learned to read this phenomenon as a "piece of the kingdom of God" from participating in the CEBs.[17]

In 1979, the bishops of Latin America gathered in Puebla and endorsed this new way of being church when they said: "As pastors, we resolutely want to promote, guide, and accompany the basic ecclesial communities, in accordance with the spirit of Medellín and the criteria of *Evangelii Nuntiandi*; to favor the discovery and gradual formation of community leaders for them. In particular, it is necessary to look at how the small communities, which are multiplying in the peripheries and rural areas, can also be adapted to the pastoral care in the big cities of our continent."[18]

Frei Betto, theologian and a strong supporter of CEBs, helps us understand how these communities work and how they can be understood.

> Basic ecclesial communities are formed by small groups organized around a (urban) parish or a (rural) chapel, on the initiative of lay people, priests or bishops. . . . They are a challenge within and for the Church, arising out of the hope of liberation of the Latin American peoples. Through the pastoral agency of their basic communities they seek to discover the most evangelical way of turning this hope into an effective practice of transforming history and seeking a world of justice and love.[19]

Founded in a prophetic and embodied spirituality, CEBs maintain the relationship between ethics and religion, spirituality and commitment to social justice. They had and still have an important role in the history of the church in Brazil. In a context of deprivation of liberty and confiscation of rights, they awakened the most vulnerable and marginalized people to take up the fight for the formation of a critical conscientiousness, through literacy and education for all.

CEBs embody a way of being church that also struggles for justice, through organized social ministry from the poor that would lead themselves to liberation and promotion of life. CEBs are at the root of several social movements and have contributed to the formation of many leaders in the social and political life. CEBs became also a space where lay leaders within the church embraced this way of living and celebrating the faith. The ecclesial hierarchy has always had a conflictive relationship with CEBs and their horizontal model of organization. Lack of official ecclesial support and sometimes deliberate action against them worked to weaken this new way of being church. However, in 2012, the National Conference of Brazilian Bishops encouraged the CEBs with the following message:

> The Basic Ecclesiastical Communities, as we said in 1982, constitute "in our country, a reality that expresses one of the most dynamic features of the life of the Church" . . . (Comunidades Eclesiais de Base na Igreja do Brasil, CNBB, doc. 25, 1). After the Conference of Aparecida (2007) and the 12th Interecclesial (Porto Velho 2009), we want to offer to all our brothers and sisters a message of encouragement, albeit brief, for the journey of our CEBs.
>
> We reaffirm that they continue to be a "sign of the vitality of the Church" (RM 51). The disciples of Christ gather in them to attentively listen to the Word of God, to seek more fraternal relationships, to celebrate the Christian mysteries in their lives, and to assume the commitment to transform society. In addition, as Medellín states, the basic communities are "the first and fundamental ecclesial nucleus . . . , the initial cell of the ecclesial structure and focus of evangelization and, currently, the primordial factor of human promotion (Medellín 15).[20]

In this same historical context, the National Conference of Bishops in Brazil created the MEB, the Basic Education Movement, in the early 1960s, with the aim of developing a popular education program (at grassroots level for low-income families) through radio schools, especially in less developed rural areas of Brazil, such regions in the Midwest, North, and Northeast of the country.

The initial proposal of the MEB was to resume the traditional UNESCO concept of basic education, taken up by the church as an educational project that became important due to its commitment to evangelization. Given the impact of poverty on many marginalized groups, education was a key instrument to overcome oppression. The development of the MEB expressed the church's attentiveness to the impoverished and oppressed social classes, their struggle, challenges, and needs.[21] This effort required a re-thinking of the relationship between church and state to enable a partnership in this educational project toward the poorest and neediest population in the country. The project suffered from its politicization and from conflicts regarding the promotion of values and ideologies, but it was an important contribution to literacy and the formation of the critical consciousness of thousands of people. This experience shows that any initiative to re-think justice must include the education and development of critical consciousness of impoverished and marginalized populations.

In the early 1960s, Brazil also saw the development of literacy projects for youth and adults initiated by Paulo Freire, who, with an innovative method, inspired the National Literacy Plan and many Catholic social initiatives, including the MEB. Due to political reasons and the military coup, this project did not last long. Yet it left a powerful legacy, showing that it was possible to move forward toward justice by educating marginalized people. But no authoritarian government wants educated and critical thinkers. The dismantling of this project by the military regime in Brazil only proved this fact. The popularization of Freire's method allowed thousands of Brazilians to experience a new way of learning and teaching. His ideas encouraged literacy students to appropriate writing and words to better understand not only the texts but the world, thus gaining an autonomy that made them agents in the transformation of the environment where they lived.[22]

Aimed at restoring justice to the poor and disinherited of the earth, these initiatives encourage us to look at our era, seeing creative possibilities for action with the vulnerable. It is from the perspective of the vulnerable, the poor, and historically marginalized groups with their creative capacity to survive in oppressive conditions that we must re-think justice and our way to a more just world.

In 1993, Brazilian sociologist Herbert de Souza, widely known by his nickname Betinho, founded the social movement ADC (Citizen Action). It fostered an immense network of national mobilization to help those who found themselves below the poverty line. Promoted by organized civil society, this action for life and against hunger and misery has become the most recognized social movement in Brazil, with the agency of local community leaders and the participation of different social sectors.[23]

In 2003, ten years later, the FZ program was created to combat hunger and its structural causes, aiming to ensure food security for all Brazilians. Luis Inácio Lula da Silva stressed:

> When I took over the presidency of the Republic, in 2003, I stressed that the mission of my administration was to ensure that all Brazilians have access to at least three meals per day. . . . Ending hunger meant including all Brazilians in a major development project for the country and freeing people to dream and to be entitled to other rights. Hunger is fought with permanent, sustainable, and broad public policies that can reach the most distant ones. These policies can and should count on the participation of various sectors of society, non-governmental organizations, the many entities and associations dedicated to study this subject and to serve planning actions to support poorer communities. . . . Then, the *Fome Zero* was developed. We were not the first to denounce hunger, but we were the first to take responsibility for radically combating it. For this reason, *Fome Zero* was a milestone in the history of Brazil, as for the first time in our history a government was willing to organize a strategy to articulate policies in various Ministries to eradicate hunger.[24]

Pope Francis's proposals highlight the possibility of revitalizing basic communities and ministry led by the oppressed at grassroots level with actions committed to justice. He encourages the church "to go forth" as a field hospital, which must focus on care for those who have fallen by the side of the road, on the existential peripheries. He rekindles this spirit that led the church in Latin America in the second half of the twentieth century. As a Latin American himself, Francis brings his experience of social ministry with the poor and marginalized to re-think justice in Catholic social teaching at the highest level of the ecclesial structure. In other words, the voices of the poor and the marginalized, alongside their creativity, offer an important contribution to the project undertaken in this volume to re-think justice in the Catholic social tradition and beyond.

A close reading of Francis's words in *Evangelii gaudium* shows us that we need to learn and commit ourselves to *primeirear*, that is, to anticipate ourselves in loving others, being the first one to love others, getting involved in caring for the lives of others and the planet. Hence, we can accompany those who are unable to advance because of the oppression and suffering; we can endure with them as long as it takes. We cannot exclude the tares if we hope to harvest the wheat we desire, so we can celebrate our achievements with the joy of the simple and humble who gratefully celebrate each small step.[25]

These small communities, strengthened by the presence and the care of the church and its leaders, constitute the people of God who walk in the search for justice and peace. "They also welcome, with joy, Pope Francis's call to modify the socioeconomic structures that dominate our planet, creating a fraternal, free, and egalitarian society, capable of enhancing the economy."[26]

Brazil currently has seen a pioneering project committed to an education for all, resulting from a grassroots group led by sociologist Jessé de Souza and economist Eduardo Moreira. ICL, Instituto Conhecimento Liberta (The Knowledge Liberates Institute), defines itself as follows:

> We are an educational and cultural institute that believes true freedom can only be achieved through knowledge. We seek to democratize essential content and materials for an integral human development, making it simple and accessible to everyone. We emerged with the certainty that learning is remarkable when it is enjoyable. We were born with the mission of showing that there are no barriers when there is a desire to think and learn. Our purpose is to show you the way to free yourself through knowledge.[27]

ICL has a highly credible board of trustees and almost fifty partner entities distributing scholarships for low-income people. Hence, historically marginalized populations have access to high-quality educational content and materials. There is a symbolic monthly fee, called the "solidarity fee," for those who can pay, with the money going to fund scholarships for students in partner institutions. They offer more than 170 courses, taught by the best professors in Brazil, who offer lectures and other materials available on a virtual platform to be accessed live and at any time. Today, ICL has more than 55,000 students in Brazil and around the world, offering 19,000 scholarships. It is a revolutionary project that helps to minimize the inequality that generates poverty in Brazil. It continues the legacy of offering education for critical consciousness, empowering low-income people to move toward justice.

Brazil is a continental, pluralistic country, where differences foster inequalities. The predatory neoliberal capitalist system creates impoverishment for most people, a lack of participation of the marginalized groups in the management of the common good, and environmental destruction of the earth in the name of greed and profit of a powerful elite. Food insecurity and the scourge of hunger are back on the scene. Plates are increasingly empty, and people's eye are increasingly sad, reflecting the situation of a country that is one the largest food producers in the world. There couldn't be a bigger contradiction.

In 2022, statistics showed that 33.1 million people did not have enough to eat. In just over a year, 14 million more Brazilians were forced into hunger. The most recent data show that more than half (58.7%) of the Brazilian people experience food insecurity to some degree—mild, moderate, or severe. The country has regressed to a level equivalent to that of the 1990s.

> In 2022 Brazil, only 4 out of 10 households manage to maintain full access to food—that is, they are in a condition of food security. The other 6 households are divided on a scale, ranging from those who remain concerned about the possibility of not having food in the future to those who are already experiencing hunger. According to a second survey, in absolute numbers, there are 125.2 million Brazilians who have experienced some degree of food insecurity. It is a 7.2% increase since 2020, and a 60% increase compared to 2018.[28]

Recent years have seen a reality in Brazil that moved us backward, with the dismantling of the social programs described above. Here is a country that needs to be rebuilt, and the ghost of hunger needs to be faced and fought against. Catholic social teaching and Pope Francis remind us that the principles of solidarity and the common good and the desire for fraternity must not be neglected. Historical consciousness leads us to the experience of grassroots social organization with broad participation beginning from the bottom of society. Here is a Brazilian contribution to re-thinking justice and engaging local communities in the movement toward a more just world.

THE ECOLOGICAL QUESTION

In a previous work published at Catholic Theological Ethics in the World Church, I suggested that we are living in a crucial moment for the survival of humanity. The presence of wars, which result in poverty, destruction, and death, bringing along the possibility of a global destruction through the use of atomic weapons, frightens us. Intolerance and hatred—produced by polarizations and prejudices that generate violence—frighten us. We live in a time of the banalization of evil, with a worrisome indifference and disregard for others. However, there is an even a more tragic situation that has long preoccupied theologians and ethical activists: environmental degradation. Climate scientists and ecologists have tirelessly spoken to people, organizations, and states about the alarming situation of irreversible degradation of the planet. They have also demonstrated, from climate catastrophes, the suffering of the earth and the consequences that are already being felt. Yet many people and global leaders have not yet awakened to the severity of this situation.

Leonardo Boff, writing from Brazil, has contributed greatly to our grasp of this issue. He has broad international recognition with his tireless voice and countless articles calling our attention to the ecological crisis. He began to address this issue even before it became widely known as it is today. He was one of the first to employ the notion of integral ecology in his works *Ética da vida* (Ethics of Life)[29] and then *Cuidar da terra, proteger a vida: Como evitar o fim do mundo* (Caring for the Earth, Protecting Life: How to Avoid the End of the World). According to Boff, "we are at the heart of a phenomenal planetary crisis that affects all cultures and all peoples." He addresses, as a singular interrelated problem, the global social crisis, climate change, and the unsustainability of the Earth-system, caused by highly predatory consumption and exploitation. Boff also affirms that this crisis "could mean a leap towards a higher state of hominization, as well as a devastating tragedy for the entire species."[30] In 1992, Brazil hosted Eco-19, one of the main international conferences and first global summit on the environment, organized by the United Nations, with the participation of 197 countries. Boff was one of the key voices at this summit calling for ecological protection and changes in our model of economic development. At the center of the discussions was the notion of sustainable development, a concept considered innovative at the time. From the conference emerged "Agenda 21," with a program of environmental actions that aims to promote so-called sustainable development.

As Moacir Gadotti, honorary president of the Paulo Freire Institute, has said, "Brazil is the birthplace of the Earth Charter. . . . In 1987, a United Nations Commission for Environment and Development recommended the drafting of a new Charter on sustainable development, but this was only at the parallel event of the Earth Summit (Eco-92), called 'Global Forum,' held in Rio de Janeiro, in 1992, where the first version of the Earth Charter was written, alongside a set of documents called 'Treaties' of the NGOs."[31] Even though it was presented at Eco-92, the Earth Charter was only ratified and assumed by UNESCO in the year 2000 at the Peace Palace in The Hague, the Netherlands, with the support of more than 4,500 nations and organizations from around the world, including Brazil. This international declaration can be considered an inspiration for the search for a society in which everyone is responsible for actions of peace, respect, and equality. It aims for the world's well-being by dealing with ethical issues of great importance to everyone today. The Earth Charter is still an important educational tool that should not be forgotten if we want to think about justice for people and the earth, our common house.

In Brazil, many other voices gathered in the struggle for environmental defense and in a search for sustainability that can promote the earth and human life. The original peoples, victims of inexcusable genocide, are still fighting for the good of the planet, fostering their harmonic relationship with the earth, always a core part of their ancestral culture. Ailton Krenak, an Indigenous leader born in a region of Brazil deeply affected by mining activity, criticizes the idea of a humanity that does not consider itself part of nature. He wrote a book, small in size but large in scope, entitled *Ideias para adiar o fim do mundo* (Ideas to Postpone the End of the World), where he says:

> Our time specializes in creating absences: the meaning of living in society, the very meaning of experiencing life. This generates great intolerance towards those who are still able to experience the pleasure of being alive, of dancing, of singing. And around the world there are small constellations of people who dance, sing, and make it rain. The type of zombie humanity that we are called to become does not tolerate so much pleasure, so much enjoyment of life. So, they preach the end of the world as a possibility to make us give up on our own dreams.[32]

Davi Kopenawa, a Yanomami shaman, born in the forest of Brazil's Northern Amazonas state and defender of the Indigenous peoples of the Americas, coauthored a book with the French anthropologist Bruce Albert, *A queda do céu* (The Fall of the Sky). They offer these words to us:

> The forest is alive. It will only die if the whites insist on destroying it. If they succeed, the rivers will disappear underground, the ground will crumble, the trees will wither, and the rocks will crack in the heat. The parched earth will be empty and silent. . . . Then we will die one after other, both white people and us. All shamans will eventually

die. When there are none of them left alive to support the sky, it will collapse.[33]

Committed to the original peoples who fight for the preservation of the forests, the journalist Eliane Brum, born in southern Brazil, made her home in the city of Altamira, in the northern Brazilian state of Pará, within the Amazon rainforest. She calls this region "the center of the world." In Altamira, she became involved in the struggle to preserve the forest and the existence of the people who live there through a journalistic investigation that denounced the escalation of devastation, rapidly taking the forest to a point of no return. This commitment generates deep reflection and mobilizes us to recognize the actions of dominant and predatory minorities, who are directly responsible for the climate collapse, the mass extinction of many species, and the killing of uncountable humans. The Amazon is a ground fertilized with the blood of many martyrs. In a terrifying testimony, Brum shares her experience with us:

> Throughout my life as a reporter, I've seen many children with eyes of an old man. I already wrote about them. They are children who live with death every day, they are children who are afraid of dying and who are at real risk of dying at any moment. . . . When we find children with eyes of an old man, we know that a crime has been committed, because children cannot have eyes of an old man.[34]

People must open their ears to hear the cry of the poor, which is a Latin American ethical tradition. The poor are the first ones to be disturbed by the cry of the earth, poor mother of impoverished children, sons, and daughters brutalized by the greed that makes poor people even poorer with more suffering in a context where suffering is already part of daily life. Their voices bring the voices of the forest. They are the first voices to be heard when we are committed to re-think justice and our path to concretely build it. As Pope Francis reminds us, we cannot pretend to be distracted![35]

Moreover, the Synod for the Amazon was an event of extreme importance for the environmental challenges and the reality of the peoples in the Amazon. Convened by Pope Francis in 2017, its main purpose was "finding new ways for the evangelization of that portion of the People of God, especially of Indigenous peoples, who are often forgotten and left behind with no prospect of a serene future, also because of the crisis that has hit the Amazon rainforest, a lung of fundamental importance for our planet."[36]

This special assembly took place between October 6 and 27, 2019, and resulted in the post-synodal exhortation *Querida amazônia,* in which Pope Francis reiterates his dreams for the Amazon:

> I dream of an Amazon region that fights for the rights of the poor, the original peoples and the least of our brothers and sisters, where their voices can be heard and their dignity advanced.
>
> I dream of an Amazon region that can preserve its distinctive cultural riches, where the beauty of our humanity shines forth in so many varied ways.
>
> I dream of an Amazon region that can jealously preserve its overwhelming natural beauty and the superabundant life teeming in its rivers and forests.
>
> I dream of Christian communities capable of generous commitment, incarnate in the Amazon region, and giving the Church new faces with Amazonian features.[37]

Francis's social dream is relevant for re-thinking justice, as it projects an Amazon that takes care not only of the forest but of all the beings that inhabit it. This dream includes the teaching offered by the existence and voices of the Amazon people, including justice in the environmental discussion as an integral participatory ecology. He stresses that "a conservationism that is concerned with the biome, but ignores the Amazonian peoples, is not useful." He urges us to develop the ability to lament and be distressed, so we can ask for forgiveness, recovering a communal way of living.

Francis's ecological dream reminds us of the wisdom of ancient peoples who "inspire care and respect for creation, with a clear consciousness of its limits, and prohibit its abuse. To abuse nature is to abuse our ancestors, our brothers and sisters, creation and the Creator, and to mortgage the future."[38] We cannot re-think justice without the wisdom of these peoples, a demand that the Latin America theology and church have recognized for decades and that now Francis, coming himself from this continental tradition, has expanded for the global church and Catholic social teaching.

Finally, we should acknowledge ISA (a Portuguese acronym for a Brazilian institute for socio-environmental initiatives). ISA is a civil organization of public interest that has been working since 1994 alongside Indigenous, *riberinhos, quilombolas,* and extractive communities (all historical marginalized populations that live in the forest and its environs). Its purpose is to develop solutions that protect their territories, strengthen their culture, and promote their traditional knowledge, raising their political consciousness and participation toward the development of sustainable economies.[39]

ISA seeks to promote public policies that result in increased protection of the environment and guarantee the rights of populations, so they can live and preserve their territories. In addition, ISA monitors Indigenous lands and conservation areas across the country, helping to create more protected areas, seeking to detect the threats that hang over them (e.g., deforestation, fires, mining, land grabbing, and prospecting). Thus, it provides information to improve the public debate. This initiative is aligned with the dreams of Pope Francis, showing that environmental justice includes social, cultural, and epistemological justice, with initiatives that grow at the bottom of marginalized communities with their participation and leadership. It is from the bottom that justice begins to be [re-]thought—that is, justice begins to be built.

CONCLUSION

In conclusion, justice is a value criterion for discerning the good that we intend, for building a prosperous, happy, and peaceful continent. Together we must take up the challenges that present themselves to us as priorities. Taking these tasks as ours is a way to guarantee that the dignity of all will be respected, that solidarity, subsidiarity, and the common good will be principles able to guide us through an authentic integration of Catholic social teaching with local values and the confrontation offered by new voices, experiences, and insights. Hence, the values of truth and freedom, allied to a merciful justice, become a foundation for a community effort toward a new world. We must address the urgent needs of those disproportionally vulnerable. We must make ourselves their partners in a common effort to open paths for re-thinking justice and establishing just structures that contribute to a social, economic, and political order without inequities and oppression.

The Catholic Church and all Christian communities, as institutionalized structures, also need to seek conversion in a penitential path. Overbearing structures, clinging to laws and norms that have already expired, do not respond to the questions that need to be heard and answered to guarantee the lives of so many people. These ecclesial structures are hostile to including voices that challenge old ways and to old hearts seeking social ministry and justice. They contribute to the maintenance of chronic injustices instead of announcing the good news of the kingdom of God, preached by Jesus of Nazareth.

In the end, we need to remember that the reconstruction of our continent, and its history of injustices and inequality, depends on our evangelical option for the poor.

Considering the experience in Latin America, especially the Brazilian one described here, there is no path for justice without the preferential option for the poor. This concept summarizes all experiences offered in this chapter for re-thinking justice in our social tradition. The option for the impoverished and needy is essential for our current world, a concept of Christological faith that guides us to join with those at the bottom of our societies to re-tell history through their eyes and, from there, to re-think justice in an historical consciousness developed from below.

BIBLIOGRAPHY

Ação da Cidadania. *"Nossa história:* Quem tem fome, tem pressa." https://www.acaodacidadania.org.br/nossa-historia.

Articulação dos Povos e Organizações Indígenas do Brasil. "Acampamento Terra Livre." https://apiboficial.org/historicoatl/.

Articulação dos Povos e Organizações Indígenas do Brasil. "Home." https://apiboficial.org/.

Assembleia Sinodal para a Pan-Amazônia. "Por que o Sínodo para a Pan-amazônia?" http://secretariat.synod.va/content/sinodoamazonico/pt/sinodo-pan-amazonico/assembleia-sinodal-para-a-pan-amazonia.html.

Beozzo, José Oscar. Pacto das catacumbas: Por uma igreja servidora e pobre. Paulinas, 2015.

Betto, Frei. *O Que é Comunidade Eclesial de Base,* 4th ed. Editora Brasiliense, 1985.

Boff, Leonardo. "CEBs: Que significa 'novo modo de toda a igreja ser'?" *Revista Eclesiástica Brasileira* 49, no. 195 (1989): 546. https://doi.org/10.29386/reb.v49i195.3102.

Boff, Leonardo. Cuidar da Terra, proteger a vida: Como evitar o fim do mundo. Record, 2010.

Boff, Leonardo. *Ética da vida.* Letraviva, 1999.

Brighenti, Agenor. "A justiça em Medellín e as categorias da tradição eclesial libertadora." In *Medellín: Memória, profetismo e esperança na América Latina,* edited by Ney de Souza and Emerson Sbardelotti, 151–66. Vozes, 2018.

Brum, Eliane. *Banzeiro Òkòtó: Uma viagem à Amazônia centro do mundo.* Companhia das Letras, 2021.

CEBs do Brasil. "Quem Somos." https://cebsdobrasil.com.br/quem-somos/.

Chirone, Alberto. "A construção de uma sociedade justa, democrática e ecologicamente sustentável: Alguns aspectos das CEBs na economia de Francisco e Clara." *Instituto Humanistas Unisinos.* https://www.ihu.unisinos.br/categorias/610544-a-construcao-de-uma-sociedade-justa-democratica-e-ecologicamente-sustentavel-alguns-aspectos-das-cebs-na-economia-de-francisco-e-clara.

Coalisão Negra por Direitos. "Carta Proposta da Coalizão Negra por Direitos." https://coalizaonegrapordireitos.org.br/sobre/.

Concílio Vaticano II. *Constituição Dogmática Lumen Gentium: Sobre a igreja.* https://www
.vatican.va/archive/hist_councils/ii_vatican_council/documents/vat-ii_const
_19641121_lumen-gentium_po.html.
Conferência Nacional do Bispos do Brasil. "Mensagem ao Povo de Deus sobre as Comunidades Eclesiais de Base." May 15, 2010. https://www.cnbb.org.br/mensagem-ao-povo
-de-deus-sobre-as-comunidades-eclesiais-de-base/.
Conselho Episcopal Latino-Americano. *Conclusões da II Conferência Geral do Episcopado.*
Latino-Americano: Documento de Medellin, na seção 1, sobre a Justiça, 3. https://pjmp
.org/subsidios_arquivos/cnbb/Medellin-1968-2CELAM-PORTUGUES.pdf.
Conselho Episcopal Latino-Americano. *Conclusões da III Conferência Geral do Episcopado Latino-
Americano: Documento de Puebla* (1979): no. 648. https://www.celam.org/documentos
/Documento_Conclusivo_Puebla.pdf.
Conselho Indigenista Missionário. "Nossa estrutura." https://cimi.org.br/o-cimi/#estrutura.
DaMatta, Roberto. *O que faz o Brasil, Brasil.* Rocco, 1986.
de Castro Millen, Maria Inês. "Grito da Terra, Grito dos Pobres." *The First.* https://catholicethics
.com/forum/grito-da-terra-grito-dos-pobres/.
EDUCAFRO. "Conheça a EDUCAFRO." https://www.educafro.org.br/site/quem-somos/.
Fávero, Osmar. "Movimento de educação de base? MEB." *Gestrado-UFMG.* https://gestrado
.net.br/verbetes/movimento-de-educacao-de-base--me.
Francis. *Exortação apostólica Evangelii gaudium: A Alegria do Evangelho.* Paulinas; Loyola,
2013.
Francis. *Exortação Apostólica Pós-Sinodal Querida amazônia,* no. 7. https://www.vatican.va
/content/francesco/pt/apost_exhortations/documents/papa-francesco_esortazione
-ap_20200202_querida-amazonia.html.
Francis. *Querida amazônia,* no. 42. https://www.vatican.va/content/francesco/en/apost
_exhortations/documents/papa-francesco_esortazione-ap_20200202_querida
-amazonia.html.
Francis. *Vamos Sonhar Juntos: Um Caminho para um Futuro Melhor.* Intrínseca, 2020.
Gadotti, Moacir. *A Carta da Terra no Brasil.* https://earthcharter.org/wp-content/assets
/virtual-library2/images/uploads/A%20Carta%20da%20Terra%20no%20Brasil.pdf.
Instituto Conhecimento Liberta. "Quem Somos." https://icl.com.br/.
Instituto Socioambiental. "Somos o ISA, Instituto Socioambiental." https://www.socioambiental
.org/sobre.
Kopenawa, Davi, and Albert Bruce. *A queda do céu: Palavras de um Xamã Yanomami.* Com-
panhia das Letras. 2015.
Krenak, Ailton. *Ideias para adiar o fim do mundo.* Companhia das Letras, 2019.
Lula da Silva, Luis Inácio. "Introduction." In Veiga Aranha Adriana. *Fome Zero: Uma História
Brasileira.* Vol 1. Ministério do Desenvolvimento Social e Combate à Fome, 2010.
Ministério da Educação. "Inspirada em célebre educador, estudante aprende sobre a vida ao
ensinar adultos a ler." http://portal.mec.gov.br/ultimas-noticias/211-218175739/39611
-inspirada-em-celebre-educador-estudante-aprende-sobre-a-vida-ao-ensinar-adultos-a
-ler. The method was developed by Paulo Freire, *Pedagogia do Oprimido.* Paz e Terra, 1979.
Nonato Dornelas, Nelito. "A identidade das CEBs." *Vida Pastoral* 50, no. 248 (2008): 3–5.
https://www.vidapastoral.com.br/artigos/eclesiologia/a-identidade-das-cebs/.
"Pacto das catacumbas da igreja serva e pobre" RELAMI. http://www.missiologia.org.br/wp
-content/uploads/cms_documentos_pdf_15.pdf.

Portal das CEBs, "O que são CEBs." https://portaldascebs.org.br/o-que-sao-cebs/.

Rede PENSSAM "2º Inquérito Nacional sobre Insegurança Alimentar no Contexto da Pandemia da Covid-19 no Brasil. https://pesquisassan.net.br/2o-inquerito-nacional-sobre-inseguranca-alimentar-no-contexto-da-pandemia-da-covid-19-no-brasil/.

Veiga Aranha Adriana. *Fome Zero: Uma História Brasileira*. Vol 1. Ministério do Desenvolvimento Social e Combate à Fome, 2010.

NOTES

1. Roberto DaMatta, *O que raz.*
2. Francis, *Vamos Sonhar Juntos*, 153.
3. Conselho Indigenista Missionário, "Nossa estrutura."
4. Articulação dos Povos, "Home."
5. Articulação dos Povos, "Acampamento Terra Livre."
6. Coalisão Negra por Direitos, "Carta Proposta."
7. EDUCAFRO, "Conheça a EDUCAFRO."
8. Social inequality and the impoverishment of the Latin American population, especially in Brazil, will be presented based on analyses made by reliable institutions including those made by the Latin American Episcopal Conferences, with their creative reception of the Second Vatican Council, plus a particular vision of contemporaneity.
9. "Pacto das catacumbas."
10. José Oscar Beozzo. *Pacto das catacumbas*, 9.
11. Concílio Vaticano II, *Lumen Gentium.*
12. Conselho Episcopal Latino-Americano, *Documento de Medellin*, na seção 1, sobre a Justiça, 3.
13. Agenor Brighenti, "A justiça em Medellín," 155.
14. CEBs do Brasil, "Quem Somos."
15. Portal das CEBs, "O que são CEBs."
16. Nelito Nonato Dornelas, "A identidade das CEBs," 3–5.
17. Leonardo Boff, "CEBs: Que significa," 546.
18. Conselho Episcopal Latino-Americano, *Documento de Puebla*, no. 648.
19. Frei Betto, *Comunidade Eclesial de Base*, 5, 7.
20. Conferência Nacional do Bispos do Brasil, "Mensagem ao Povo de Deus."
21. Osmar Fávero, "Movimento de educação de base?"
22. Ministério da Educação, "Inspirada em célebre educador." The method developed by Paulo Freire can be found in Paulo Freire, *Pedagogia do Oprimido* (Rio de Janeiro: Paz e Terra, 1979).
23. Ação da Cidadania, *"Nossa história."*
24. Luis Inácio Lula da Silva, "Introduction."
25. Francis, *Evangelii gaudium*, no. 24.
26. Alberto Chirone, "A construção."
27. Instituto Conhecimento Liberta, "Quem Somos."
28. Rede PENSSAM "2º Inquérito Nacional."
    The research was carried out by the Rede Brasileira de Pesquisa em Soberania e Segurança Alimentar e Nutricional (Rede PENSSAM), made up of a diverse group of researchers, teachers, students, and professionals. The study was carried out in the field

in partnership with the Vox Populi Institute. The organizations Oxfam Brasil, Ação da Cidadania, ActionAid Brasil, Fundação Friedrich Ebert Brasil, Ibirapitanga, and Sesc São Paulo are also supporting organizations and partners in this initiative.

29. Leonardo Boff, *Ética da vida*, 31.
30. Leonardo Boff, *Cuidar da terra*, 11–12; 17.
31. Moacir Gadotti, *A Carta*.
32. Ailton Krenak, *Ideias*, 26–27.
33. Davi Kopenawa and Albert Bruce, *A queda do céu*, 6.
34. Eliane Brum, *Banzeiro Òkòtó*, 222.
35. This section in the article presents an updated version of a text previously published at the website of Catholic Theological Ethics in the World Church. See Maria Inês de Castro Millen, "*Grito da terra, Grito dos pobres.*"
36. Assembleia Sinodal para a Pan-Amazônia, "Por que o Sínodo."
37. Francis, *Querida amazônia*, no. 7.
38. Francis, *Querida amazônia*, no. 42.
39. Instituto Socioambiental, "Somos o ISA."

CHAPTER 4

Scripture as a Resource for Re-thinking Justice in Catholic Social Thought

Anathea Portier-Young

Re-thinking justice in Catholic social thought requires attention to the diversity of forms of injustice today and the various theological and philosophical analyses of injustice. Equally essential is a careful consideration of the scriptures, where ancient responses to injustice provide vital insight for Christians today.

WHO INTERPRETS FOR JUSTICE

Context shapes our understanding of justice. Biblical interpretation is likewise shaped by interpreters' unique historical and cultural horizons, attitudes, social location, personal experience, and commitments, and even their exposure and responses to earlier interpretations. Scripture has no meaning apart from interpretation and can only be interpreted by actual humans within actual contexts. For biblical interpretation to speak adequately to the character of justice in the diverse contexts of people today, Catholic social teaching must be informed by diverse interpretive perspectives. As a result, interpreting for justice must be a conversation, not a monologue. To this end, at various points in this essay, I incorporate the insights of interlocutors with diverse backgrounds who are doing the work of justice "on the ground" in a way that is sustained and shaped by the witness of scripture.[1]

HOW WE INTERPRET FOR JUSTICE

It matters not only who interprets but how. I do not mean that one approach or methodology is superior to another—key insights emerge from historical critical, literary, social-scientific, postmodern, and interdisciplinary approaches alike. Instead, a hermeneutic of justice, whatever its methods, commits to self-criticism and mutual accountability. It shares interpretive power and authority. It is multiperspectival and privileges voices and perspectives that have been marginalized. This hermeneutic thus echoes the commitment to read the scriptures "with the poor," as Maria Inês Castro Millen advocates in her chapter in this volume. It owns up to histories of harmful interpretation and seeks interpretations that heal and promote flourishing. It grapples honestly with difficult texts and learns from neglected ones. It does not cherry-pick or proof-text but attends to the full breadth of scripture's witness, including diverse genres with differing conventions and functions and the full context of each biblical text. It refocuses attention from classical protagonists of biblical narrative to minor characters and those portrayed as "other," and recognizes that no characters in scripture are straightforward moral exemplars. Consistent with Daniel Finn's argument in chapter 9 in this volume, a hermeneutic of justice expands focus from individual action to broader systems, commits to deep analysis of ancient and present-day social structures and systems, and allows the complexity of biblical narrative to illuminate complex contemporary realities.

Self-criticism entails a willingness to examine our own assumptions, recognize our complicity in systems of oppression, and acknowledge the injustices we have perpetrated while also asking how these shape our reading and how we might challenge our assumptions. But self-criticism must be accompanied by accountability, a surrender of interpretive power-over, and a commitment to shared interpretive power and authority. As argued by Agnes Brazal in her chapter, such a commitment must bridge differences of gender, race, ethnicity, citizenship, language, education, socioeconomic status, professional credentials, and ecclesial role. This requires cultural and social humility and a recognition of our shared fragility.[2]

Such a hermeneutic of humility and mutual accountability can help the church own up to histories of harmful interpretation. Biblical interpretation has justified genocide, colonialism, conquest, violence toward and exclusion of LGBTQ+ people, the systemic denigration and disempowerment of women, and the slavery of African peoples and their descendants. It is not enough to offer a new reading that simply avoids repeating those violations. Social justice happens in history. Past interpretations contribute to unjust realities in the present. Owning up to the church's sponsorship of such interpretations allows it to historicize and dismantle the systems, structures, and attitudes it has propped up with harmful interpretations. This awareness further equips the church to choose interpretation that more authentically promotes justice and healing, openly admitting, as Lisa Cahill proposes in chapter 7, that the church has had only limited success in the struggle against injustice.

Origen believed that the Holy Spirit seeded scripture with textual problems that would cause interpreters to stumble.[3] In this view, the difficult texts are the ones we most need to spend time with. Yet the lectionary has conditioned many to glide over the surface of the scriptures and approach them more willfully and selectively. Preference is accorded passages that inspire; portray the goodness, grace, and glory of God; unfold a story of salvation and redemption; and explicitly teach virtuous attitudes and behavior. But the scriptures are far more complex. The scriptural texts that have contributed to Catholic social teaching in centuries past remain vitally important resources. But operating from a limited canon-within-a-canon (e.g., the Sermon on the Mount, the great commandments, the decalogue) too easily allows us to see what suits us or to default to received interpretations that support the status quo.

New wine bursts old wineskins.[4] Activist Luverta Gilchrist and Rev. Dr. Fatimah Salleh emphasize the need to learn from scripture's "forgotten stories."[5] Some passages will turn a person's stomach, elicit anger or deep sorrow, and raise more questions than answers. And it is so with our world. All of the ugliest and most painful realities are contained in scripture, alongside the most beautiful and joyful. Justice requires that we attend to both. Our engagement with difficult and neglected texts will not provide easy answers but will advance the work of honest grappling with the most complex moral issues we face today. If we are to learn to see what we have failed to see in the past and imagine a just future we have not yet realized, we must engage with the whole scriptural canon.

As we expand our canonical awareness, there must be greater recognition of how distinctive genres function—literarily, socially, and even politically. Scripture's diverse genres range from story and prayer to proverb, dialogue, law, oracle, and apocalypse. They contribute distinctive types of resources and function in different ways. These genres interact with each other in a dynamic textual economy.

Literary context, composition, and framing offer further clues for interpretation. When attention is given to the immediate literary context, passages in Leviticus commonly interpreted as forbidding same-sex sexuality take on a different meaning—namely, prohibition of incest and protection of vulnerable members of the extended household. The covenant code in

Exodus is framed on one side by a story of slavery and liberation and on the other by detailed instructions for building the tabernacle. This framing positions Israel's future polity as an alternative to an exploitative social system and Israel's worship as the telos of just social praxis. The social teachings of Leviticus appear after instructions for the communal rite of atonement and precede instructions for agricultural festivals, yoking together accountability to God, human community, and the land.

Expanded focus on neglected texts, context, and genres can be supplemented by shifting attention from traditional protagonists to minor characters and those portrayed as "other."[6] In biblical narrative and in the history of interpretation, many characters are used as narrative props.[7] Their marginalization, minoritization, or "othering" can reflect cultural biases on the part of writers. Training ourselves as readers to attend to the ways classes of people are used, obscured, caricatured, or silenced in biblical texts can help to shape what and whom we attend to in the world we inhabit and help us interpret today for the welfare of all. Here we see the advantage of the cross-cultural perspective advocated in Agnes Brazal's chapter.

A justice hermeneutic must also resist looking for moral paragons in the pages of scripture. The stories in scripture rarely show us unambiguous models of virtue. Unlike the genre of saints' lives, which are offered to the faithful as exemplary models of moral virtue to imitate, scripture's protagonists are morally complicated. Moses becomes a murderer when he strikes a slave driver in anger at the oppression of his people. Elijah delivers the Lord's condemnation of Jezebel and Ahab for their abuses of power; he also slaughters 450 prophets of Baal. Solomon asks the Lord for a hearing heart and receives the gift of wisdom that allows him to administer justice for Israel; he also conscripts Israelites into forced labor to build his palace. Moments after declaring that a person is defiled by what comes out of their mouths, Jesus calls a foreign woman a dog. We may yet emulate these characters' virtues and acts of courage and justice, but we must see a portrait of a whole person in each of them. This includes the shaping and sometimes distorting force of social settings, systems, and structures; of cultural biases, prejudices, and histories of conflict; and of personal and social trauma, temptations to anger, fear, self-righteousness, greed, lust, or glory. These stories do not provide a template for just praxis so much as they invite deep reflection on the complexities of social systems and moral agency. They show us that the path of justice is not always clear. They give to us, the readers, an opportunity to acknowledge our complicity with systems of injustice, to consider factors that previously eluded our awareness, and to discern pitfalls and temptations to which we, too, are susceptible.

Beyond character analysis, a narrow focus on individual actions and responsibilities (e.g., in focusing on what the decalogue, Sermon on the Mount, or great commandments require a person to do and not do) has often implicitly exonerated corporations, governments, and other collective bodies, including the church. These collectives are not simply people multiplied or writ large; they are systems and, as such, require a different kind of analysis and re-thinking of accountability. Other types of systems and structures require a similarly expanded focus. A justice hermeneutic thus analyzes both ancient and present-day structures and tests what one may teach us about the other.

Finally, as a resource for Catholic social thought, scripture requires not simply appropriation but critical engagement. Catholic theology has often employed proof-texting, whether at the snippet level or in a manner more sensitive to literary context. But engagement with scripture as a resource for Catholic social thought must grapple with the character of scripture as divine word in human words, divine revelation mediated through human experience, perception, limitation, culture, creativity, and sinfulness. Interpreters must, therefore, recognize that the writers of scripture (highly educated and thus in some measure elite, typically male, often vested with significant power in political and/or religious domains) were shaped by such dynamics and structures as colonialism, nationalism, monarchy, and patriarchy; the personal and social effects of trauma; time-bound cultural norms pertaining to gender and sexuality, inheritance, and criminal justice; and the limited range of social locations and perspectives. These shaping factors mean that the witness of scripture will sometimes more fully represent the interests of those in power and perpetuate the subordination and oppression of vulnerable members of society. Several other chapters in this volume have stressed this same problem, from traditional African culture (Agbonkhianmeghe Orobator in chapter 1) to the contemporary critique of gender bias in modern Catholic social teaching (Agnes Brazal in chapter 8 and Lisa Cahill in chapter 7).

Recognizing the intermingling of these distorting characteristics with scripture's insistence on justice and its witness on behalf of the vulnerable, interpreters have adopted various strategies, ranging from reading scripture against itself to sifting timeless truths from time-bound cultural norms. These strategies are important, but we have a further opportunity: to see in this mixed scriptural testimony a mirror of our own sinfulness, a prompt for critical self-awareness and reflection that can facilitate our thinking theologically about the myriad ways our own commitments to justice are implicated in sinful systems.

DEMOCRACY AND TOTALITARIANISM

Catholic social thought today speaks into a world that is partly democratic, partly totalitarian. Biblical texts do not portray democracy. They describe covenantal theocracy adapted to diverse political structures. These include a loose and shifting federation of tribes governed by charismatic warlords and judges, independent monarchy, monarchy in fealty to an empire, satrapy, and colony within an empire. The closest analogs to modern democracy within biblical texts may be various bodies of elders functioning in judicial, executive, representative, and advisory capacities (e.g., Exod 3:16–18, 24:1; Ezra 5:4–17; Jer 29:1; Matt 26:57–59; Ruth 4:2–12; etc.). Yet such bodies of elders were typically male, may have been limited to landholders or other individuals of means, and may have typically excluded people not considered to be native Israelite or Judean. The designation "elders" also implies that membership was limited to older adults. This recognition of both the promise and limitations of ancient cultures is also identified in the description of the African palaver in chapter 1 by Agbonkhianmeghe Orobator.

These caveats notwithstanding, Exodus 18:13–27 and Numbers 11:16–25 provide one model of shared governance. In Exodus, Jethro criticizes Moses's attempt to be the sole judge of the people, arguing that Moses will wear out both himself and the people he is attempting to serve (18:18). Jethro outlines a more limited role for Moses and calls him to identify men of valor (and/or "of means," חיל), honesty, and integrity (18:21) who will share in judging and governing the people (v. 22). In a parallel passage, Moses complains about the burden of leadership, and God instructs him to assemble elders (Num 11:14–15). God then takes "some of the spirit" that is on Moses and puts it on the elders (11:25). They are to "share the burden" of leadership (11:17); they also prophesy (11:25). Both narratives emphasize the impossibility of one person acting as judge for an entire population. While the stories focus attention on the burden of leadership and decision-making, Exodus 18:18 also stresses the people's right to timely legal recourse.

Moses's dialogues with Jethro and God underscore the importance of revising existing models of governance to ensure equity, access, and justice. Jeremiah's temple sermon (Jer 7:1–15) challenges those who imagine that a primary institution that afforded certain social benefits in the past will continue to do so in the face of corruption and abuse. The reform that is needed is summarized by the command "do justice for real" (עשׂו תעשׂו משפט 7:5, AT). While the abuses are wide-ranging, special attention is given to the welfare of society's most vulnerable members: "Do not oppress the alien, the orphan, and the widow, or shed innocent blood in this place" (7:6 NRSV).

In the book of Acts, concern for the material needs of widows prompts a re-thinking of the roles and structures that provide social services within the community of early Jesus followers (Acts 6:16).

A scene from the book of Daniel leans in the direction of democracy. The book critiques imperial regimes, revealing as monstrous a series of kingdoms built on domination, displacement, and exploitation of conquered peoples (Dan 7:3–8).[8] Justice takes a seat beside God, and the end of these atrocious empires is decreed (Dan 7:10–12). In the scene that follows, one like a human being receives power and dominion (7:13). A ministering angel interprets the vision for Daniel, explaining that justice or judgment would be given for "the holy ones of the Most High" and the holy ones would "possess" the kingdom (7:22). He later adds that the kingdom and dominion (מלכותא ושלטנא) will be given to the "people of the holy ones of the Most High" (7:27).

The human form of this fifth kingdom contrasts sharply with the composite beasts that precede it, suggesting that where the four empires were rapacious and violent, the final kingdom is humane. Moreover, while the "holy ones" may or may not refer to angels, their "people" are a human collective. Giving the kingdom and dominion not to one ruler alone but to a body of people bears some resemblance to the democratic ideal of governance "by the people." Yet it would be wrong to assert that Daniel articulates a vision of a democratic society. The people of the holy ones are to receive dominion *over* other population groups, who will "serve [or worship] and obey" them (7:27). And the divine rule that grants this dominion is imagined by analogy with that of an emperor on a mobile throne, with the result that the vision of just governance in Daniel remains heavily inflected by the structures and culture of empire.

It has been common for later polities to identify themselves as the fifth kingdom of Daniel.[9] While that human kingdom exemplifies some features worth aspiring to, modern nations should resist self-congratulatory identification with an idealized polity that exceeds the boundaries of history. Daniel's visions of the rise and fall of nations and empires underscore the precarity of all forms of government, including democratic ones. A more appropriate engagement with Daniel's visions might focus on its critique of existing, exploitative systems of government and the deceptive rhetoric and symbols that prop them up. The book shines a revelatory spotlight on totalitarian regimes, urges diverse modes of nonviolent direct action, and helps its readers imagine, claim ownership of, and live into more just alternatives. Jesus's self-identification with the human one in Daniel 7 (e.g., Mark 13:26; 14:62) further shapes and challenges our understanding of such an alternative polity.

Two key Hebrew terms for "justice" are צְדָקָה (*ṣĕdaqă*) and צֶדֶק (*ṣedeq*). Among the texts where these terms appear most frequently, Proverbs emphasizes justice in human governance, praxis, and civic speech (Prov 8:15, 16; 12:17; 16:12–13; 25:5; 31:9). For this reason, Proverbs can be an important resource for re-thinking justice in a democratic society. It identifies wisdom as both source and precondition of justice generally and of just conduct, legislation, and judgment specifically (2:9; 8:15, 18; cf. 8:20). Accordingly, it accentuates the need for instruction in justice (1:3). This emphasis on needed instruction in virtue is, of course, also prominent in the virtue ethics tradition from Aristotle through Aquinas, as described in Jean Porter's chapter.

Justice has high intrinsic value (Prov 16:8) but also produces positive outcomes for nations (15:9) and individuals, including a smooth and safe path, reward, salvation from death, long life, and honor (10:2; 11:4–6, 18–19; 12:28; 13:6; 16:31; 21:21). God desires justice (21:3) and loves the person who pursues it (15:9). The emphasis on education, intrinsic value, desirable outcomes, honor/shame, and pleasing God underscores the importance of persuasion, perspective, and framing. Proverbs speaks from a standpoint of pragmatism and realism, cautioning against alternatives to justice that may be appealing in the short term because they are easier or more immediately profitable. Instead, it encourages its audience to adopt a broader and longer horizon for their decision-making. For Proverbs, justice is "long" work, whose gains will not always be immediately apparent. Teachers, advisers, and civic leaders have a duty to help others expand their horizons and choose the harder, longer path of justice.

The practitioners I spoke with found three key assets in scripture: a template for shared power and advocacy, assistance in focusing on the long view, and strength in the face of challenges. A touchstone for several of the activists I spoke with is Micah 6:8: "You have been told, O mortal, what is good, and what the LORD requires of you: Only to do justice [*mišpaṭ*] and to love goodness [*ḥesed*], and to walk humbly with your God" (NAB). Sarah Jobe, chaplain with the Interfaith Prison Ministry for Women, attends a Baptist church where this verse has a liturgical function within the altar call, shifting the focus of that call from "individual salvation to what the Lord requires."[10] For Salleh, the brevity of this saying is a key to its power. It demands that we "do the work."

The understanding of justice set forth in this verse is closely linked with ḥesed and humility. English translations of ḥesed vary greatly, each capturing some but not all of the texture of its meaning in Hebrew. Among translations are "covenant loyalty," "faithfulness," "steadfast love," "loving care," "loving-kindness," "kindness," and "mercy." Whatever the translation, ḥesed is relational, locating the work of justice within a framework of mutual care and responsibility. It also tempers the demands of justice with those of mercy. The pairing of justice and mercy can appear contradictory, but these very qualities are fundamental to God's character and actions (Hos 2:21; cf. Isa 30:18; Jer 9:24; Ps 33:5; 89:15).[11]

A closely parallel passage in Isaiah instructs people to "learn to do good. Make justice your aim: redress the wronged, hear the orphan's plea, defend the widow" (Isa 1:17 NAB; cf. Amos 5:14–15; Hos 12:7). The pairing of broad directives with advocacy for the injured and those bereft of providers and protectors reminds us that justice cannot be pursued in the abstract. It also draws attention to how systems purporting to enact justice often favor those with higher social status and power. For Angela MacDonald, system director for mission integration at Christus Health, and for Salleh, founder of A Certain Work, Jesus's instruction to care for "the least of these" is a vital corrective (Matt 20:40–45). For Sarah Jobe, "the least of these" are not only the recipients of justice but are agents called and empowered to enact change.[12]

Tiffney Marley, senior vice president for practice transformation for the National Community Action Partnership, finds a model of advocacy and shared power in 2 Kings 4. Marley explains that "maximum feasible participation," "local solution-making," "engagement," "shared governance and power," and "partnership" are foundational to Community Action's approach "to connecting all people to opportunity and building strong, resilient communities." Agbonkhianmeghe Orobator outlines similar commitments in chapter 1, describing the importance of Ubuntu in traditional African life.

In her analysis of 2 Kings 4, Marley focuses on the agency and power of the Shunammite woman who, bereaved of her child, saddles her donkey, rides to find the prophet, and grabs hold of his feet. She vows that she will not let go until he agrees to return with her to restore life to her child. Marley states: "In the moment of adversity and in the face of the greatest loss, she is mobilized to go to the prophet and advocate for herself. She speaks truth to power. She has full agency and shifts the narrative and the outcome."[13]

God requires God's people to *do* justice. It is not an easy charge. People in power often succumb to the temptation to betray justice in favor of self-interest. The universality of this insight is made clear in the chapters by George Kodithottam (on Hinduism and Buddhism) and Agbonkhianmeghe Orobator (on African traditions). Systems of domination that serve the interests of the powerful often convince others that sidelining justice is in their self-interest too, even though it is not. This means that those who remain committed to doing the work of justice will find themselves up against forces they cannot comprehend or control. They will subject themselves to gaslighting, ridicule, and petty meanness. They will sacrifice health without meaning to and put their lives at risk to advocate for the lives of others. They will need not only those scriptures that help us tease out what justice is but also the scriptures that tell us that the God of justice and mercy is with us. God is listening. People do not do this work alone. People who do justice face lies, danger, and complexity, and they need scriptures that help them hold fast to faith, courage, and clarity. They need scriptures that empower and sustain.

Two passages help ground MacDonald in the face of internal and external resistance to the work of justice. There are days, she says, when she feels "sad, unheard, shut out, frustrated." In these moments, she identifies with Jeremiah, who openly voiced "his frustrations and desires." Jeremiah acknowledges that God is just (צדיק ṣaddîq 12:2) but recognizes, too, the flourishing of the wicked and the resulting suffering of nonhuman creation (12:1–4). God's response to Jeremiah is a word of challenge: if you get tired of racing people on foot, how will you run with the horses? (12:5). God shifts the focus from small-scale, short-term responses to the bigger picture, helping MacDonald to recognize the true dimensions of the work that God has called her to and the ways that today's challenges prepare her for future ones.

Psalm 27 similarly turns directly to God in search of strength and clarity in the face of violence and deceit. When MacDonald wonders "what is the endgame?" or whether her justice work is really making a difference, this psalm emboldens her belief in a greater purpose and greater good: "I believe that I shall see the goodness of the LORD in the land of the living. Wait for the LORD; be strong, and let your heart take courage; wait for the LORD!" (27:13–14 NRSV). The command to hope reminds her that she is sowing seeds and won't always see the full bloom of change. She may have to move on before justice comes to fruition, but she will trust and keep going.[14]

Luverta Gilchrist, a formerly incarcerated person and activist with the North Carolina NAACP, Moral Monday Movement, and Second Chance Alliance, identifies a similar dynamic in her reliance on Psalm 119. The psalm's first-person voice creates a framework for her own conversation with God, allowing her to articulate her questions and frustrations and name the challenges she is confronting, while also asking for God's help. "How long are we gonna have to sustain all this pain and negativity and name calling? I didn't make a difference today so you gotta help me. I thought you were supposed to be there. I still trust you." This particular psalm does something more: it repeatedly affirms the primacy of God's law. This structuring feature of Psalm 119 makes it an especially powerful resource for those who work to reform legal, judicial, and carceral systems and enfranchise those deprived of their rights. Gilchrist paraphrased the way that Psalm 119 frames this work in relation to *God's* laws: "I obey your commands. You're God; I'm not. But I keep the faith. We keep on fighting."[15]

MacDonald's and Gilchrist's reliance on the psalms and Jeremiah highlights the ways scripture not only describes the character and work of justice but also facilitates it. Democracy today emphasizes shared responsibility in the face of polyphony, inaction, bias, or organized resistance to change. First-person prayer texts and dialogues with God help practitioners process difficult experiences and frame their day-to-day work within a larger agenda and in relation to a God whose power exceeds the human resistance and structural challenges they may face.

ECONOMY

The Re-thinking Justice project highlights certain characteristics of economic life today, including shifts from a predominantly agricultural society to a predominantly wage-based economy with heavy reliance on banks and financial markets, and urges attention to the just wage, the just price, a just interest rate, and economic inequality.

In the scriptures, workers join the familiar triad of widows, orphans, and resident aliens whose rights and welfare God is especially concerned to protect. (This is a commitment still important in twenty-first-century papal teaching, as made clear in chapter 7, by Lisa Cahill.) God promises judgment against employers who use intimidation or deceit to deprive workers of what is due to them (Mal 3:5).[16] A fair rate of pay for all hours worked is not the only concern, however. Wages should also be paid promptly, especially to those with financial need. To this end, employers should pay a worker at the end of the workday (Deut 24:14–15). In Leviticus, the command to pay wages on the day work is performed is paired with a command against fraud and robbing a neighbor, suggesting that withholding wages is a form of theft (Lev 19:13). These commands occur within a section of the holiness code that overlaps considerably with the decalogue, echoing and expanding key teachings while framing them as an imitation of divine holiness (19:1). Within this opening portion of the holiness code, 19:9–16 specifically focus on economic justice.[17] The parallel structure of 13a, focused on wage theft, and 13b, focused on fraud and robbery, highlights how the relation between employer and laborer is similar to the relationship of neighbors.

Both relations are sanctified by imitating God's holiness. Proverbs similarly deploys parallel structure to assert commonality between those to whom money is owed and neighbors who deserve honesty and prompt payment: "Do not withhold good from those to whom it is due, when it is in your power to do it. Do not say to your neighbor, 'Go, and come again, tomorrow I will give it'—when you have it with you" (Prov 3:27–28).

The rhythm of labor and rest is a crucial concern of the Torah. The Genesis creation story introduces sabbath—rest from labor—as foundational to the very structure of created time. Sabbath observance is stressed multiple times, in the decalogue (Deut 5:12–15; Exod 20:8–11), the holiness code (Lev 23:3, 26:2), and numerous other passages (e.g., Exod 23:12; 31:13–17; 34:21; 35:2; Isa 58:13–14; Neh 13:15–22). The two versions of the decalogue (in Deut 5 and Exod 20) offer different rationales for sabbath observance, one grounded in creation, the other in Israel's history as a people freed from slavery. Exodus enjoins human and nonhuman laborers alike to observe a rhythm of work and rest that mirrors God's own, implicitly asserting that creaturely labor participates in divine creative work (Exod 20:8–11). Deuteronomy, by contrast, motivates sabbath observance through cultural memory of slavery in Egypt and God's work of liberation (Deut 4:15). Jesus's statement that "the sabbath was made for humanity, not humanity for the sabbath" (Mark 2:27) emphasizes that sabbath observance is not an end in itself but should promote people's welfare and flourishing.

While the dual rationale for sabbath in Exodus and Deuteronomy links the ordering of life at creation to a social order that rejects slavery as a primary economic engine, it nonetheless fails to exclude all forms of slavery from its vision of a just economy.[18] Both decalogic articulations of the sabbath commandment list slaves among those who should rest on the sabbath day (Deut 5:14; Exod 20:10), yet neither enjoins their liberation. The failure of key biblical legislation to reject slavery outright draws attention to the persistence of slavery today, which can function as a hidden component of economic systems in "free" and democratic societies. Critical areas for attention today include increased human trafficking resulting from globalization, mass migration, mass incarceration, and the reliance by many corporations on underregulated overseas labor to increase profit margins.

Although no biblical text categorically condemns slavery, the jubilee legislation of Leviticus 25 expands the application of sabbath principles to the rejection of debt slavery among Israelites (25:39–40). The jubilee year amplifies (increasing scale from days to years), multiplies (seven times seven, plus one), and expands the scope (to include the land) of sabbath (Lev 25:2–12), culminating now in a proclamation of liberty (דרור *děrôr*) to all inhabitants of the land (25:10). (This is a view of liberty different from that in the modern liberal tradition described in Francis Fiorenza's chapter, but it stands as a religious precursor.) Yet while the jubilee legislation prohibits enslavement of Israelites, it continues to make provision for enslavement of foreigners and inheritance of human chattel (25:45–46). James Watts has argued that Leviticus 25:39–46 likely helped "naturalize and justify ... differential treatment of White indentured slaves and Black chattel slaves" in the modern era, contributing to "structural racism" that persists even where slavery has been officially abolished.[19] It is thus vital that in engaging with a passage such as Leviticus 25, Catholic social teaching not ignore this enduring legacy of harm but rather confront it directly.

Numerous passages from the Hebrew Scriptures are concerned with fair and consistent prices, commonly expressed concerning weights and measures (Amos 8:5; Ezek 45:10; Lev 19:36; Mic 6:10). Deuteronomy 25 prohibits variable weights and measures (vv. 13–14), identifying a correct, whole, or wholesome (שלמה) weight or measure as a "just" (צדק) one (v. 15) and declaring the practice of falsifying weights and measures an "abomination" (v. 16).[20] Amos lists dishonest measures and scales with debt slavery and sale of adulterated food products among economic abuses by which the wealthy oppress the poor (8:4–6), a precursor of the "preferential option for the poor," discussed in chapter 7, by Lisa Cahill, and in chapter 3, by Maria Inês de Castro Millen. Micah identifies the use of false weights and measures as a form of violence the Lord condemns (6:10–12).

David Pleins urges attention to the differing social contexts of the prophetic books and their resulting visions of social justice: Amos "exposed the pervasive decay of moral sensibilities throughout Israel that accompanied the economic prosperity experienced under Jeroboam II."[21] This included building programs, increased trade, and accelerated economic growth in urban centers that contributed to a widening wealth gap.[22] While Amos places this greater focus on urban centers, Micah "defend[s] the cause of the residents of the countryside, both villagers and farmers."[23] To this end, Micah is also concerned with practices of land seizure and fraudulent dishoming of residents. He recognized that women and children were particularly vulnerable in these situations (2:1–2, 9).[24] These practices were part of a shift from subsistence farming to "revenue-driven agriculture" for trade and tribute.[25] Analyzing differing social contexts for these superficially similar prophetic texts should guide engagement with their vision for just economic practices.

Another key area for economic justice is equitable access to resources and opportunity. Among these, food, shelter, clothing, and health care meet the basic needs of the body. Sarah Jobe urges an understanding of justice animated by "the fleshiness of . . . familiar words."[26] The Hebrew word *nephesh*, commonly translated as "soul" or "life," literally means "throat," underscoring embodiment as fundamental to what God's justice demands of us. The metonym "throat" invokes a range of basic needs: nourishment, water, warmth, clean air, and freedom to breathe.[27] A set of interrelated scriptures emphasizes justice for the whole, embodied person: Psalms 146:7–9; Isaiah 58:6–10; 61:1–3; James 2:15–16; Luke 4:18; 7:22; and Matt 25:31–46, among others. Breana van Velzen, executive director of Durham Congregations in Action, identifies Isaiah 58:6–10 as central to her understanding of justice. God chooses a fast of liberation that shatters every yoke, breaking bread with the hungry, opening homes to the homeless, and clothing the naked.[28] This vision of justice marries liberation with an imperative to meet basic needs in a way that strengthens bonds of community. Access to food is a crucial concern of numerous other biblical texts, including instructions for the tithe (Deut 14:28; 26:12), directions to share festival meals (Exod 12:4; Neh 8:10), provisions for gleaning (Deut 24:19–22; Lev 19:9–10; 23:22; Ruth 2), and stories of miraculous provision (Exod 16; John 6:1–14; 1 Kgs 17:2–16; 2 Kgs 4:1–7; Num 11:1–9; Mark 6:31–44 and parallels; Mark 8:1–9; Matt 15:32–39). Access to care is a frequent theme in healing accounts (e.g., 2 Kgs 4; Mark 5:25–34 and parallels). Stories such as the healings of Naaman the Syrian (2 Kgs 5; Luke 4:27) and the Syrophoenician woman's daughter (Mark 7:24–29) highlight the disparities in health care access and outcomes between members of different ethnic groups and social classes.

ECOLOGICAL JUSTICE

"Pour down from above, O heavens, and let the clouds rain justice [צֶדֶק]. Let the earth open so that they may bear fruit—salvation—and let [earth] cause justice [צְדָקָה] to spring up in unity. I the Lord have created this" (Isa 45:8 AT). In this stunning apostrophe, God's unique character (45:5–6) becomes known in the ordering of creation toward justice. Though clearly different from the Hindu view of the order of the cosmos described in George Kodithottam's chapter, one nonetheless hears an echo of a similar commitment to ecological responsibility grounded in an objective order. Heavens, waters, earth, and vegetation are active participants in a responsive, organic, and creative network of justice that extends far beyond human knowing or purview (45:9–11). The fruit of justice takes concrete form in the lives of God's people, extending beyond the natural world into the workings of history, leading to urban redevelopment, liberation, and repatriation for captives and refugees (45:13). This passage exemplifies biblical portrayals of nonhuman creation as part of divine justice and partners of it. Nonhuman creation has agency, worshiping, prophesying, witnessing, and crying out for redress.[29] This insight is particularly important in a time when global capitalism, consumer culture, and population growth, among other factors, have stripped natural resources, destroyed habitats, poisoned waterways, and driven species to extinction.[30] The present climate crisis has antecedents in biblical narrative. Other biblical texts can help chart a path to healing and accountability that recognizes creation as an active partner in the work of justice.

God sees that creation is "good" (Gen 1:4, 10, 12, 18, 21, 25), not because it is good for humans but good in itself, before humans exist.[31] Nonhuman creatures are not simply "for" humans, as indicated in God's determination that they are not "help corresponding to" the human (Gen 2:20). This realization emerges from a process of naming (2:19) akin to divine speaking and of seeing that acknowledges the intrinsic goodness of each nonhuman animal, not contingent on whether they satisfy the needs and desires of human beings. Similarly, the dominion that God grants to human beings (Gen 1:28) is not license to exploit but custodianship.[32] (Here we can recognize a distinction between what centuries later Thomas Aquinas identified as just and unjust dominion, as Jean Porter's chapter explains.) Psalm 72, a prayer for justice, provides a crucial intertext for this commission. The psalmist asks God to equip the ruler with justice and righteousness. Just dominion (72:8) is portrayed as custodial, championing the welfare of the afflicted and the needy and redeeming from oppression (Ps 72:4, 12–14; cf. Lev 25:43, 53). The psalmist names mountains and hills as collaborators, as agents of prosperity and righteousness (Ps 72:3). The custodial commission of Genesis 1:28 regards creation not as instrument but agent. The Earth Bible Team thus proposes a "principle of mutual custodianship" characterized by partnership rather than hierarchy.[33] Similarly, the charge to the first human to "serve and guard" God's garden (Gen 2:15) enjoins that agricultural practices preserve and promote the land's integrity.

Narrative, legal, prophetic, and hymnic texts in the Old Testament emphasize the relationship between justice among humans and the welfare of the rest of creation. The flood narrative portrays destructive consequences for nonhuman creation arising from human violence and sin (Gen 6:5–7, 12–13, 17; 7:4; 7:17–24; 8:21). God commissions the surviving human beings to ensure the continued existence and flourishing of nonhuman animal species

(6:19–21; 7:2–3; 8:17). God also establishes a covenant with the earth (9:13) and all its creatures (9:10, 16–17).

Through Noah, humans are given a role in helping to maintain God's covenantal obligation to the earth. This first biblical covenant story helps to situate human relationship with God within a wider set of relationships. Humans are not alone in covenant relation with God. God entrusts them to promote the welfare of all God's covenant partners.

Various other scriptures recognize that human sin pollutes the land or brings guilt upon it (Deut 24:4; Ezek 36:18; Jer 2:7; Lev 18:25, 28; Num 35:34).[34] The land itself exercises agency by expelling the people who defile it, vomiting them out like food that poisons the body (Lev 18:25, 28). The plague narratives similarly reveal consequences of human sin for the rest of creation, focusing more pointedly on systems of oppression (Exod 7–12). The pharaoh has enslaved a vulnerable population of climate refugees who came to Egypt in search of food. The forced labor of the Israelites created the physical structures for hoarding grain in time of famine and produced prosperity for Egyptian elites. God demands that the pharaoh "let my people go" (5:1, 7:16, 8:1, 20; 9:1, 13; 10:3), but the pharaoh refuses. God responds to pharaoh's refusal with a series of plagues. Psalms 78 and 105 locate the memory of this event within the worship life of the people, rehearsing a litany of devastation that included pollution of waterways (78:44; 105:29); lack of potable water (78:44); ecological imbalance (78:45–46; 105:30–31, 34); crop failure (78:46; 105:33, 35); extreme weather (78:48; 105:32); pandemic (78:50); and death of fish (105:29), livestock (78:48), and human children (78:51).[35] While God is identified as the "efficient cause" of these consequences, they are the explicit consequence of pharaoh's refusal to liberate those he has enslaved.

The Sinai covenant establishes an alternative polity oriented toward justice that includes nonhuman creation. Domesticated animals are to have rest from their labor (Exod 23:12). The same sabbath principle provides fallow time for fields, orchards, and vineyards every seventh year (Exod 23:11; Lev 25:2–7, 34, 43). During that time, the earth continues to sustain life: the poor are to eat freely of the fruits that the earth produces in sabbath years; wild animals have a right to the food the poor do not require (Exod 23:11). This sabbath for the land and earth's provision for the needy punctuate a cyclical calendar whose goal is liberation and restoration (Lev 25). Restoration of land to families who invest in and care for it is not only a matter of economic justice; it promotes mutual custody and care between people and land.[36]

The earth also exercises prophetic agency in service of justice. Following Cain's murder of his brother, Abel, the earth "takes" the blood of Abel from the hand of his brother, exposing Cain's crime and participating in divine justice by withholding "strength" (vegetation) from him (Gen 4:10–12).[37] In Amos, "the cosmos works along with YHWH to expose those who are attempting to flee [divine] judgement" (Amos 9:2–3).[38] Earth speaks prophetically for God and helps "to execute YHWH's judgement," fulfilling divine decrees of destruction and restoration alike.[39] Isaiah summons earth and heavens to witness God's complaint against Israel (1:2), while heavens, depths, mountains, and trees testify to Israel's redemption from captivity (44:23). Such passages show that nonhuman creation is an active stakeholder and participant in the work of justice.

MacDonald highlights environmental racism as a critical justice concern.[40] This includes access to clean water, a topic that has received increasing attention in the twenty-first century.[41] Two passages portray the healing of water as a prophetic act: Exodus 15:22–26 and 2 Kings 2:19–22. When Israelite refugees from Egypt are unable to access potable water (Exod 15:22–23), Moses intercedes for them, and God instructs the prophet on how to make the water sweet (15:25). God's subsequent speech requires adherence to God's laws and statutes, identifies God as healer, and makes freedom from disease contingent on following God's teachings. This speech is only the second time in scripture and the first time in Exodus that divine commandments are mentioned (15:26; the first instance is Gen 26:25). In this instance, it anticipates the giving of the law at Sinai. Implicit in the pairing of this speech with the story of the bitter and sweet water is the recognition that clean water is necessary for public health, and both are contingent on a polity oriented toward justice. Like the Israelites, displaced populations today and communities that have experienced systemic racism are especially vulnerable in this regard.

In 2 Kings, the people of Jericho make known that their city's water is bad. As a result, the land miscarries and causes miscarriage and childlessness (מְשַׁכָּלֶת *mĕshakkālet* 2 Kgs 2:19). The piel participle מְשַׁכֶּלֶת (*mĕshakkālet*) holds a dual meaning that recognizes the interrelationship of the health of the land and the health of the people; it also highlights the vulnerability of children and the lingering effects of loss. Elisha performs a rite that heals the water, attributing this act of healing to the Lord and declaring that the water will no longer cause death or childlessness (2:21). Elisha's healing of the water occurs within a series of prophetic interventions that include providing food and locating a tool needed to build houses and produce heat. While Elisha also interacts with political leaders, these direct prophetic actions address the daily needs of the people, including water. Ezekiel 47 similarly recognizes the importance of clean water for all forms of life and names water as a source of healing (47:9, 12). Revelation develops this vision further, promising that the water of life will sustain fresh produce every month (Rev 22:2). Isaiah 35 recognizes the need for extraordinary interventions to provide water for displaced peoples and those in arid regions.

CONCLUSION

A hermeneutic of justice commits to mutual accountability, self-criticism, and sharing of interpretive power and authority. It shifts focus from classical protagonists to marginalized characters and expands attention from individual action to broader systems and structures, ancient and modern. It does not shy away from difficult texts but engages with the whole of the scriptural canon; it does not proof-text but attends to literary and sociohistorical context, genre, and history of interpretation. As part of a ground-up approach to re-thinking justice in Catholic social teaching, I have included throughout the essay the interpretive perspectives of interlocutors who are today doing the work of justice "on the ground." I also focused on three topics crucial for re-thinking justice in the twenty-first century: democracy, economy, and ecological justice.

First, while the scriptures do not portray democracy as we know it today, they provide models of shared governance and social and political reform while critiquing totalitarian regimes and underscoring the precarity of human polities. An analysis of justice in Proverbs highlights its relation to wisdom and education, portraying justice as long, incremental work. Interlocutors engaged in this long work found inspiration, strength, assurance, and clarity in passages ranging from 2 Kings 4 to Psalm 119.

Second, the need to re-think justice today—at a moment Pope Francis has called a "change of era"[42]—is partly spurred by changing economic realities such as a wage economy. In addition to scriptural perspectives on just wages and prices, teachings regarding the Sabbath speak directly to the rights of workers, delineating a rhythm of labor and rest that participates in the rhythm of God's own creative activity and refreshment. Yet engagement with these texts also highlights scripture's failure to condemn slavery. A hermeneutic of justice must confront scripture's enduring legacies of harm on this issue and others.

Third, the scriptures extend the scope of justice and covenant relationship to include nonhuman creation, which is portrayed as agent and partner in the work of justice. God entrusts humans to promote the welfare of the earth and its creatures; human sin, by contrast, pollutes the land and brings guilt and destruction upon it. Teachings regarding sabbath for the land and jubilee promote liberation, restoration, and mutual custody and care between people and land. The accessibility of life-giving water within Ezekiel's and Revelation's visions of renewal similarly presents not merely a hope for the future but a mandate for the present.

These three topics do not exhaust scripture's insights for re-thinking justice in Catholic social thought, as it offers a treasury of resources that can help to reframe, deepen, and sharpen our thinking while simultaneously shaping faithful praxis. Equally vital are the questions concerning who interprets for justice and how. A hermeneutic of justice that commits to conversation with diverse practitioners can help to ensure that Catholic social thought addresses the full range of contexts and issues facing the church and world today.

BIBLIOGRAPHY

Bauckham, Richard. "Dominion Interpreted—A Historical Account." In *Living with Other Creatures: Green Exegesis and Theology*, edited by Richard Bauckham, 14–62. Baylor University Press, 2011.

Bauckham, Richard. "Human Authority in Creation." In *God and the Crisis of Freedom: Biblical and Contemporary Perspectives*, edited by Richard Bauckham, 128–77. Westminster John Knox Press, 2002.

Collins, John J. *What Are Biblical Values? What the Bible Says on Key Ethical Issues.* Yale University Press, 2019.

Coomber, Matthew. "Women and Land Seizure in Micah." In *Micah*, by Julia O'Brien, 25–26. Wisdom Commentary 37. Liturgical Press, 2015.

The Earth Bible Team. "Guiding Ecojustice Principles." In *Readings from the Perspective of Earth*. Vol. 1 of *The Earth Bible*, edited by Norman C. Habel, 38–53. Sheffield Academic Press, 2000.

The Earth Bible Team. "The Voice of Earth: More than Metaphor?" In *The Earth Story in the Psalms and the Prophets*. Vol. 4 of *The Earth Bible*, edited by Norman C. Habel, 23–28. Sheffield Academic Press, 2001.

Francis. "Pastoral Visit of His Holiness Pope Francis to Prato and Florence," on the occasion of the Fifth National Convention of the Italian Catholic Church, November 10, 2015. https://www.vatican.va/content/francesco/en/travels/2015/inside/documents/papa -francesco-prato-firenze_2015.html.

Gomez y Paloma, Sergio, Laura Riesgo, and Kamel Louhichi, eds. *The Role of Smallholder Farms in Food and Nutrition Security.* Springer, 2020.

Hamilton, Clive, Christophe Bonneuil, and François Gemenne, eds. *The Anthropocene and the Global Environmental Crisis: Rethinking Modernity in a New Epoch.* Routledge, 2015.

Harrison, Peter. "Having Dominion: Genesis and the Mastery of Nature." In *Environmental Stewardship: Critical Perspectives—Past and Present*, edited by R. J. Berry, 17–31. T&T Clark, 2006.

Hens-Piazza, Gina. *The Supporting Cast of the Bible: Reading on Behalf of the Multitude*. Lexington/Fortress Academic, 2020.

Hill, Andrew. *Malachi: A New Translation with Introduction and Commentary*. The Anchor Bible 25D. Doubleday, 1998.

Joerstad, Mari. *The Hebrew Bible and Environmental Ethics: Humans, Nonhumans, and the Living Landscape*. Cambridge University Press, 2019.

Kamionkowski, Tamar. *Leviticus*. Wisdom Commentary 3. Liturgical Press, 2018.

King, J. Christopher. *Origen on the Song of Songs as the Spirit of Scripture: The Bridegroom's Perfect Marriage-Song*. Oxford University Press, 2005.

Kletter, Raz. "Vessels and Measures: The Biblical Liquid Capacity System." *Israel Exploration Journal* 64, no. 1 (2014): 22–37. https://www.jstor.org/stable/44473980.

Lyons, Michael A. "The Book of Ezekiel: A Help or a Hindrance for Environmental Ethics?" *Horizons in Biblical Theology* 43, no. 1 (2021): 1–22. https://doi.org/10.1163/18712207-12341420.

Marlow, Hilary. "The Other Prophet! The Voice of Earth in the Book of Amos." In *Exploring Ecological Hermeneutics*, edited by Norman C. Habel and Peter Trudinger, 75–84. Society of Biblical Literature, 2008.

Meyer, Esias Engelbertus. "The Jubilee in Leviticus 25: A Theological and Ethical Interpretation from a South African Perspective." PhD diss., University of Stellenbosch, 2004.

Mitchell, David T., and Sharon L. Snyder. *Narrative Prosthesis: Disability and the Dependencies of Discourse*. University of Michigan Press, 2000.

Newsom, Carol, with Brennan Breed. *Daniel*. Old Testament Library. Westminster John Knox Press, 2014.

O'Brien, Julia. *Micah*. Wisdom Commentary 37. Liturgical Press, 2015.

Parker, Julie Faith. *Valuable and Vulnerable: Children in the Hebrew Bible, Especially the Elisha Cycle*. Brown University, 2013.

Pleins, David. *Social Visions of the Hebrew Bible: A Theological Introduction*. Westminster John Knox Press, 2001.

Portier-Young, Anathea. *Apocalypse against Empire: Theologies of Resistance in Early Judaism*. Grand Rapids, MI: Eerdmans, 2011.

Portier-Young, Anathea. "'Bless the Lord, Fire and Heat': Reclaiming Daniel's Cosmic Liturgy for Contemporary Eco-Justice." In *Full of Your Glory: Liturgy, Cosmos, Creation. Papers from the 5th Yale ISM Liturgy Conference, June 18–21, 2018*, edited by Teresa Berger, 45–67. Liturgical Press Academic, 2019.

Portier-Young, Anathea E., and Gregory E. Sterling, eds. *Scripture and Social Justice: Catholic and Ecumenical Essays*. Lexington Books/Fortress Academic, 2018.

Towner, Sibley. "Were the English Puritans 'The Saints of the Most High'? Issues in the 'Pre-Critical' Interpretation of Daniel 7." *Interpretation* 37, no. 1 (1983): 46–63. https://search.ebscohost.com/login.aspx?direct=true&AuthType=ip,sso&db=lsdar&AN=ATLA0000921572&site=ehost-live&scope=site&custid=s8996485.

Toynbee, Arnold. "The Religious Background of the Present Environmental Crisis." *International Journal of Environmental Studies* 3, no. 1–4 (1972): 141–46. https://doi.org/10.1080/00207237208709505.

Watts, James W. "The Historical Role of Leviticus 25 in Naturalizing Anti-Black Racism." *Religions* 12, no. 8 (2021): 1–10. https://doi.org/10.3390/rel12080570.

White, Lynn, Jr. "The Historical Roots of Our Ecologic Crisis." *Science* 155, no. 3767 (1967): 1203–07. https://www.jstor.org/stable/1720120.

Zenner, Christiana. *Just Water: Theology, Ethics, and Global Water Crises*. Rev. ed. Orbis, 2018.

NOTES

1. Breana van Velzen urges representation of perspectives across a range of "education levels, life experiences, race, geography, culture, and class." "Justice," she insists, "wells up from the ground." Re-thinking justice thus requires we "listen to people on the ground. Get to know the communities that need the most justice and deeply listen." This deep listening includes ecumenical and interfaith dialogue, openness to theology "from the street," and learning through relationship that is not "patronizing or charitable" but fully collaborative. Interview by the author, August 24, 2020.
2. Tiffney Marley, interview by the author, August 15, 2020.
3. For discussion, see King, *Origen on the Song of Songs*, 149–60.
4. Luverta Gilchrist proposes Mark 2:21–22 as a guideline for interpretation. Interview by the author, August 25, 2020.
5. Gilchrist, interview; Fatimah Salleh, interview by the author, August 24, 2020.
6. See Hens-Piazza, *Supporting Cast*, and Parker, *Valuable and Vulnerable*.
7. Mitchell and Snyder, *Narrative Prosthesis*.
8. For more detailed treatment, see Portier-Young, *Apocalypse against Empire*.
9. Towner, "Were the English Puritans 'The Saints of the Most High'?" Newsom with Breed, *Daniel*, 243–45. Breed writes, "This radical political trajectory culminates in the nationalism of the modern era, captured well in Presbyterian millenarian David Austin's 1794 discussion of the United States' role in dethroning European powers and instilling universal peace . . ." (*Daniel*, 245).
10. Sarah Jobe, interview by the author, October 22, 2020.
11. Salleh, interview.
12. Salleh, interview; Angela MacDonald, interview by the author, January 15, 2021; Jobe, interview.
13. Marley, interview.
14. MacDonald, interview.
15. Gilchrist, interview.
16. For discussion of the Hebrew text and its possible range of interpretations, see Hill, *Malachi*, 282.
17. See the treatment in Kamionkowski, *Leviticus*, 203–9.
18. For an overview of biblical attitudes toward slavery and later interpretations for and against slavery, see Collins, *What Are Biblical Values?* 126–46.
19. Watts, "Historical Role of Leviticus 25," 1, 10. See also Meyer, "Jubilee in Leviticus 25."
20. On the topic of the complete measure, see Kletter, "Vessels and Measures," 26–27.
21. Pleins, *Social Visions*, 368.
22. Pleins, 369.
23. Pleins, 390.
24. Note, however, Julia O'Brien's caveat that the prophet may have included an appeal to the fate of women and children as a rhetorical strategy to fan outrage in the audience. "The appearance of a concern for the oppressed can often mask the details of what

causes oppression. Not discussed in this chapter of Micah are the social conditions of women and children that make them a ready symbol for 'the weak,' the land rights of women, or the effects on women of the confiscation of family land" (O'Brien, *Micah*, 23–24).

25. Coomber, "Women and Land Seizure," 25–26.
26. Jobe, interview.
27. Jobe connects the fully embodied anthropology implicit in the usage of the Hebrew term *nephesh* to the Black Lives Matter movement through Eric Garner's repeated statement at the time of his murder in 2014, "I can't breathe."
28. Van Velzen, interview.
29. Joerstad, *Hebrew Bible and Environmental Ethics*; See also The Earth Bible Team, "The Voice of Earth," 23–8.
30. See Hamilton, Bonneuil, and Gemenne, eds., *Anthropocene and the Global Environmental Crisis*.
31. This corresponds with the first of the Guiding Ecojustice Principles of the Earth Bible, "The Principle of Intrinsic Worth." See The Earth Bible Team, "Guiding Ecojustice Principles," 42–4.
32. For a discussion of the ways interpretation of this passage has contributed to or authorized ecological destruction, see Bauckham, "Dominion Interpreted"; Bauckham, "Human Authority in Creation"; Harrison, "Having Dominion"; Toynbee, "Religious Background"; and White, "Historical Roots."
33. Earth Bible Team, "Guiding Ecojustice Principles," 50.
34. Lyons, "Book of Ezekiel," argues that Ezekiel offers a resource for environmental ethics only when read alongside a broader range of biblical texts.
35. The cosmic liturgy of Daniel 3 recognizes the participation of all creation in a worship that is oriented toward justice and resistant to imperial liturgies that celebrate systems of exploitation and domination. See Portier-Young, "'Bless the Lord, Fire and Heat.'"
36. For ways smallholder farming contributes to economic welfare more broadly, see Gomez y Paloma, Riesgo, and Louhichi, *Role of Smallholder Farms*.
37. Joerstad, *Hebrew Bible and Environmental Ethics*, 58–65.
38. Marlow, "The Other Prophet!" 75–83.
39. Marlow, 83.
40. MacDonald, interview.
41. On water, see Zenner, *Just Water*. Zenner discusses water in Catholic social teaching and in the work of organizations like Catholic Relief Services, the National Catholic Rural Life Conference, and the Catholic Agency for Overseas Development and distills eight insights about fresh water from the Catholic tradition.
42. Francis, "Pastoral Visit."

CHAPTER 5

Thomas Aquinas's Theory of Justice

Jean Porter

Any effort to re-think justice in Catholic social thought must contend with Thomas Aquinas's theory of justice, as it is the primary intellectual influence on official Catholic teaching on justice today. As other chapters in this volume make clear, several limiting characteristics of medieval thinking—for example, silence concerning human rights and social structures—characterize Aquinas's account as well. Nonetheless, in spite of the nine centuries that separate our world from his, his account is open to such ideas and provides principles that can guide re-thinking that account today.

According to Aquinas, justice is a virtue, one of the four cardinal virtues (along with prudence, fortitude, and temperance). It is the only cardinal virtue directly concerned with the individual's relationships with others and the community at large. Aquinas's approach to justice as a personal quality rather than a feature of institutions or social systems poses a challenge for anyone attempting to draw on his thought as a resource for thinking about justice today. As Francis Schlüsser Fiorenza explains in the case of John Rawls in his chapter in this volume, for many of our contemporaries, justice is a quality of institutions or social structures because of which they preserve and promote a certain standard of fairness, respect, and equality.[1] This way of looking at justice reflects critically important insights into the causal effects of structures and the moral significance of material equality that contemporary Catholic reflections on justice cannot afford to set aside. And we must admit that Aquinas, together with his interlocutors, has little to offer directly on justice seen as a quality of social structures or institutions.

At the same time, social structures and legal norms alone are insufficient to bring about a just society or just relations among individuals. Institutional norms are put into place, enacted, and carried out by individuals. For a community to sustain its commitments to equality and care for the most vulnerable, its members and especially its leaders must be personally committed to the ideals that these norms embody. Aquinas's detailed account of justice offers one way of spelling out the ideals and the overall orientation that characterize the just individual. While his account may strike us as dated in some ways, his critics today may be surprised to know that for Aquinas, the just individual is committed to ideals of equality, political freedom, and respect for the claims of others.

Furthermore, justice, like every other virtue, is defined by reference to its object, in this case, the *jus*, or the right. Here we find a critical point of contact between Aquinas's conception of justice and our own. Aquinas, following Aristotle, identifies the right with an ideal of equality of exchange, but he goes beyond Aristotle to affirm the equality of all persons.[2] He spells out the meaning of equality by reference to the touchstones of free status, political rule, and common participation in a shared human nature. Although controversial, I would also claim that at specific points he interprets the notion of right as a basis for a subjective claim, resonating with later theories of natural or human rights.

To investigate these themes, this chapter will begin with an overview of Aquinas's theory of justice in the *Summa theologiae* and will then address the relation between general justice and the common good. It will examine how Aquinas's treatment of the actions of individuals in the face of injustice anticipates features of later theories about human rights possessed by all individuals. Last, the chapter will clarify some implications of these features of Thomistic thought for re-thinking justice today.

AQUINAS'S ACCOUNT OF JUSTICE: AN OVERVIEW

Aquinas begins his account of justice by examining the proper object of justice (*Summa theologiae,* II–II 57.1). Together with most other scholastic theologians of the time, he accepts Justinian's definition of justice as "a constant and perpetual will rendering to each that which is his right" (II–II 58.1), a definition still useful in the twenty-first century, as Lisa Cahill's chapter in this volume indicates. Aquinas correlatively identifies the object of justice as the *jus*, the right (II–II 57.2). Yet, in contrast to his immediate predecessors, he does not identify the right with the claims and duties arising between unequals, for example, between parent and child, or servant and master. On the contrary, justice is paradigmatically exercised through equal exchanges, in accordance with a norm of equality determined by some relevant criterion. That is, someone renders to another that which is their right through an exchange that preserves some kind of equality between them (II–II 57.1).

Of course, a norm of equal exchange in itself does not imply equality of persons. However, Aquinas elsewhere says that justice pertains to exchanges between equals, and since the obligations of justice are comprehensive in scope, it would seem that justice presupposes that human persons are in some way equal (I–II 114.1). In fact, Aquinas says that human persons are naturally equal, in such a way as to rule out any kind of natural dominion of one person or class of persons over another, in contrast to the angels: "The demons are not equal with respect to nature, and so there is among them a natural precedence. This is not the case among human beings, who by nature are equal (I 109.2, A.D. 3).

Aquinas begins his account of the virtue of justice proper with a defense of Justinian's definition, reformulated in formal terms: "Justice is a habit in accordance with which someone, through a constant and perpetual will, renders his right to each one" (II–II 58.1). Here is a fundamental difference between justice and the other cardinal virtues. Because the right implies a relation between two agents, justice is always directed toward another. It takes shape and operates in and through the agent's external actions (in contrast to purely internal acts of will or passions [II-II 58.2]). As such, it is a distinct virtue, and its subject is the will (II–II 58.4).

Aquinas distinguishes general (or legal) justice from particular justice, which itself has two distinct forms: distributive and commutative justice (II–II 61.1). General or legal justice, which is oriented toward the common good, is in a sense a general virtue insofar as it directs the operations of the other virtues toward its own proper end, the common good (II–II 58.5, 6). Nonetheless, general justice is a specific virtue with a delimited object and cannot be identified with virtuousness in a generic sense (II–II 58.6).

Particular justice orients the agent rightly toward other individuals, and it is still more clearly a discrete virtue with a specific field of operation (II–II 58.7,8). Distributive justice presupposes a communal context since it pertains to the fair allocation of honors, rewards, shared benefits, punishments, burdens, and the like. Nonetheless, it pertains directly to relations between individuals, namely, between those in charge of distribution and its recipients. Thus, it is a species of particular rather than general justice (II–II 61.1 A.D. 4). Aquinas does not focus on any one paradigmatic act of distributive justice. Still, he does devote considerable attention to the characteristic sin against it, namely, "respect for persons," defined as the conferral of some benefit or burden for the wrong reason, that is, not related to the purpose of the benefit or burden being distributed (II–II 63).

Commutative justice pertains to individuals' relations to one another as individuals and not as representatives or members of a community. It is paradigmatically identified with buying and selling, but Aquinas extends it to include every kind of interaction between individuals through an expansive interpretation of exchange. He identifies restitution as the paradigmatic act of commutative justice, understanding restitution to include both the return of what has been voluntarily handed over and compensation for unjust appropriations of all kinds (II–II 62).

Aquinas's treatment of the sins against commutative justice is especially significant from our standpoint today because it represents his clearest and most developed account of the normative implications of equality among persons as he understands it. These sins include every kind of exchange between individuals involving the infliction of unjustified harm or loss (II–II 64 introduction), whether brought about through harmful acts, damaging speech, or unfairness in voluntary transactions. In some instances, it would seem to be stretching a point to describe these kinds of actions as "transactions"; while the victim obviously suffers a kind of loss through such actions, it is not always clear that the perpetrator gains at the victim's expense. Nonetheless, Aquinas builds on the idea of unfair exchange in such a way as to tie central norms of non-maleficence to an expansive ideal of equality.

This point is made explicit in the context of a discussion of verbal offenses committed, including invective, detraction, and the like. He begins with the observation that these sins all imply a kind of disrespect. He then goes on to compare this disrespect embodied in words with that shown by actions directed against the person, the associates, or the possessions of another. The critical point is that in each case, Aquinas associates this disrespect with dishonor: "Contumely implies dishonor to someone. This can happen in two ways. For since honor follows from some excellence, someone can dishonor another by depriving him of an excellence on account of which he had honor. This comes about through sins of deeds, which we treated above. In another way, when someone brings that which is contrary to the honor of another to his attention and that of others. And this properly pertains to contumely" (II–II 72.1). To appreciate the full significance of these remarks, we need to keep in mind that the sins of deeds to which Aquinas refers include assaults on the person, the associates, or the property of another, for example, murder, adultery, or theft (II–II 64–71). These kinds of actions are strictly prohibited, no matter the status or circumstances of the intended victim. Thus, when Aquinas characterizes these as deprivations of excellence, what he has in mind can only be some natural excellence, on account of which every man and woman should be honored. In this way, Aquinas draws on the language of personal fealty and differential status to articulate a very different set of ideals, according to which human individuals relate as equals on the shared ground of mutual respect.

After his treatment of the kinds of justice, Aquinas considers the integral parts of justice, those qualities or actions jointly necessary to the full expression of the virtue (II–II 79.1). These he identifies as "to do good and avoid evil." This presents us with a puzzle because it is nothing other than the first principle of practical reason, which serves as the fundamental principle for all virtue (I–II 94.2, I–II 58.4, II–II 47.6). Yet, as Aquinas has already established, general and particular justice are both specific virtues, implying an orientation toward delimited kinds of goods and aversion to definite kinds of evils. That is exactly what "do good and avoid evil" implies in this context. After noting that this principle, generally understood, applies to all virtue, he explains that it is qualified with respect to justice. Particular justice aims at the good, formally understood as that which is due to another, and avoids evil, understood as injury to another. In contrast, general justice aims at the obligatory good in relation to the common good and avoids the contrary (II–II 79.1). Thus, Aquinas regards the integral parts of justice as a specification of the first principle of practical reason—more limited in scope and yet similarly foundational to the processes of practical reason, operating within the sphere of right relations.

GENERAL JUSTICE AND THE COMMON GOOD

In contrast to particular justice, which aims at the good of the individual, the object of general justice is the common good (II–II 58.5,6). For this reason, it is distinctively a virtue of lawgivers and rulers, although private individuals also possess general justice, expressed through their respect for just laws (II–II 58.6). What is more, political authority for Aquinas is legitimate only insofar as it is oriented toward the common good. A ruler who acts contrary to the virtue of general justice is not thereby illegitimate. Still, he is to be regarded as a tyrant rather than a just ruler (II–II 42.2 A.D. 3).

Aquinas's strong views on general justice and legitimacy are grounded in a distinction, taken from Aristotle, between just political dominion and unjust dominion (that correlates with servitude). In the first part of the

Summa theologiae, Aquinas asks whether authority and subordination would have existed in Paradise if our first parents had never sinned. He addresses this question by distinguishing two kinds of dominion. Understood in the first sense, dominion is exercised for the sake of the one holding power over another. This is servile dominion, and it would not have existed in Paradise. But there is another kind of dominion, grounded in human nature as such, that respects the free status of its subject: "Someone exercises dominion over another as a free person, when he directs him to the proper good of the one being directed, or to the common good. And such dominion of a human person would have existed in a state of innocence" (I 96.4). A similar distinction concerning a responsible dominion of humans in the natural world is apparent in Anathea Portier-Young's articulation of Hebraic ecological commitments in her chapter.

Understood in this way, the common good is contrasted with the ruler's private good or with the good of any one individual or faction. For this reason, the common good provides a rationale for a political authority that preserves the free status, and by implication the equality of status, of its subjects. Political authority does not compromise the free status of its subjects because it does not place one individual at the service of the private interests of another. Men and women are subject to political rule and legal authority for the sake of a greater good, for which they are jointly responsible and from which they all benefit (II–II 47.10). But a ruler or political official can take certain actions on behalf of the common good, including the use of coercive or punitive force, which are closed to private citizens (see, for example, II–II 64.2,3; 65.1). This ancient distinction is also clear in George Kodithottam's chapter on the Hindu view of justice. A ruler can employ force because they act as a minister of the state and not as a private person inflicting harm on another, in violation of the fundamental norms of commutative justice. This line of analysis implies that the common good is understood and pursued in such a way as to preserve the free status and fundamental equality of each member of the community.

Nonetheless, Aquinas recognizes that equity and respect for innocence stand as limits against unjust appeals to the common good. In his discussion of the validity of human law, he observes that an enactment that imposes burdens inequitably is not a just and valid law, even it if otherwise promotes the common good (I–II 96.5). Even more importantly, considerations of common good do not justify harming those who are innocent of any wrongdoing because "the life of the just conserves and promotes the common good, since they themselves are the most significant part of the multitude" (II–II 64.6). Society exists for the sake of its members, and especially for the sake of those good men and women whose lives sustain the moral integrity of the community. A supposed love for the common good that subjected the members of the community to unfair burdens or injury turns out, on this showing, to be something other than a love for the common good—a love of one's image of society, perhaps, or a love for those elements of society that promote one's own sense of self-worth or security.

DOING WHAT IS RIGHT AND HAVING A RIGHT TO DO IT

In 1948, the UN Declaration of Human Rights proclaimed, "All human beings are born free and equal in dignity and rights." Although there are debates about how best to implement and protect human rights, few today would deny they "exist." Yet we know this is not how the Greeks and Romans thought about things. An individual—the emperor, the mayor, the owner of a farm—had rights, but there were no rights that everyone possessed simply by being human.

Scholars have long regarded natural or human rights as a late medieval or early modern idea. However, over the past several decades, leading historians have been convinced that at least some scholastic canon lawyers in the thirteenth century had a conception of natural rights, understood as a kind of moral power to claim some benefit or forbearance from another at the individual's discretion.[3] It is not clear that Aquinas has such a conception of rights as moral powers of the individual. Still, at the very least, he does associate the right—"that which is right," the object of justice—with the moral power of the individual to claim immunity from punishment or freedom of action in certain spheres of life.

Aquinas does not generally refer to someone's right in possessive terms, as the jurists do, except at one point. But that point is critically important. In citing Justinian, he says that the object of justice is to render *jus suum unicuique*, to each their own right. He goes on to say that the right includes both natural and positive right, a distinction that can be traced to Aristotle, but that was by then generally incorporated into legal theory (II–II 57.2). For Aristotle himself, the categories of what is right by nature and what is right by convention are associated with generally applicable normative claims rather than individual powers. But by placing Aristotle's distinctions within the context of Justinian's definition, Aquinas at least leaves open the possibility that the claims of right to which Aristotle refers ought to be understood as grounds for the claims of individuals, which remain to some extent within individual discretion.

Yet even if Aquinas *could* have thought of the right in this way, do we have good, textually grounded reasons for thinking that he actually *does* understand the right in these terms? I believe that we do. Consider, first, his argument that in dire and urgent need, it is licit to take what is another's in order to sustain one's own life (II–II 66.7). Some jurists in this period resolve this question by appealing to the right of the poor individual to the necessities of life.[4] But Aquinas's analysis of the case would seem initially to fit squarely within the paradigm of an objective order of justice and right:

> Those things which depend on human right cannot restrict natural right or divine right. Now according to the natural order instituted by divine providence, lower things are directed to this end, that human necessities are to be supplied by them. And therefore, the division and appropriation of material things, which proceeds from human right, does not prevent human necessities from being supplied by things of this kind. . . . [He adds that ordinarily, human needs will be met through such practices as almsgiving.] Nevertheless, if the need be so urgent and evident that it is manifest that the immediate need must be relieved by whatever things occur, as when some danger to the person is imminent and cannot be relieved in another way, then someone may licitly relieve his necessity from another's things, whether taken openly or in secret. Nor does such an action have the rational character of theft or robbery. (ST II–II 66.7)

In other words, the primary purpose of material things, as determined by a providentially instituted natural order, sets limits to the claims that can be made on the basis of human right, property claims grounded in positive law. This analysis by Aquinas is consistent with biblical commitments to the poor (outlined in Anathea Portier-Young's chapter) and is foundational for modern papal teaching on property ownership (in chapter 7, by Lisa Cahill). Normally, the necessities of those in need should be met through almsgiving. However, in some circumstances, someone can literally take matters into their own hands in order to relieve their urgent need. Aquinas goes on to say that "the use of another's things taken secretly in the case of extreme necessity does not have the rational character of theft, properly speaking, because, through such necessity, that which someone takes to sustain his own life is made his own" (II–II 66.7 A.D. 2). He adds that the same considerations apply when someone takes what is another's to meet the immediate needs of a third party (II–II 66.7 A.D. 3).

Clearly, the claims generated by natural right in this context go beyond the imperatives of an objective order of obligations. The critical point is that in some circumstances, the primary purpose of material things, which is a matter of natural right, is put into effect through someone's free choice and action. In the case of extreme and urgent necessity, someone can take what they need from the property of another to sustain their life, and what they take is regarded as their own. It was a commonplace that the goods of the rich should be regarded as belonging to the poor, generically considered. Still, for Aquinas, the specific goods taken by this particular desperate person belong to them. Thus, they cannot be said to be guilty of theft or robbery. By implication, they can claim immunity from punishment, a plausible extension of the category of subjective rights.

Consider, secondly, Aquinas's response to the question concerning whether the children of Jews and other unbelievers can be baptized against the will of their parents (II–II 10.12). He begins by asserting, in the strongest terms, that this practice is contrary to the universal custom of the church, which has greater authority than any individual theologian, however eminent. He goes on to say that this custom is justified on two grounds, the second of which is relevant here. That is, it is repugnant to natural justice to baptize a child against the will of its parents because before the child attains the use of reason, they are under the care of their parents by natural right (*de jure naurale*). On a first reading, it seems that Aquinas is asserting that it would be contrary to the objective duties set up by the order of justice and right to baptize a child against its parents' will. But his way of framing the case implies that something more is at stake. Aquinas says it would be contrary to natural justice to baptize the child of unwilling parents, implying that these parents, as individuals, are asserting a claim to raise their child as they see fit. The general considerations that Aquinas sets out are only salient because these individuals are asserting a claim, as individuals, pertaining to the upbringing of this specific child. Once again, what Aquinas seems to have in mind is a claim to an immunity that is grounded in an objective natural right but takes the form of a specific claim pertaining to one's freedom of action concerning a particular object, in this case, this specific child.

In addition to these examples, we can identify other texts in which Aquinas defends immunities from coercion or punishment by appealing to some aspect of our shared human nature without invoking natural right explicitly. For example, those who are accused of a crime are entitled to appropriate judicial procedures, and those who are convicted of a crime retain immunities for harm from other private individuals in virtue of the claims of humanity that they hold in common with the rest of us (II–II 64.3, especially 2 CE).

Someone can defend themselves against attack, even by lethal force, because, in these circumstances, the natural inclination toward maintaining one's life justifies them in placing their self-preservation ahead of the claims of their attacker (II–II 64.7). In the former case, Aquinas formulates the claims of judicial procedure in terms of the duties of public officials and private individuals to those accused of crimes. Yet it is difficult to believe that these particular duties would not be closely correlated with the claims of the accused—to be heard, to enjoy immunity from private vengeance, and the like.

Aquinas's formulations do not imply a purely objective conception of rights, but they do suggest that he has some notion of rights as claims imposing duties, as well as rights understood as immunities. At any rate, in the latter example, he clearly sees the individual's natural inclination to self-defense as a basis for a claim to act in a certain way and to be vindicated in the confessional or in a court of law.

Furthermore, Aquinas places clear limits on the obligations of obedience in such a way as to reinforce the general tendency to protect individual freedom and self-determination. When we come to II-II 104.5, "Whether subordinates are bound to obey their superiors in all things?" we find that this is indeed the case. First, no one is bound to obey another if doing so would contravene God's law—on the contrary, one is positively obliged not to obey in such a case. This is, of course, what we would expect. However, Aquinas goes on to qualify the obligation of obedience in another way. "No inferior is held to obey a superior if he commands something in which [the inferior] is not subordinated" (ST II–II 104.5). This implies, first of all, that no one is obliged to obey another human being with respect to those things that pertain to the inner motions of the will. Secondly, even with respect to external actions, the scope of authority and the obligations of obedience are further limited in particular contexts by the rationale for the authority in question. For example, a soldier is required to obey his commander in military matters but not in other spheres of life. Finally, just as the obligation to obedience is grounded in nature, so nature sets limits on the extent of this obligation:

> With respect to those things which pertain to the nature of the body, a human person is not obliged to obey another human person, but only God, because human persons are equal by nature, for example, in those things which pertain to the sustaining of the body and the generation of children. Hence, those in a state of servitude are not obliged to obey their lord, nor are children obliged to obey their parents, with respect to contracting matrimony or preserving virginity, or anything else of this sort. (ST II–II 104.5)

Here we see Aquinas asserting a general claim to freedom in certain fundamental aspects of human life, including most centrally those having to do with marriage and celibacy. We are all equal insofar as we share in a common human nature, and for Aquinas, this natural equality places strict limits on the scope of human authority. This is by no means equivalent to the view of these matters in liberalism (addressed in Francis Fiorenza's chapter), but it does move the Catholic tradition toward a greater respect for the individual person.

By now, it appears that Aquinas does have something like a conception of subjective rights, insofar as his moral analyses depend at critical points on individual claims, grounded in some consideration of natural right or nature. Generally, although not always, these are claims to some kind of immunity, implying that no one has a right to constrain the individual's freedom in specific ways. The predominance of immunity claims in Aquinas's analysis implies that he associates claims of right with the human capacity for free judgment and self-governance. Men and women can claim certain immunities because they are by nature free, and as we have already seen, the needs and desires intrinsic to our shared nature provide the field within which claims of natural right operate.

At this point, we can begin to see how Aquinas integrates an Aristotelian ideal of equality of exchange with Roman-juridical ideals of right. We have already observed that he associates basic norms of non-maleficence with the ideal of equality proper to commutative justice, on the grounds that actions that violate these norms are acts of dishonor that violate the respect due to someone's excellence (II–II 72.1). Since he is referring here to acts that are generally prohibited, no matter what the status or particular qualities of the victim may be, it is clear that the excellence in question can only be the excellence proper to human nature itself. With most of his interlocutors, he acknowledges that this natural status is qualified, and to some extent compromised, through social arrangements that introduce division and dominion into human society. Nonetheless, natural right cannot be set aside by human law, as he explicitly says at II–II 66.7. The claims of private ownership, a creation of human law, are to be set aside in favor of a claim based on the natural right to sustain one's life through the appropriation of material goods. Similarly, for him, the claims of dominion and the disabilities attached to servitude are inextricably part of our fallen world. Still, they are also limited in scope by claims of natural right, including critically the right either to marry or to refrain from marriage. In short, for Aquinas, natural right, natural equality, and the fundamentally honorable status of each man and woman are expressed and qualified but not set aside by human law.

Seen from this perspective, natural equality and the capacity to claim certain things by right are inextricably tied together. Men and women have the authority to claim certain things by right because in certain fundamental respects, we share equally in the same status, an honorable status attached to the human estate itself. More specifically, the fundamental equality enjoyed by all men and women is an equality of status as free, self-directed rational agents. For Aquinas, this is not just a matter of status, having no practical implications. Instead, it implies that individuals ought to be free to act as they see fit in certain critical respects and to claim certain immunities and certain kinds of sustenance for themselves. The ideal of equality, as Aquinas understands it, is not limited to an equality concerning claims of right, since it also integrates broader considerations of equity and general claims of non-maleficence. Nonetheless, natural equality is centrally connected to claims of right. Equal regard, as we would express the normative ideal, is bound up with respect for the honorable status of men and women, who are equally free by nature.

Of course, like political authority, individual authority is limited. Individuals can be constrained for good reasons. But if the authority of individuals is to be meaningful, they must be able to claim certain immunities and freedoms over against those who would constrain them unjustifiably. These claims are grounded in the same kinds of considerations that ground legislative activity. The general concept of *jus*, right, is a legal concept, and as such, it carries practical implications.[5] Understood in its broadest sense, the right refers to a principle of justice or a basis for a legitimate claim of some kind. As such, it is frequently contrasted with *lex*, written law, which is said to be an authoritative formulation of some principle of right or justice. The correlation between the right and legal enactments is critically important for the jurists in this period. Still, they never lose sight of the broader sense of the right, seen as conventional or natural grounds for some kind of claim.

This latter way of construing the right is central to Aquinas's moral analysis. For him, the critical moral power inhering in individuals is an authority to pursue one's natural aims and overall beatitude independently, in accordance with one's own best judgments. This authority cannot be exercised without restraint because without some framework of mutual obligations and constraints, no society could exist at all. At the same time, however, the individual has to have the authority to set certain limits on the constraints imposed by others since otherwise, our human capacities for judgment and self-determining freedom would be worthless. Aquinas assumes that individuals exercise their authority through claims, and these claims are grounded in considerations of natural right, which he believes to be generally accessible to all.

Aquinas does not seem to think of rights as discrete moral powers, and in that respect, his approach would differ from that of many theories of natural or human rights today. Nonetheless, he holds that the individual possesses the authority to determine the course of their own life in certain critical ways. This authority implies moral powers to claim certain immunities and performances by right. The individual does not possess discrete rights as discrete powers, but they do possess a general moral power for self-determining action, which they can exercise preemptively on the basis of some claim of right.

IMPLICATIONS FOR RE-THINKING JUSTICE

This chapter has briefly reviewed some of the features of Aquinas's account of justice. This account is the primary intellectual forbear of the view of justice articulated in official Catholic social teaching since 1891. As a result, the effort to re-think justice undertaken in this volume entails re-thinking various elements of that account and could be misunderstood as nothing more than a critique of its limitations. Yet a more careful reading of Aquinas indicates that constructive critique can move in both directions.

At the beginning of this chapter, I noted that Aquinas's account of justice differs from many contemporary theories of justice as a virtue of society or other social structures. Nonetheless, our examination of his views reveals a more fundamental similarity between his conception of justice and that of our contemporaries. For both, justice is grounded in a commitment to preserving both the equality of individuals in relation to one another and the equal standing and political freedom of each individual in relation to the community. This fundamental commitment links the social conceptions that informed Aquinas's account of justice and our own social world. Admittedly, he seems to have little sense of institutional and social structures as something distinct from individual relations. So it is not surprising that he does not address issues of structural justice in his account. But that does not mean that his account of justice has nothing to offer to contemporary reflections on justice, even the structural analysis addressed by Daniel Finn in chapter 9. Aquinas's account of justice as a virtue of the will provides both a corrective to the secular accounts of justice proposed today and a starting point for engaging them.

Aquinas's account is a corrective insofar as he gives a central place to the overall stance of the will that characterizes justice. Unless individuals, especially political leaders, are committed to respecting the claims and the equal dignity of all, institutional and social norms will not guarantee a just and equitable society. This would be true even if all the social norms of a society were just, and it is even more true in our own, far-from-ideal society. Similarly, his account offers a starting point for engagement with contemporary theories of justice. For Aquinas, true justice presupposes equality and respects the equal dignity of all. Thus, it would seem that a truly just individual would be disposed to preserve and promote equality through institutional structures, as well as respecting claims of right in their individual actions. In other words, the normative stance of justice, as Aquinas understands it, implies criteria for evaluating institutional and social structures. Furthermore, he insists that the obligations of justice are accessible to all and binding on all. We should expect to find that his insights are relevant to secular perspectives on justice and open to correction by them.

Much of what Aquinas says about the norms of commutative justice is immediately relevant to our contemporary situation. His detailed discussion of justice in the courtroom can be applied to the widespread breakdown of procedures of criminal justice, and his remarks on honor, reputation, and public respect offer valuable perspectives on the evils of racism and other forms of prejudice. We recognize, of course, that Aquinas does not seem to have much sense of race, class, or other forms of collective identity as morally salient in themselves. This is a limitation, but it can also prompt valuable reflections on the relation between individual and collective claims, such as reparations for past injustices.[6]

For Aquinas, both distributive and general justice are primarily exercised by those in authority. However, in modern democratic societies, all citizens share to some extent in responsibilities for the distribution of social wealth and for maintaining the common good. From this perspective, his remarks on distributive justice take on fresh relevance since we are all to some degree responsible for just distributions. As we noted above, Aquinas gives special attention to the sin opposed to distributive justice, namely, a disregard for rational criteria in favor of what he calls "respect for persons." Clearly, this kind of unjust regard for personal qualities is at work in our own society, in racism, sexism, and other kinds of discrimination, and in the systematic preferences that sustain economic inequalities, injustices addressed in the chapters by Maria Inês de Castro Millen and Agnes Brazal. If we are to be fair and just distributors of social goods, we need to identify these forms of "respect for persons" for what they are, violations of justice.

This is the context within which to consider Aquinas's often-cited claims that the goods of the earth are meant for the use of all, and correlatively, those in urgent need may take what they need to sustain life. This claim is essential in itself, and even more important because of its implications for systems of property and financial systems more broadly. In Aquinas's view, private property is a social convention set up to attain naturally sanctioned aims, primarily, the distribution of material goods in such a way as to sustain human life. The critical point from our perspective is that for him, the distribution of private property rights is properly a political choice, which ought to be guided by due consideration of the natural aims that the institution of property is meant to serve (II–II 66.2 A.D. 1). Unlike John Locke and libertarians today, he does not seem to recognize anything like a natural right of acquisition, which could serve as a basis for a natural right to private property. The distribution of property is, therefore, a public trust, governed by considerations of common well-being, and above all, justice.

This leaves open the critical question of justice in the distribution of material resources, which is, of course, a central question for our contemporaries. Aquinas has little to say on this question beyond observing that material things are meant to sustain the life of all. This remark suggests that the criterion for just distributions should be sufficiency (meeting human needs) but not necessarily equality—in contemporary terms, it would imply an approach similar to Amartya Sen and Martha Nussbaum (as recommended by George Kodithottam and Agnes Brazal in their chapters) rather than that of John Rawls and Ronald Dworkin. However, Aquinas's overall emphasis on equality, as, in two different senses, both a presupposition of justice and its aim, should at least raise doubts about relying on sufficiency as the sole or chief normative criterion for the distribution of material resources. It goes well beyond the scope of this chapter to consider this question further, but it is worth noting that this question arises within the context of a Thomistic approach to justice.

CONCLUSION

In this chapter, we have surveyed Thomas Aquinas's theory of justice. Like his premodern contemporaries, Aquinas does not attend to the justice of social structures or to the rights of individuals as do theories of justice today, both secular and religious. Yet we find that his concern for the common good has important implications for a theory of just institutions today, and his fundamental commitment to fairness, respect, and equality of persons provides a basis for the justice claims of individuals both then and now. Thus, Aquinas himself provides resources helpful in re-thinking justice in the twenty-first century.

And, of course, Aquinas tells us all that there is more to life than justice. On the one hand, we need to appeal to other principles for an appropriate response to some problems, for example, the demands of care for the environment. On the other hand, seen from the vantage of Christian commitment, there is a limit to justice, as it is transcended by charity. Nonetheless, Aquinas would remind us that whatever other aims and ideals we pursue, we need always to be mindful of the demands for justice, which set the boundaries for individual morality and the common good alike.

BIBLIOGRAPHY

Bartlett, Robert C., and Susan D. Collins. "Interpretative Essay." In *Aristotle's Nicomachean Ethics*, translated by Robert C. Bartlett and Susan D. Collins, 237–302. University of Chicago Press, 2011.

Dworkin, Ronald. *Sovereign Virtue: The Theory and Practice of Equality*. Belknap Press, 1986.

Leo XIII. *Rerum novarum*. 1871. https://www.vatican.va/content/leo-xiii/en/encyclicals/documents/hf_l-xiii_enc_15051891_rerum-novarum.html.

Porter, Jean. *Ministers of the Law: A Natural Law Theory of Legal Authority*. Eerdmans, 2010.

Rawls, John. *A Theory of Justice*. Harvard University Press, 1971/ revised edition, 1999.

Reid, Charles J., Jr. *Power over the Body, Equality in the Family: Rights and Domestic Relations in Medieval Canon Law*. Eerdmans, 2004.

Reid, Charles J., Jr. "The Canonistic Contribution to the Western Rights Tradition: An Historical Inquiry," *Boston College Law Review* 33, no. 37 (1991): 37–92. https://core.ac.uk/download/71458665.pdf.

Tierney, Brian. *The Idea of Natural Rights: Studies on Natural Rights, Natural Law, and Church Law 1150–1625*. Scholars Press, 1997.

NOTES

1. Contemporary work on justice among political theorists takes its starting points from John Rawls, *A Theory of Justice*; he asserts that justice is a virtue of institutions on 3. Similarly, Ronald Dworkin remarks that "Justice is an institution we interpret," *Sovereign Virtue*, 73.
2. I do not attempt to determine whether Aquinas is reading Aristotle accurately; for a good overview of Aristotle's account of justice seen in the context of his overall theory of virtue, see Bartlett and Collins, "Interpretative Essay," 237–302. Aristotle's discussion of justice comprises the fifth book of the *Nicomachean Ethics*, 90–114, in the Bartlett/Collins translation.
3. In particular, this view is defended by Brian Tierney in *The Idea of Natural Rights*, 43–77, and Charles J. Reid Jr. "The Canonistic Contribution," 37–92, and in greater detail, *Power over the Body, Equality*.
4. For further details, see Tierney, *The Idea of Natural Rights*, 65–6.
5. I defend this claim in more detail in *Ministers of the Law*, 76–8.
6. By the same token, we should not assume that the ideal of mutual and complementary social classes proposed by Leo XIII in *Rerum novarum* reflects Aquinas's own social ideal, even though it is often presented in that way.

CHAPTER 6

How Liberalism Can Contribute
to Re-thinking Justice in Catholic
Social Thought

Francis Schüssler Fiorenza

Catholicism viewed liberalism as an intellectual attack on true faith for more than 200 years. Only in the twentieth century did papal teaching approve of democracy, human rights, and religious freedom. Official church teaching has not publicly acknowledged its adoption of elements of liberalism, but most Catholic theologians have long recognized the debt.

Nonetheless, many of those same scholars have also argued that liberalism is seriously flawed by its individualism and the lack of a foundational idea of the good. This chapter analyzes and defends liberalism—in particular, the perspective of John Rawls—as well warranted in itself and helpful for theology. It examines some of the shortcomings of relying on the notion of the common good in discerning what justice requires. And it briefly examines failures of recognition of minorities when "the community" is allowed too significant a role. It finishes with an exploration of a conception of the common good that liberalism can sustain.

Because of its past contributions and the importance of its insights for further improvements, it makes perfect sense to ask what liberalism can contribute to the project to which this volume is dedicated—re-thinking justice in Catholic social thought.

JOHN RAWLS: JUSTICE IN A PLURALISTIC WORLD

One of the most fundamental differences between liberalism as a political philosophy and Roman Catholic social thought concerns the audience. Catholic social thought sets out to articulate the political, social, and economic implications of Catholic faith. It rests on the theological convictions of a particular religious group. In contrast, liberalism historically has not wanted to limit itself to the views of any specific religious or cultural group. Liberalism argues that no one religious perspective can provide a sufficient warrant for its religious view of justice in a pluralist society, especially where such a perspective animates only a minority of citizens. It simply won't be persuasive to enough people.

The Right and the Good

In *A Theory of Justice,* the classic work on justice of the twentieth century, John Rawls explicitly designs his theory to set aside many of the most contentious issues debated in religion and culture to address justice separately. He distinguishes "the right" from "the good." "The right" is for him a synonym for justice. "The good" refers to whatever leads to human happiness or fulfillment, a contentious issue. One person sees a sixty-hours-a-week career as most fulfilling, while another minimizes work to spend time with family. One prefers Bach and red wine, while another listens to rock and drinks beer. One is Buddhist, another an atheist. There are many alternative views of a good life.

Rawls argues that democratic political life requires an "overlapping consensus" on the requirements of justice but that once society comes to an agreement on justice, there would be no problem with different individuals and groups leading their lives with quite different convictions about what constitutes "the good." The tension here with Catholic thought is evident. The common good is a fundamental element of Catholic views of social life, and any Catholic view of justice must be intimately related to concern for the common good.

Liberalism's problems with this notion of the common good are many. For now, we simply note that Rawls seeks to take diversity seriously in a way Catholic theology does not—by refusing to rest his theory of justice on any specific foundational conception of the common good. As he puts it, "the right precedes the good."[1] Still, as we will also see, Rawls does propose a liberal version of the common good for a pluralist society.

The Two Principles
of Justice

Rawls proposes two principles of justice. The first guarantees equal basic liberties, and the second specifies when inequalities are just. He first reformulated these in *A Theory of Justice* (1971) and later reworked them in *Justice as Fairness: A Restatement* (2001). The first principle is that "each person has the same indefeasible claim to a fully adequate scheme of equal basic liberties, which scheme is compatible with the same scheme of liberties for all." Put more simply, society should maximize liberties as long as everyone has the same liberties. The second principle is: "Social and economic inequalities are to satisfy two conditions: first, they are to be attached to offices and positions open to all under the conditions of fair equality of opportunity; and second, they are to be the greatest benefit of the least-advantaged members of society (the difference principle)."[2] Fair equality of opportunity means that society should improve the opportunities of those who, by the luck of natural abilities and social position at birth, grow up with disadvantages. The difference principle says inequalities (e.g., that physicians have higher incomes than dishwashers) are just if the inequality helps out the worst-off group in society (in our example, higher incomes for doctors induce some people to spend years in medical school, and dishwashers are then better off due to the availability of medical care).

Significant changes have occurred in Rawls's understanding and application of justice. These changes involve the difference between liberty and equality, specifics of the difference principle, the role of an overlapping consensus, his views on the structures of society and the accumulation of wealth, his understanding of primary goods, the complementary of the good and the right, and his view of public reason. Any criticism that Rawls's position is individualistic overlooks the interrelationship of the principles of justice within Rawls's work, his reflections on their interaction in society, and his later developments.

Even though Rawls has been inaccurately criticized as individualistic, his position does entail several warnings about too great a reliance on the notion of the common good as central to an understanding of justice, as this chapter will investigate. The caution about overemphasizing and, at times, idealizing the common good represents a fundamental contribution from liberalism to the project of this volume to re-think justice in Catholic social thought.

Reciprocity:
A Third Principle

Although the above two principles of justice have garnered most of the attention, it has become increasingly obvious that Rawls has a third principle of justice in mind: reciprocity, which requires taking into account the views of other people. Reciprocity initially appears as an element of the difference principle[3] but then increasingly gets a more distinct independence and importance. It gains prominence as part of Rawls's "political conception of justice" in association with the ideas of overlapping consensus and public reason. A political conception of justice is different from the moral conception developed in the hypothetical "original position" in *A Theory of Justice*. This political approach rests on fundamental convictions shared in a democratic culture by reasonable citizens. In *Political Liberalism*, Rawls suggests that through reciprocity, citizens holding distinct and even contrasting comprehensive doctrines of the good can reach a stable conception of justice. He further develops the notion of reciprocity in his *The Law of Peoples*, where he revisits the idea of public reason.[4] He suggests that his liberal political conception of justice, with its discussion of the constraints of public reason, is one that "holders of both religious and nonreligious comprehensive views can reasonably endorse."[5]

The principle of reciprocity accomplishes many of the same goals implicit in the notion of the common good in Roman Catholic theology. Rawls advocates his understanding of justice as "fair reciprocity."[6] The importance of reciprocity and public reason comes to the fore in dealing with differences. Rawls writes: "The fact of reasonable pluralism raises this question sharply, since it means that the differences between citizens arising from their comprehensive doctrine, religious, and nonreligious, may be irreconcilable. By what ideals and principles, are citizens who share equally in ultimate political power to exercise that power so that each can reasonably justify his or her political decisions to everyone?"[7] His answer appeals to reciprocity; one should be prepared to offer others cooperation in terms of their most reasonable understanding of political justice. "The criterion of reciprocity requires that when those terms are proposed as the most reasonable terms of fair cooperation, those proposing them must also think it at least reasonable for others to accept them, as free and equal citizens."[8] We can detect here an echo of one of the Buddhist foundations for justice articulated in George Kodithottam's chapter, that it is not rational to expect others to respect my interests if I don't respect theirs.

Rawls further develops the criterion of reciprocity with his notion of "civic friendship," again nearing goals implicit in the Catholic sense of the common good.[9] Related to his natural duty of mutual respect, civic friendship requires not simply civility in political discourse. It also entails a sort of intellectual sympathy, an effort to overcome mutual suspicion by striving to understand the other's point of view. In this way, Rawls's conception of justice aims not only to attain a just political order but also to stabilize this order over time.[10]

PROBLEMS WITH THE NOTION OF THE COMMON GOOD

The idea of the common good is fundamental to Catholic moral theology, as Lisa Cahill makes clear in chapter 7 on the development of modern Catholic social teaching on justice. Catholic scholars have criticized liberalism for not having a sufficiently robust notion of the common good. Yet Catholic scholarship has some critical things to learn from liberalism's skepticism about the idea, in four distinct ways.

Civic Good, Public Good, and the Common Good

In Catholic theology, God is the true common good of all humanity. This sense of the common good as most basically transcendent often stands in unexamined conflict with other uses of the term "common good" in Catholic analysis of more concrete moral questions. Often, goods better described as civic or public or political goods are identified with the Catholic notion of the common good, inappropriately linking these goods with transcendent moral obligations.

I live in Boston, and I know that the citizens in Boston want the city to make sure the Department of Public Works clears the street of snow and fixes the potholes resulting from the weather. In New York City, the failure to remove snow quickly enough cost one mayor his job at the next election. Snow removal is a political and civic good but only locally applicable to those cities with snow. Other communities have different goods as more central. The point here is that we should not too quickly universalize civic and political goods or elevate them to the transcendent common good but rather acknowledge the particularity and limits of such civic goods. Much of government consists in dealing with such limited societal and civic goods.

And, of course, a lot is wrong with our society. There is inadequate emphasis on goods for the benefit of the health of its members. Quite often, economic interests prioritize profit over the well-being of individuals. Cigarette companies knew for years that smoking caused cancer. Major fossil fuel companies had research years ago that showed that using fossil fuels increased global warming. Food companies realize that increasing the salt and sugar content of processed food leads people to eat them in abundance. In these and other cases, society has to confront the destructive effects of the profit motive in economic life.

Yet these examples raise the question of whether they can best be resolved by appealing to the common good or by a different sort of analytical assessment of justice provided by liberalism. One has to deal with the limited problem of the economic structures of our society. We have learned from the critical theory of the Frankfurt school that the experience of injustice often comes prior to the grasp of the common good.[11] To make progress in our society, the experience and awareness of the suffering and harm caused by certain structures is a more helpful starting point than an abstract conception of the good.

One might assert that certain natural goods, such as water, air, and food, are part of the common good. No one wants lead-contaminated water or water from a source that has not been purified. Yet there can be some debates about what is healthy. Should water be fluoridated, and how much? Aging lead water pipes challenge many communities to meet the common good. Yet such problems are often tolerated (or deliberately located) in poor areas, racially and ethnically different from wealthier neighborhoods. Are these problems better resolved by appealing to the common good or by recognizing that economic inequality and societal racism exist? Liberalism argues that even for Catholics, the response should be focused not so much on the common good but rather on why the problems disproportionately affect neighborhoods whose members are poor or racial minorities. So many of our problems entail civic or public goods, and the larger notion of a common good is less helpful than analyzing justice claims at stake.

Common Good and Christian Belief

Classic Christian texts have understood the common good in relation to God and the dominant beliefs and values of specific religious traditions. This point has come up for discussion in some contemporary literature because John Rawls, in defending his view on the relation between the right and the good, has quoted a well-known statement of Thomas Aquinas in his *Summa theologiae*, "Therefore, if a man be dangerous and infectious to the community, on account of some sin, it is praiseworthy and advantageous that he be killed in order to safeguard the common good" (ST II–II, q. 64, a.). For centuries, Catholic doctrine approved of capital punishment for serious offenses.

Recent papal teaching has finally rejected that judgment, but the issue does raise a significant question about contemporary experience. Infectious diseases are currently in the news. If people are contagious, as, for example, with Ebola hemorrhagic fever in some West African nations, the medical political-civic reaction is to quarantine those who are ill so that they do not infect others. Statements in the Christian tradition used to suggest something similar should be done to contain heresy or prevent the spread of religious error. Such containment, it is argued, is for the common good.

The appeal to the common good in medical quarantine is likely persuasive to most within and beyond the Christian community. Yet can one in a multireligious world prioritize a religious appeal to the common good for social exclusion or isolation? The situation is more complex in the face of the COVID-19 pandemic, where a significant portion of the population, including some religious leaders, objects to a vaccine on religious grounds and hence supports the refusal of vaccination that many recommend for the common good.

The Supreme Court now allows the marriage of two persons of the same sex. Yet the Catholic Church in the United States invested millions of dollars and much time and energy opposing the change. The ethical claim advanced was that maintaining marriage as heterosexual would foster the common good. Same-sex marriage, even if only a civil (and not a sacramental) marriage, would undercut the stability of marriage. The Catholic dioceses argued that their defense of heterosexual marriage was based on the common good and natural law rather than on a sectarian religious doctrine. They advocated the common good of society, not only the church.

Similarly, many religious adoption agencies, both Catholic and Protestant, have refused to place children with same-sex couples because doing so would undermine the common good. In response to laws forbidding such exclusions in some states, some agencies have had to cease operations altogether. How does one evaluate this issue? The Barna Group, a source of evangelical research, notes that practicing Christians adopt twice as many children as others do.[12] The Williams Institute, associated with the University of California at Los Angeles, has determined that of 114,000 same-sex couples raising children, 25 percent are foster or adopted children.

That percentage contrasts with 3 percent of heterosexual couples with children.[13] Often children with disabilities or developmental issues are adopted by LGBTQ+ couples. The act of adoption should be considered a worthy moral and religious act. Yet specific religious groups argue that a caring and loving same-sex couple should not adopt children for the sake of the common good. Can one legitimately argue from the common good when a society has a different ethical and religious view on the nature of family?

Life Preferences and Common Good

Sometimes disagreements about civic goods are not rooted in differences about traditional norms or moral values but life preferences. One example is the path of Interstate 95, whose purpose was to unify the nation, linking states and cities as a highway along the East Coast, roughly 2,000 miles from Florida to Maine. In Massachusetts, I-95 would have run along the Charles River between Cambridge and Boston. The citizens of Cambridge fought it and won. As a result, Memorial Drive still exists, and on Sundays, no traffic at all is allowed there for several hours. Instead, parents can stroll with their children and enjoy the free space beside the river. In many cities across the United States, the construction of interstate highways demolished thousands of homes and divided historic communities.

What is the common good in these cases? Is it to have a highway that runs through cities and provides a quicker transportation route, or is it the life preferences of those living in the cities who prefer to maintain their local community intact? I do not believe there is an ethical or moral ground to decide which options better serve the common good. Theoretically, embracing the whole East Coast is more inclusive than the preferences of the citizens of a city. At stake is not merely the geographical location of superhighways but the good life in a concrete way. With the increasing density and growth of cities, many are concerned about how urban life can be made livable. How can it bring open spaces with greenery and trees to where people live to recreate and enjoy life? Should the "common good" of interstate transportation override a more particular good of a specific community? Is the category of the "common good" even helpful in such cases?

Does a cross-country gas pipeline serve the common good by providing energy to areas that don't produce it, or does it contradict the common good because it would run through Native American areas and violate culturally important religious grounds? Should city zoning laws set minimum lot sizes and building standards that preserve "the character" of a neighborhood but often mean less expensive housing cannot be built there? Given debates about what's good for society, does the "common good" suffice? Or would not Rawls's principles of justice provide a better way forward?

The Ambiguity of Communitarianism and the Common Good

Often, communitarianism is advocated in response to the individualism that critics attach to modern liberalism. David Hollenbach argues that "the ability of people to identify just what is 'good' or 'noble' depends on their being part of a community with a shared tradition, a *paideia* through which they are educated in virtue. But this is just what we do not have in contemporary society."[14] Quoting Alasdair MacIntyre's statement that barbarians are already present, Hollenbach nevertheless argues that values are formed in communities, and through communities, a value underscored in communitarianism. He does not attack rights. He emphasizes that those rights not only have an individual focus but also have social implications for others.[15]

Communal identity based on a sharing of values and traditions can indeed be very meaningful and positive. Yet communal identity also involves drawing lines between what constitutes a community's identity and what fractures or destroys that identity between those who are in and those who are not. The emphasis on specific traditions and practices creates identity. But it often leads to the exclusion of others and their values. Elsewhere in this volume, Agbonkhianmeghe Orobator cautions that the communitarian strength of traditional African views of justice is plagued by the abuses of tribalism, and George Kodithottam reports a similarly glaring problem in the Hindu commitment to the relatedness of all humans in the midst of an unjust caste system.

Western modernity exhibits not only the awareness of an individual's autonomy and self-authenticity but also the growth of nations and nationalism. In modernity, the development of nationalism often went hand in hand with colonialism or with fascism—and has included extreme acts of exclusion and even genocide. Josef Pieper, the renowned Roman Catholic philosopher, in his autobiographical reflections on his life in Nazi Germany, wrote: "The new masters' slogan, 'the common good before the good of the individual' which was proclaimed at all turns and like everything [the Nazis] took up, was quickly worn-out and denatured, rapidly unmasked itself as a mere pretext and a propaganda trick."[16]

Today, we see the resurgence of the emphasis on communal and national identity in the United States that takes the form of resistance to immigration and calls for the United States to be a Christian nation. Some groups advocate their community values so strongly that they want them to be applied to everyone. Communitarianism and communal identity too often justify a restricted common good that violates justice because it prioritizes the values and virtues of a particular community.

In sum, the four preceding issues articulate why an emphasis on the common good—and on the communal character of justice in many traditional religious cultures—should call for caution in the efforts in this volume to re-think justice in Catholic social thought.

RECOGNITION AS A PROBLEM IN CATHOLIC SOCIAL THOUGHT

The strong emphasis on redistribution and equality in Rawls's understanding of justice has been expanded by underscoring the connection between social-economic inequality and "misrecognition" based on racial, ethnic, national, gender, and sexual status. The development of recognition theory has clarified how asking "who counts?" is a fundamental part of any theory of justice. In chapter 7, Lisa Cahill makes a parallel argument in pointing out that most political disagreements about justice are not about what qualifies as a fundamental good for persons but about which people deserve to receive them if they cannot secure them on their own.

Thus, the issues of recognition and redistribution are "co-fundamental and mutually irreducible dimensions of justice."[17] Nancy Fraser argues that "tradition" often overlooks issues of recognition, an insight that applies to the history of Catholic conceptions of justice as well. Fraser argues that in our post-Westphalian situation, "we must ask: given the class of rival views of the bounds of justice, how should we decide whose interests ought to count? Faced with competing framings of social conflicts, how should we determine which mapping of political space is just."[18] The problem of recognition within the pluralism of multicultural societies has, in the last decades, become increasingly important and focuses on the respect for the dignity of individual persons irrespective of natural abilities, societal position, ethnicity, gender, or race. The emphasis on recognition and equality, though in quite distinct theories, poses a counterpoint to a more abstract interpretation of the common good and the natural law.

As Maria Inês de Castro Millen makes clear in her chapter, liberation theologians have been making a similar claim for half a century now.

Talking about justice without recognizing those harmed by injustice is not adequate. The preferential option for the poor entails not only an obligation to recognize and assist the poor in their struggle for justice. Importantly, it understands the poor to be in a "privileged" position epistemologically regarding the character of justice and injustice. Those who suffer injustice daily know what justice requires in a way that others who are socially and economically privileged (including most authors and readers of this volume) do not.

In his early writings, Jürgen Habermas argues that ethical norms should be formed based on a communicative reciprocity in which ethical and normative relationships are established.[19] For Habermas, a critical social theory needs to take seriously the mutual demand to reach an understanding communicatively. This entails the recognition of both the self and the other as participating in reciprocal criticism and justification. The formation of norms occurs through a communicative discourse conducted, in principle, by everyone affected by them.

In "The Politics of Recognition,"[20] Charles Taylor deals with multiculturalism within Canada and underscores the importance of the recognition of equal rights not simply in a homogeneous culture or tradition but also in different cultures. In a politics of recognition, one must accept equality across diverse cultures rather than making the identity of a single culture or community identity normative.

This raises an important question for Catholic social thought due to its dependence not only on the notion of the common good but on "community" as well. Critics argue that a recognition of others as holding equal rights in a pluralist society requires speaking of "the public" rather than "community." Nancy Fraser and Iris Marian Young suggest that the notion of community points to a homogeneous group. Young suggests that in the United States, the term "community" often refers to the people with whom I identify in a particular local, neighborhood, church, or with a particular ethnicity or race. Members of a community share a common heritage, common self-identification, common culture, and a common set of norms. One could say a common good. Young suggests that "racism, ethnic chauvinism, and class devaluation grows partly from a desire for community; that is from the desire to understand others as they understand themselves and from the desire to be understood as I understand myself."[21] Young does not claim that the ideal of community is necessarily racist, but rather that "such appeals within a racist and chauvinistic society can validate the impulses that reproduce racist and ethnically chauvinistic identification."[22] In contrast, the term "public" is the locus of a discourse that is open-ended and has a diversity of fundamental perspectives. The notion of a public is more open than "community" to a deep diversity of views.

My point in referencing the current debates about recognition is to underscore that any understanding of a political public good or the common good must be brought into dialogue with contemporary reflections on the need for diversity and especially the recognition of people, groups, and values that often are at the periphery of usual discourse, especially where the value of community is emphasized.

LIBERALISM AND THE GOOD

As we have seen in the work of Rawls, liberalism strives to develop a workable political consensus on justice without requiring a consensus on a definition of the good. As a result, a closer look at how liberalism addresses the good will be helpful.

Isaiah Berlin and Inevitably Conflicting Values

Isaiah Berlin is most widely known for his interpretation of human freedom, especially the difference between negative freedom, the absence of constraints, and positive freedom, the ability to pursue and achieve one's goals. However, concerning the common good in pluralist societies, Berlin argues that multiple points of view can legitimately coexist even if the values of some people are radically different from those of others, and this need not entail moral relativism. Berlin argues that pluralism is "the conception that there are many different ends that men may seek and still be fully rational, fully men, capable of understanding each other and sympathizing and deriving light from each other."[23] He assumes that in any pluralist society values will often conflict, an implicit criticism of the irenic assumptions that typify most papal discussions of ideal political life. "Since some values may conflict intrinsically, the very notion that a pattern must, in principle, be discoverable in which they are all rendered harmonious is founded on a false a priori view of the world."[24] This faulty worldview, for Berlin, entails transferring the transcendent metaphysics of Parmenides to the political and social sphere.

Berlin suggests that classical political theory from ancient Greece (and, for our purposes, Catholic assumptions about political life) is like a tripod that rests on three central assumptions, each of which is false. The first is that questions about values, ends, rightness, and desirability of human actions are genuine questions to which uniquely correct answers exist. "These answers are objective, universal, eternally valid, and in principle, knowable. To every genuine question, only one answer can be true, all other answers being necessarily false. . . ."[25] The second assumption is that the answers, if correct, do not clash with one another. The third assumption is that humans have a nature that is discoverable, describable, and inherently social.[26]

Berlin counters the accusation that the pluralism of modern societies is morally imperfect by arguing that, on the contrary, the pursuit of a single ideal can be and often is ethically treacherous. The greatest evils in history have typically been perpetuated for the sake of a particular goal or a religious and cultural result. The final solution, the classless society, inquisitions, class purges, and cultural revolutions are performed in the pursuit of a specific ideal. In developing this critique, Berlin takes aim at the underlying myth common to Western utopias. They envision a society that lives in pure harmony and all its members love one another. In it, individuals do not face insecurity, degrading work, envy, injustice, or violence. Instead, they live in peace.[27] The title of Berlin's book *The Crooked Timber of Humanity* illustrates his critique. The phrase and sentiment are taken from Immanuel Kant's observation, "out of the crooked timber of humanity no straight thing was ever made."[28]

Recently, Luke Bretherton has written that one can talk about the common good of a family, workplace, or small community, but to talk about the common good of a nation or the globe is antipolitical. "It denies the plurality and contestability of moral visions in complex societies and the conflicts that arise in pursuit of divergent moral goods."[29] This stands in sharp contrast with what the Catholic critics of modern liberalism are arguing and instead acknowledges the existence of genuine moral diversity.

The Common Good for Rawls

This chapter proposes that liberalism's contributions to re-thinking justice in Catholic social thought are twofold. First, as the previous criticisms have made clear, the common good should not be overrated. It brings with it significant moral risks. Second, Rawls himself accomplishes much of what the Catholic notion of the common good entails in his principles of justice, especially the second.

In response to a question about the common good in his work, Rawls answers, "you hear that liberalism lacks an idea of the common good, but that's a mistake." In his view, despite different comprehensive doctrines, citizens desire that every other citizen have justice. "In my language, they're striving toward one single end, the end of justice for all citizens."[30]

In raising the issue of the different interests among individual groups and the search for the common good, Rawls answers, "Yet since we cannot maximize with respect to more than one point of view, it is natural given the ethos of a democratic society, to single out that of the least advantaged and maximize their long-term prospects consistent with the liberties of equal citizenship."[31] This commitment to the least advantaged in society spells out the meaning of the goal of justice for all citizens. The second principle accomplishes more precisely than what the common good in Catholic social thought is typically said to require.

The first part of the second principle requires that all offices and positions be open to all in accord with fair equality of opportunity. Rawls's fair equality of opportunity aims to address the lack of favorable opportunities in life faced by those disadvantaged by the luck of birth, either genetically or socially. He illustrates this by saying that two children with roughly equal ability and willingness to work should have roughly equal chances to succeed in life. This will require, for example, greater resources expended on children born in inner-city neighborhoods than on those born in the suburbs so that later, when both apply for the same job, they have had truly equal opportunity. Catholic social thought has rarely addressed the issue of accessibility to particular jobs, but the church supports a vast network of schools, hospitals, and social service agencies to meet the fundamental needs of impoverished people, a prerequisite for gainful employment. But the closure of inner-city Catholic elementary schools around the United States indicates the practical limits of a commitment to the common good in the lives of prosperous Catholics living in the suburbs.

The second part of the second principle of justice is the difference principle: that systemic inequalities in life are just only if they conduce to the well-being of the least-well-off group. I would like, if I may, to illustrate this difference principle with reference to some published research by our daughter, a medical doctor. It is obvious that people are equal, but some people have limitations and handicaps. She points out that people with handicaps often delay going for medical care and, as a result, are seen by a doctor in a later stage of medical need. As a result, they more frequently need hospitalization, and their recovery becomes much more challenging. Consequently, public means of obviating these handicaps through ramps in buildings and public transportation are necessary. This kind of public treatment illustrates what Rawls's difference principle includes if justice is to be taken seriously.[32]

For Rawls, the right precedes the good, but the right and the good are complementary. Any conception of justice, including a political conception of justice, is related to the common good. "The general meaning of the priority of the right must fit within its framework as a political conception."[33] In distinction to those who appeal to the common good specified by the natural law, Rawls suggests six ideas of the good in the context of justice as fairness: goodness as rationality, the primary goods, comprehensive conceptions of good within the priority of the right, the political virtues of an ideal citizen, the political good of a society well ordered by principles of justice, and the good of society as a social union of social unions.

CONCLUSION

This chapter has presented ways that liberalism can contribute to re-thinking justice in Catholic social thought. The first part entailed a brief outline of the view of justice presented by John Rawls. This included his two famous principles of justice and a third that has emerged in his later thinking: reciprocity.

The second part of this effort was an outline of shortcomings that attend to emphasis on the common good. In chapter 7, summarizing papal teaching on justice, Lisa Cahill reports, "One is tempted to say that the common good *is* the definition of social justice in Catholic social teaching." She immediately resists that temptation by adding, "Yet, the danger is that this could be misunderstood to overemphasize the communal character of the good for humans." This is true, but the problems extend beyond a simple overemphasis on the communal character of the good, as she herself makes clear. The term "common good" in Catholic thought resists easy definition, is often of little practical help when confronted with concrete issues where goods compete, arouses suspicions by others who don't share Catholic commitments, and can too easily enable a community to insist that its own view of the common good should be recognized by or even imposed on others who see things differently.

The chapter has also lifted up the problem of recognition, the tendency in both individuals and systems of abstract thought to fail to address difference in society, whether based on personal or group characteristics. Because the common good is so often understood to be tied to a particular community with a particular view of what is good for humanity, the perspectives of resident minorities and of different cultures globally tend to be discounted or ignored altogether.

Finally, the chapter addressed a liberal view of the common good: how justice can be sustained even in a pluralist society where multiple conflicting foundational views of the good are present.

There is little doubt that the traditional elements of justice in Catholic social thought, including the common good, will remain essential. The hope articulated in this chapter is that justice will be understood more critically—and more adequately—due to an appropriate attention to the insights of the liberal tradition.

BIBLIOGRAPHY

Adorno, Theodor W. *Negative Dialectics,* translated by E.B. Ashton. Suhrkamp, Verlag, 1966.

Berlin, Isaiah. *The Crooked Timber of Humanity*, edited by Henry Hardy. Princeton University Press, 1990.

Berlin, Isaiah. "Two Concepts of Liberty." 2002. https://doi.org/10.1093/019924989X.003.0004.

Bretherton, Luke. *Christ and the Common Life: Political Theology and the Case for Democracy.* Eerdmans, 2019.

Buchanan, Allen. "Justice as Reciprocity Versus Subject-Centered Justice." *Philosophy and Public Affairs* 19, no. 3 (1990): 227–52. https://www.jstor.org/stable/pdf/2265395.pdf.

Christian Alliance for Orphans. "New Barna Research Highlights Christian Adoption & Foster Care Among 3 Most Notable Vocational Trends." https://cafo.org/new-barna-research-highlights-christian-adoption-foster-care-among-3-most-notable-vocational-trends.

Fraser, Nancy. "Who Counts? Dilemmas of Justice in a Postwestphalian World." *Antipode* 41, no. 1 (March 2010): 281–97. https://doi.org/10.1111/j.1467-8330.2009.00726.x.

Fraser, Nancy, and Axel Honneth. "Introduction: Redistribution or Recognition?" In *Redistribution or Recognition?*, edited by Nancy Fraser and Axel Honneth, 1–6. Verso, 2003.

Habermas, Jürgen. *Knowledge and Human Interests,* translated by Jeremy J. Shapiro. Beacon Press, 1971.

Hollenbach, David. *The Common Good and Christian Ethics.* Cambridge University Press, 2002.

Hollenbach, David. "The Common Good Revisited." *Theological Studies* 50, no. 1 (1989): 70–94. https://journals.sagepub.com/doi/10.1177/004056398905000104.

Kelly, Erin, ed. *Justice as Fairness: A Restatement.* Harvard University, 2001.

Pieper, Josef. *No One Could Have Known: An Autobiography, the Early Years*, 1904–1945. Ignatius, 1987.

Rawls, John. *A Theory of Justice.* Harvard University Press, 1971.

Rawls, John. *Collected Papers.* Harvard University Press, 1999.

Rawls, John. *Justice as Fairness.* Belknap Press, 2001.

Rawls, John. *Political Liberalism.* Expanded ed. Columbia University Press, 2005.

Rawls, John. *The Law of Peoples: With The Idea of Public Reason Revisited*. Harvard University Press, 1999.

Schüssler-Fiorenza, Rose, S. M. et al. "Potentially Avoidable Hospitalizations Among People at Different Activity of Daily Living Limitation Stages." *Health Services Research*. 52, no. 1 (2017): 132–55. https://doi.org/10.1111/1475-6773.12484.

Taylor, Charles. "The Politics of Recognition." In *Multiculturalism: Examining the Politics of Recognition*, edited by Amy Gutmann, 25–73. Princeton University Press, 1994.

Williams Institute of the UCLA School of Law. "LGBTQ Parenting in the US," July 2024. https://williamsinstitute.law.ucla.edu/publications/same-sex-parents-us/.

Young, Iris Marion. "The Ideal of Community and the Politics of Difference." *Social Theory and Practice* 12, no. 1 (1986): 1–26. http://www.jstor.org/stable/23556621.

NOTES

1. Rawls, *A Theory of Justice*, 25.
2. Kelly, ed., *Justice as Fairness*, 42–3
3. Rawls, *A Theory of Justice*, 102–103, where reciprocity is treated in relation to the difference principle. A more extensive role is given in *Justice as Fairness*, 122–24, and much more detailed in later books and essays.
4. Rawls, *The Law of Peoples*, 122–4.
5. Rawls, 129–80.
6. Buchanan, "Justice as Reciprocity," 227–52.
7. Rawls, *Collected Papers*, 577–78.
8. Rawls, 578.
9. Rawls, 579.
10. Rawls, 305.
11. See Adorno's *Negative Dialectics*.
12. Christian Alliance for Orphans, "New Barna Research."
13. Williams Institute of the UCLA School of Law, "LGBTQ Parenting in the US."
14. Hollenbach, "The Common Good Revisited."
15. Hollenbach, *The Common Good and Christian Ethics*.
16. Pieper, *No One Could Have Known*, 95.
17. Fraser and Honneth, "Introduction," 3.
18. Fraser, "Who Counts?"
19. Habermas, *Knowledge and Human Interests*.
20. Taylor, "The Politics of Recognition," 25–73.
21. Young, "The Ideal of Community," 12–13.
22. Young, 13.
23. Berlin, *The Crooked Timber of Humanity*, 11.
24. Berlin, *Liberty*, 43.
25. Berlin, 290.
26. Berlin, 280–91.
27. Berlin, "The Decline of the Utopian Ideas in the West," in *Crooked Timber*, 20–48.
28. Berlin, 48.
29. Bretherton, *Christ and the Common Life*, 48.
30. Rawls, *Collected Papers*, 622.
31. Rawls, "Distributive Justice," in *Collected Papers*, 153.
32. Schüssler-Fiorenza et al., "Potentially Avoidable Hospitalizations", 132–55.
33. Rawls, *Justice as Fairness*, 141.

CHAPTER 7

Justice in Catholic Social Teaching

Lisa Sowle Cahill

Today we are more aware than ever of the variety and extent of injustice around the world. And we are similarly more conscious of the multiplicity of competing conceptions of justice in the world today, each attempting to understand and make moral claims about what justice requires. The effort to re-think justice in Catholic social thought in this volume must attend to the diversity in both those realities and those theories. Yet Catholic thinking is part of a living tradition and, as such, responds not only to contemporary ideas and events but also to the long history of Christian views of justice, from the scriptures to the twenty-first century. Much of that history is addressed in other chapters in this volume.

This chapter summarizes the understanding of justice in modern Catholic social teaching, the official teaching of the popes and bishops of the Catholic Church, typically reckoned from 1891, the date of Pope Leo XIII's encyclical *Rerum novarum*. Catholic social teaching is a subset of Catholic social thought, including both the official teaching and the work of many others without formal ecclesiastical authority. But since modern Catholic social teaching has developed in response to both events and ideas of the day, it will be helpful to begin with a question about justice more generally before turning to official teaching about it.

WHAT IS JUSTICE?

The meaning of justice is hard to capture—not only in Catholic social teaching. David Miller, a political theorist of social and global justice, remarks that justice is sometimes defined so broadly that it is indistinguishable from rightness or virtue or morality as such.[1] Plato and Aristotle—followed by Augustine and Aquinas—defined justice as a virtue, one of the cardinal four (along with prudence, fortitude, and temperance). Modern theorists, following John Rawls, add that justice is a virtue not only of individuals but of social institutions as well.

A core definition of justice can be drawn from the sixth-century codification of Roman law, the *Institutes of Justinian*: "the constant and perpetual will to render to each his due."[2] This definition suits the idea that justice is a virtue, a habit, and a disposition to act. Justinian's phrasing implies that the virtue of justice deals with the treatment of individual persons and suggests that the agent in justice is a justly willing individual. In summary, according to Miller, the concept of justice encompasses three elements: an agent to enact justice, an obligation to do so, and the expectation of impartiality and consistency in so doing.[3] It should be added that the recipient of just treatment can be a group, treated individually for the purpose of allocation. And the agent of just treatment—whether toward individuals or groups—might be a collective entity, establishing, sustaining, and working through social structures.

John Rawls has most famously articulated this broadening of justice beyond a virtue of an individual: "Justice is the first virtue of social institutions, as truth is of systems of thought."[4] As Paul Ricoeur explains, remarking on Rawls's definition, "'the just' marks the extension of interpersonal relationships to institutions," with respect to "the good."[5] As we will see, Catholic social teaching has come to adopt this perspective.

Yet to present justice as a virtue—an individual virtue and a virtue of social institutions—and as a disposition to "render each his due" does not move the definition of justice very far toward the specific content of justice. What are the specific acts to which the virtue of justice disposes? "To render to each his due" defines the requirements of justice only formally. What is "due" can be specified by several competing criteria, such as equality, merit, need, or entitlement. And what any one of these would require in practice varies with time, place, and circumstance: justice always "takes different forms . . . in different practical contexts."[6] Another complicating issue is that the acts proper to justice can be envisioned either as ideals against which actual states of affairs are judged (e.g., adequate nutrition for every human being), or as practicable standards given existing resources, laws, and expectations (e.g., free school lunches for all low-income children in the United States).

The three goods or principles that in contemporary Catholic social teaching most frequently and prominently indicate the kinds of actions to which the virtue of justice is disposed, understood to apply consistently across contexts, are the common good, the dignity of the person, and the preferential option for the poor. Here the formal criteria of justice as "what is due" are defined indirectly—as equality, need, and comprehensive social good. And since these criteria are frequently in tension with each other, if not mutually exclusive, much more must be done to define justice coherently.

Perhaps the most formidable barrier to a successful theorization of justice in Catholic social teaching is the problem that the "disposition" to act justly is even harder to come by than knowledge of what justice requires. Each historical place, era, and culture presents myriad evolving disincentives to act justly. This problem demands a more profound solution than what philosophical concepts of justice typically envision.

Modern and postmodern developments have made the job of defining justice, its acts, and its practices immeasurably more daunting by modern and postmodern developments since 1891. Some of these factors are the emergence, prevalence, and subversion of democratic political systems worldwide; pluralism, secularization, and the resurgence of religion in the global South; renewed attention to the social conditions of justice in liberal societies and to the value of individuals within communitarian, hierarchical ones; the growth of global financial systems and markets, generating inequality; increased attention to the interdependence of individual and structural agency; and complex, locally actualized yet globally interconnected ethical and political challenges around the environment, armed conflict, religious freedom, political corruption, and both gender- and race-based violence.

To assess justice in Catholic social teaching, let's briefly consider two highly influential approaches: the views of Thomas Aquinas, the primary theological-ethical forebear of the Catholic justice tradition (treated more thoroughly in Jean Porter's chapter), and those of John Rawls (examined carefully in the chapter by Francis Fiorenza), considered by many to be the foremost modern secular theorist of justice and thus representative of the environment in which Catholic teaching has evolved.

Aquinas endorses the formal definition of Isidore (a habit or disposition to give each their due), which Aquinas confirms with Aristotle's *Ethics* ("justice is a habit whereby a man is said to be capable of doing just actions according to his choice").[7] Reflecting this medieval environment, Aquinas envisions what is "due" more in terms of the common good of society than of individual dignity.[8] However, the latter, as Porter argues, is not left out of account (the *polis* is not the final end of the person). For example, in discussing when and why homicide is murder, Aquinas establishes the principle that "every part is directed to the whole, as imperfect to perfect, wherefore every part is naturally for the sake of the whole. . . . Now every individual person is compared to the whole community, as part to whole." Therefore, "it is praiseworthy and advantageous" that people who are a danger to the community "be killed in order to safeguard the common good."[9] Anyone familiar with "the new Jim Crow"[10] and mass incarceration in the United States will readily see here the truth in Miller's claim that justice "takes different forms . . . in different practical contexts," as well as in the proposition that this virtue is easily corrupted by vice. Yet Aquinas's priority of the common good resonates with cultures in Asia and Africa, where individual identity is embedded in social relations, as chapters by Agbonkhianmeghe Orobator and George Kodithottam indicate. Nonetheless, Catholic social teaching can also be helpful in these contexts precisely to assert individual dignity against excessively powerful social goals.

John Rawls, on the other hand, is a liberal theorist of justice.[11] His most influential work, *A Theory of Justice* (1971), defines justice as fairness within a worldview in which equal and free individuals have primacy over the common good and whose basic rights are its condition of possibility.[12] Social and economic inequalities must be attached to opportunities open to everyone and are acceptable only insofar as they work to the advantage of all, especially the least well-off.[13] Here we see that Rawls incorporates considerations of societal justice that resemble the requirement of Catholic social teaching that community benefits be shared by all, as Fiorenza argues in his chapter. A Rawlsian argument on capital punishment would not make the individual subordinate to the common good but would ask whether capital punishment were justified as a penalty for severe violations of social norms that are to everyone's advantage and whether everyone benefits from the availability of this ultimate sanction. Because of this principle of fundamental equality, Rawls might have room to consider more readily than Aquinas whether and how some groups are disadvantaged in relation to basic social opportunities, norms, and protections in the first place and whether that negates the justice of capital punishment.

Though Rawls does prioritize individual dignity and might oppose the death penalty, he would not be disposed as a philosopher to say, with Elias Opongo and Orobator, that every life is "sacred" because "we are all created in the image and likeness of God."[14] Aquinas would appreciate the religious orientation of Opongo and Orobator and the transcendent validation of human dignity. But especially as a premodern thinker who relates person and community as part to whole, Aquinas does not give the individual "sacred" value such that killing is always unjust.

In the twenty-first century, however, modern Catholic social teaching has gradually come to reject the death penalty altogether, after accepting it for centuries as a just response to certain grave crimes and as a necessary means of safeguarding the common good. The past century has seen two world wars, the invention of ever more powerful and indiscriminate means of warfare, global media exposing the violence of war, revolutions, societal violence, and even humanitarian intervention. These realities have heightened Catholic skepticism about state-sanctioned killing. Critical studies of political systems, judiciaries, and the law have revealed the rarity of true "due process" and the relative frequency with which capital punishment is inflicted on the poor, the racially marginalized, and the mentally impaired. In 1995, Pope John Paul II restricted the conditions under which capital executions could be justified[15]; in 2018, Pope Francis altered the *Catechism of the Catholic Church* to teach that "the death penalty is inadmissible because it is an attack on the inviolability and dignity of the person."[16]

The example of killing illustrates that today's official Catholic social teaching on justice is indebted both to the long Judeo-Christian tradition on justice (beginning with the biblical sources examined in Anathea Portier-Young's chapter) and to the secular cultures (primarily European) within which it has developed and continues to evolve over time. As a result, this volume's effort to re-think justice today includes voices from that tradition, from those secular cultures, and from traditions and cultures of the Global South.

JUSTICE IN CATHOLIC SOCIAL TEACHING

Justice in Catholic social teaching includes, at least implicitly, the common good, the dignity of the person, and a "preferential option for the poor."[17] If justice is defined as a virtue, these three terms name the criteria and content of the acts, practices, and social institutions to which justice disposes agents. They are the measures of whether individual acts and collective practices are habituated by the virtue of justice or by its contrary vice, injustice.

The Common Good

First, the common good has been an indispensable criterion of justice in modern Catholic social teaching since at least the end of the nineteenth century, and can be seen in the analysis of justice provided by Aquinas, as Jean Porter's chapter makes clear. Catholic social teaching has expanded the concept's sphere of reference from the nation-state and its constitutive communities (e.g., families, neighborhoods, towns, cities, provinces, states, and regions) to the "universal common good" of all nations and peoples. Pope John XXIII's *Pacem in terris* (1963) uses this phrase ten times, primarily to validate the authority and mandate of a global "public authority."[18] Pope Francis expands the universal common good to include the entire planet: "everything is connected," the recurring refrain of *Laudato si'*.[19]

For Catholic social teaching, the common good defines the just society (a society disposed to give each their due) and entails the equal participation of every member of society in basic material, social, and political goods, both as a contributor and as a beneficiary. The common good is a form of dynamic, participatory, and mutually supportive community that is a good in itself. It is not enough to say that the common good provides benefits to individuals, to which just social processes are instrumental. Instead, the social relationships and processes that sustain common good conditions and benefits are already realizations of the common good.[20] Justice *is* the justly functioning society as a historical reality. Society is never fully just, yet it *is* just to the extent that it corrects, rebalances, and reforms its institutions, practices, and relationships to increase the personal and social virtue of justice.

Dignity of the Person

One is tempted to say that the common good *is* the definition of social justice in Catholic social teaching. Yet the danger is that this could be misunderstood either to overemphasize the communal character of the good for humans or to overlook the tensions that can arise between the common good at different levels of society, as cautioned by Francis Fiorenza in his chapter. Thus, the second defining value of Catholic social teaching is the dignity of the person. The Catholic standard of the common good has developed in tandem with the various liberal democratic political traditions that began to emerge in the Enlightenment. John Locke gave these a distinctive formulation in terms of natural rights and the social contract, and they furnish a fundamental and indispensable place to individual freedom and rights, in contrast to earlier Roman Catholic political teaching. Like liberalism, modern Catholic social teaching has come to espouse individual freedom, democracy, human rights, freedom of religion, and a restrained market economy. But individuals—and their rights and freedom—are understood in Catholic thought within the web of social relations that are their condition of possibility and mode of fulfillment.

From papal Catholic social teaching's earliest expressions, the common good incorporates the individual and individual rights as essential components or points of reference for justice. This emphasis became markedly stronger during and after the Second Vatican Council.[21]

Preferential Option for the Poor

A third signature contribution of modern Catholic teaching on justice is the priority given to the needs of the most vulnerable or oppressed, often expressed (in the phrasing of liberation theology) as "the preferential option for the poor," a commitment that extends beyond charity, philanthropy, and targeted social welfare programs. The priority of the poor is distinctively highlighted and mandated by Christian love and the scriptures, investigated in depth in Anathea Portier-Young's chapter and in Maria Inês de Castro Millen's contribution from Brazil. The preferential option gives special visibility to the poor as a matter of systemic justice across the institutions of society, and it forms a critical responsibility of democratic governments and their constituents.

Nonetheless, it is important to recognize that this option for the poor could not have come into view as a matter of systemic, structural, and public justice within church teaching without the "modern" or "liberal" premise of equality or equal respect as the foundation of democratic institutions and civil law. Affirmative action for those historically excluded (e.g., by gender or race) is a measure of justice in liberal democracies too. Catholic social teaching's priority of the poor bears a resemblance to Rawls's "difference principle" (that systemic social and economic inequalities are just only if they benefit the most disadvantaged group).[22]

The special emphasis on the priority of the poor in Catholic social teaching was already visible in *Rerum novarum*: national governments must consider the welfare of the poor equally with the rich, "or else that law of justice will be violated which ordains that each shall have his due." "Justice, therefore, demands that the interests of the poorer population be carefully watched over by the administration."[23] Yet the phrase "the preferential option for the poor" arises from the bishops of Latin America (CELAM) and their public statements issued at their international meetings in the decade from 1968–78, as we will see in more detail later in this chapter.

Recognizing the importance of the preferential option for the poor as Catholic social teaching's criterion of justice helps refocus attention on a critical fact about justice in general. Disagreements about justice do not have to do primarily with stipulations of the basic human goods or of what basic social institutions are necessary for human and political flourishing. The same *fundamental* requisites of human flourishing are recognized virtually everywhere. Instead, disagreements concern who deserves or is entitled to flourish and thus is entitled to the basic conditions of human well-being.

Political disagreements and conflict have to do with relations of *access* to essential human goods, or in other words, with hierarchies of power and mechanisms of inclusion and exclusion in the primary institutions. Debates about access—whether both material and political goods can be called fundamental rights; whether housing, education, or employment are rights at all; or whether only citizens and not refugees have rights within a nation-state—stem from philosophical or cultural disagreements not about what counts as a good but about who is entitled to have that good.

Debates about rights stem from advocacy for and resistance to changes in the status quo of power relationships. Controversies about cultural relativity and objective truth in relation to political systems, economic systems, marriage and family, or sex and gender can operate as "red herrings" to distract from the real justice question: Does a culture, structure, system, or politics prioritize and empower the most marginal or vulnerable stakeholders, "the poor"? Or does it not? The common good in Catholic social teaching, which incorporates the equal dignity of persons as mandating a preferential option for the poor, is an essentially prophetic and subversive concept. "Common good" in Catholic social teaching does not refer to the community status quo of social benefits and lines of access but to the ongoing process of seeking inclusive benefits and access, including the disruptive relations and actions required by constant, reforming attention to those whom the status quo marginalizes or excludes.[24] This is precisely what adds the dispositional problem of justice (what is the level of commitment to justice by persons and systems?) to those we can call epistemological (what is justice?) and criteriological (what does justice require?).

Subsidiarity and Other Requirements of Justice

In addition to the common good, the dignity of the person, and the preferential option for the poor, other justice-related concepts of Catholic social teaching include solidarity, the rule of law, just participatory political institutions, reciprocal rights and duties, and the principle of subsidiarity.

Subsidiarity provides both that higher authorities do *not* interfere unduly with arrangements at the local level and that they *do* intervene when local institutions cannot or do not fulfill the requirements of justice. Importantly, responsibility for the common good includes not only government but also civil society, private institutions, and religious bodies. Somewhat paradoxically, the authors of the modern social encyclicals have often seemed to hope that the United Nations or a like body will step in to handle intransigent structural injustices, such as war, violence, economic inequality, development, forced migration, and climate change.

On the other side, Pope Francis has turned ever more emphatically to the necessity of popular pressure to produce social change,[25] an approach strongly endorsed in Maria Inês de Castro Millen's chapter. In *Laudato si'*, Francis decries the failure of national governments to restrain the environmentally destructive behavior of transnational corporations and praises "the commitment of international agencies and civil society organizations which draw public attention to these issues and offer critical cooperation, employing legitimate means of pressure, to ensure that each government carries out its proper and inalienable responsibility."[26] In 2020, he called the members of popular movements an "invisible army" and praised "social poets, because from the forgotten peripheries where you live, you create admirable solutions for the most pressing problems afflicting the marginalized."[27] In 2021, he addressed the Fourth World Meeting of Popular Movements. This event draws Catholic activists from marginalized communities to support the rights of workers, including street vendors, artisans, fishermen, farmers, builders, and miners. He called for solidarity, subsidiarity, and hope to challenge governments and corporations who devastate the common good by destroying the natural world and turning a deaf ear to those struggling on the peripheries of society.

JUSTICE AS SOCIAL JUSTICE

The phrase "social justice" enters official Catholic social teaching with the 1931 encyclical of Pius XI, *Quadragesimo anno*.[28] Forty years earlier, Leo XIII addressed "the social question" and began the papal engagement with pressing social and economic problems. But the language of "social justice" represents, in an inchoate manner, the idea to be developed later that justice as a social virtue is concerned with a complex field of ethical-political agency, comprising social institutions and structures, cultures, and responsibilities of individual agents within a dynamic "social" whole. This identification of "social justice"—requiring multiple, intersecting forms of agency and informed by a "social charity" that inspires a genuine disposition to seek justice—is a new development. It widens the meaning of the common good and opens Catholic social thought to the kind of analysis of social structures provided in chapter 9, by Daniel Finn.

For nearly a century now, modern Catholic social teaching has employed the term "social justice" interchangeably with "justice."[29] This phrase reminds us of the complexity of justice as a social virtue. As David Hollenbach stresses, the virtue of justice engages a "web of social interdependence." To specify what justice requires entails "examining the social relationships, patterns of mutuality and structures of interdependence which bind human beings together in communities."[30] "Social justice" implies similarly that the coherence of justice is attained in specific practical realizations more than in theoretical accounts that must leave the door open to the different intersecting responsibilities that any virtuous person will encounter. Thus, even amid a deeply philosophical engagement with justice in Catholic social teaching, there stands a concern for its practicalities, attending to both the *nīti* and the *nyāya* approaches to justice identified in George Kodithottam's chapter on Hinduism and Buddhism.

The tradition of Catholic magisterial political and social thinking that preceded modern Catholic social teaching relied on the definition of justice provided by Thomas Aquinas.[31] Jean Porter notes, referencing Aquinas, that "the virtue of justice is oriented toward right relations with other people, the community, and God."[32] This part of the definition of justice has not changed. But Aquinas sorts this virtue into three types, which regard primarily the obligations of and among individuals within a justly ordered society. While each type may *imply* social, structural, and institutional sustainability by just or unjust means and to just or unjust ends, Aquinas does not directly address such structures as subjects of justice.[33] The types are commutative justice (rectitude in individual relationships), distributive justice (rectitude in sharing or apportioning the benefits and duties belonging to the community as a whole), and legal or general justice (orienting social relationships to their highest end, the common good).[34] This typology still appears in contemporary Catholic social teaching, but, as indicated by the term "social justice," the field on which it is envisioned and realized has changed.

Aquinas's definition of the virtue of justice presumes a divinely ordained social order within which rightly ordered relations will be stable and more or less clearly defined. Justice or equity takes due regard of natural dignity (and, in that sense, equality, as described in Jean Porter's chapter) of human beings as such, as well as of the shared basic "inclinations" and needs of persons.[35] Yet for Aquinas, practical equality is channeled by the hierarchy of social roles, with socially normative gender roles being a case in point.[36] Of course, commutative, distributive, and general justice vary in the concrete due to the variability and contingency of circumstances. Yet it would be hard to call Aquinas's view of society dynamic and open-ended or his view of the virtue of justice geared to the standpoint of "the poor."

The changes implicit in adopting the phrase "social justice" are critical. But of more *practical* importance to the unique character of justice in Catholic social teaching are changes in the church's presence, voice, activity, and influence in the political sphere. The Roman Catholic Church in the sixteenth through eighteenth centuries supported wars of religion, sought territorial precedence in Europe through alliances with state and imperial governments, used colonial expansion to extend influence, and opposed the rights-advocating French and American revolutions. (Ahead of their time, thinkers like Francisco de Vitoria and Bartolomé de las Casas were the exceptions that proved the rule.) Encyclicals from the late nineteenth century onward, in contrast, championed social cooperation in more pluralistic societies and affirmed universal rights. Yet until the mid-twentieth century, they still defined the common good and dignity of the person within a presumed hierarchical and organic society. In the first modern social encyclicals (by Leo XIII and Pius XI), the princes of the church advised princes of government and industry to be more just to the dependent classes.

Nevertheless, these early social encyclicals reveal a new social consciousness about what justice will involve. First, they are marked by what would later come to be called "the preferential option for the poor." Second, they recognize that overcoming injustice and approximating justice means engaging a complicated international social, political, cultural, and economic reality. Multiple institutions and their participatory stakeholders interact, overlap, work at cross-purposes, and reinforce one another, all in motion and constantly morphing. The term "social justice" (accompanied by "social charity") identifies and replies normatively to this reality.

THE ENCYCLICAL HISTORY

After the American and French Revolutions, the nineteenth century saw the spread of democracy and liberal government across Europe and North America. Similar ideals inspired twentieth-century resistance to colonial power in Asia, Africa, and Latin America. These developments coincided with the beginning of modern papal Catholic social teaching in 1891. This emerging Catholic tradition incorporated liberal values of individual dignity and freedom while retaining the older Aristotelian-Thomistic conviction that persons are social by nature, that the common good is the condition of individual rights and flourishing, and that persons must be formed by the gospel virtue of love of neighbor.

Both *Rerum novarum* and *Quadragesimo anno* identify the plight of the poor as the most urgent social priority. For Pius XI, the "non-owning worker" and "rural wage worker" pushed to "the lowest level of existence" are in intolerable situations.[37] In this context, the pope introduces the term "social justice" (appearing nine times) to gesture toward the profound and far-reaching realignments of social order that justice involves. He asserts that the "huge disparity" of wealth in the present economic system must be brought to "conformity with the norms of the common good, that is, social justice."[38] "The public institutions of the nations" should conform to "the common good, that is, the norm of social justice."[39]

Pius is well aware that the reforms he envisions require a comprehensive mandate, social-institutional capacity, and political power. Social justice means the "penetration" by justice of the "institutions themselves of peoples" and of "all social life." And justice can only be "effective" with "a juridical and social order" that can reshape the economy.[40] The many institutions that constitute that order are neither free-standing nor impersonal; they are created, upheld, and changed by morally colored cultures, relationships, and practices in which personal agency and collectively patterned agency intersect and affect one another. At stake in the reform of the economic order is the complete reorientation of a social system in which "capital hires workers, that is, the non-owning working class, with a view to and under such terms that it directs business and even the whole economic system according to its own will and advantage."[41] Pope Pius states directly what is implicit yet generally avoided in *Rerum novarum*: this restoration will require a massive redistribution of resources, at odds not simply with the hegemonic industrial system. It challenges the fundamental values, motives, and interests of those who established that system, benefit from it, and hence collaboratively sustain it with the social-structural and institutional consolidation and enlargement of their agency.[42] Instilling individual virtues does not go far enough; collective action and holistic conversion of intersecting, culturally embedded, and mobile institutions are what social justice means.

Like later popes, but unlike some other Christian social theorists of the day, such as Reinhold Niebuhr, Pius XI does not question whether such massive change is possible. Still, he does envision that it will require supernatural help. "Social justice" requires an infusion of "social charity."[43] Social charity confirms and empowers justice as a genuine disposition to act in the face of the countervailing power of distorted self-interest and the social structures through which people and groups perpetuate and facilitate it. As Pope John Paul II would later express, social charity (which he renames as "solidarity") is "a firm and persevering determination to commit oneself to the common good; that is to say to the good of all and of each individual."[44]

For Pius XI, social charity can become a widely operative social virtue, but its spread depends on the political influence of Christian citizens working in and through the social order. Lay Christians are commissioned to convey gospel values into the social-structural sphere. Christine Hinze explains that the "practical centerpiece" of Pius XI's social agenda (in education, family, and the socially embedded economy) was the lay movement Catholic Action, subject to episcopal supervision and cooperating with clergy. The mission of Catholic Action was "infusing Christian values and spirit" into public and private life, especially via concern for the working classes.[45] This focus on Catholic citizens was, of course, practical. The popes of the first half of the twentieth century did not yet address themselves "to all people of good will" as later papal encyclicals would. But there were theological reasons as well. Charity as a theological virtue was not seen as equally available to all. It is not until *Nostra Aetate* (1965), and most especially *Dominus Iesus* (2000), that magisterial teaching incorporated the (Rahnerian) claim that God is present in all major religious traditions and that the grace of Christ can awaken every human heart.

Parts of *Quadragesimo anno*'s vision and social program are today outdated and even failures. These include Pius XI's aspiration to "Christianize the social order," his wholesale condemnation of socialism and socialist ideas, and his disconnect from the upwardly mobile aspirations of "the working class" themselves. Nonetheless, this encyclical was groundbreaking, and its influence on later Catholic social teaching has been immense and long-lasting. *Quadragesimo anno*'s interpretations of the common good, social justice, and subsidiarity; its denunciation of economic disparities and the excessive self-interest propelling them; its aspiration to a "multi-associational" inclusive society; its diagnoses of structural evils and the need for structural reforms; its relocation of poverty alleviation to the ground of justice, not charity alone; its reinforcement of the virtue of justice by a kind of social grace; and its call to Catholics at all levels of society to renovate cultures and institutions—all these determine the meaning of justice for the subsequent Catholic social teaching tradition.[46] Pius XI's emphasis on practical and energetic Christian and public action across the sectors and structures of society becomes even stronger as the tradition progresses, for example, in *Populorum progressio* (Paul VI, 1967), *Justitia in mundo* (Synod of Bishops, 1971). and *Laudato si'* (Francis, 2015). His insight that genuine commitment to justice exhibits charity and that both virtues can be socially-structurally operative resounds throughout the whole subsequent tradition. This is especially important in light of twenty-first-century challenges to (and defeats of) justice and the possibility of transformative political hope. Social charity is redefined in significant ways by John Paul II, who in renaming it as "solidarity" makes it more inclusive (*Sollicitudo rei socialis*); and by Francis, with his direct appeal to the compassionate and "connected" spirituality of all religious believers, not only Catholics or even all Christians (*Laudato si'*).

Human Rights

The occasion of *Rerum novarum* was the exploitation of workers and the responsibilities of the privileged classes (also the primary concern of the Protestant social gospel, arising around the same time). But at least until the Second Vatican Council, Catholic social teaching was a Eurocentric tradition that envisioned reform rather than reversals of the status quo. *Rerum novarum* was designed both to champion the rights of the working classes against unaccountable industrialists and to avoid the systemic social change called for by (atheist) Marxist socialism.

From modern papal social teaching's earliest expressions, the common good incorporated the individual and individual rights as essential components or points of reference for justice. This emphasis became markedly stronger during and after the Second Vatican Council. As David Hollenbach stresses, John XXIII's *Pacem in terris* (published in 1963, during the council) took a significant step forward in affirming the modern rights and freedoms that the Catholic Church had long opposed. "*Pacem in terris* moved the leadership of the Church from a position of staunch opposition to modern rights and freedoms to activist engagement in the global struggle for human rights. This shift was one of the most dramatic reversals in the long history of the Catholic tradition."[47] In fact, Catholic social teaching is problematically "liberal" when it frequently prioritizes the individual *over* the common good, even seeing the common good as essentially the protection of individual dignity and liberty. *Pacem in terris*, for example, proclaims, "in our time the common good is chiefly guaranteed when personal rights and duties are maintained." Securing the "inviolable" rights of the individual is even the "chief duty" of government.[48] The problem with such oversimplifications is that the common good is not an aggregation of individual goods, nor simply the social attainment and provision of goods to individuals. The common good can only be realized cooperatively, and individual well-being and happiness require participation in the processes that realize the common good for and with all.[49]

Nonetheless, balancing its stress on rights, *Pacem in terris* also affirms building up the common good, for human beings are "social by nature."[50] *Gaudium et spes* (Vatican II) insists on the "need to transcend an individualist morality."[51] Importantly, the common good means affirming and sustaining social and material (primarily economic) rights equally with civil and political rights. This is a critical move against the individualistic understanding of rights and justice prevalent in liberal and Western human rights ideologies.

The Preferential Option for the Poor

In pre–Vatican II expressions of Catholic social teaching, care for the poor is presented as a responsibility of elites and leaders, not as the empowerment *of* the poor.[52] Yet the message takes on new dimensions, including the agency of the poor, with *Gaudium et spes*: all the goods of the earth have a common destiny; no one has a right to appropriate more than their share; relief of the poor is a duty of justice; in cases of extreme necessity, people have a right to take from the riches of others; both individuals and nations should be furnished "the means necessary to helping and developing themselves."[53]

As implied by the preferential option for the poor, the agency and empowerment of the poor themselves receive more overt and frequent endorsement in Catholic social teaching with the advent of Latin American liberation theology, as Maria Inês de Castro Millen examines in her chapter. Meetings of the Latin American Conference of Catholic Bishops (CELAM) in 1968 in Medellín, Colombia, and in 1979 in Puebla, Mexico, accentuated the misery of the majority of people in their countries, diagnosed grinding poverty as the result of structural injustices and "institutionalized violence," and coined the phrase "preferential option for the poor." As Hollenbach notes, this phrase and the responsibility it denotes "has become a leitmotif in Catholic social thought on the level of the magisterium, in social theology and ethics, and in much of the Church's pastoral discourse."[54]

It would be difficult to find a social encyclical since then that does not in some way allude to this theme. One of the most important expressions is John Paul II's *Sollicitudo rei socialis* (1987), which presents "the option or love of preference for the poor" as an expression of Christian charity, yet an obligation that "applies equally to our social responsibilities . . . and to the logical decisions to be made concerning the ownership and use of goods."[55] John Paul II recognizes, moreover, the growing solidarity among the poor themselves, who together take action for their own futures with the support and help of the church.[56] Immediately after his election, Pope Francis named his aspirational Catholic Church as a "Church of the Poor" and "a poor Church for the poor." The Synods on the Family (with their parish-level diagnostic questionnaires), the Synod on the Amazon, Pope Francis's invitation to Sr. Veronica Openibo to address assembled bishops regarding the plight of African women sex abuse victims, as well as his (limited) outreach to LGBTQ+ Catholics represent efforts—still in process—to give voice and power to the "poor."

Sinful Social Structures

Quadragesimo anno began an important development in Catholic social teaching's understanding of justice as structural, with implications for moral agency, responsibility, and reform. John Paul II, in *Sollicitudo rei socialis*, addresses structural sin,[57] targeting, for example, "the structures of ownership, especially with regard to the so-called means of production while limiting agency and responsibility to individual persons"[58] As we have seen, Pius XI had already critiqued these same structures in a way that acknowledged that, as structures, they incorporate and organize personal agency in systems of collaboration: capital "directs business and even the whole economic system according to its own will and advantage."[59] Because human persons create, sustain, and continually constitute structures as forms of collective agency, structures include, depend on, yet transcend individual powers.

As Daniel Finn investigates in chapter 9, sinful structures and those advantaged within them exert power to perpetuate a status quo that favors the interests of the privileged. This is one reason why Pope Francis turns to local peoples and popular movements to counteract entrenched economic structures. Local communities and popular movements can form new economic and environmental cultures and generate new solidaristic structures that empower appropriate forms of agency. Like *Quadragesimo anno, Laudato Si'* identifies fundamentally personal yet socially structured self-interest as the power that impedes efforts to achieve environmental reforms, such as the UN climate accords.[60] Structures of destruction (e.g., transnational corporations and complicit national governments) and structures of reform (international institutions and national regulations) embody different agential "mindsets,"[61] for one, the technological paradigm, and for the other, integral ecology. But to date, the latter mindset is taking shape mostly in top-down endeavors and has been "ineffectual."[62] Pope Francis thus turns to broad-based ecological education, to conversions of spirituality and imagination, and to mobilization from below. Structural reform is possible because local individuals and local groups, and the social innovations they create, "are able to instill a greater sense of responsibility, a strong sense of community, a readiness to protect others, a spirit of creativity and a deep love for the land. . . . Because the enforcement of laws is at times inadequate due to corruption, public pressure has to be exerted in order to bring about decisive political action."[63] Pope Francis is demonstrably right that popular pressure is sometimes necessary to persuade self-interested politicians and corporate executives to act virtuously or at least to realize that their own interests won't ultimately be served by a course of action inimical to the common good. However, as white supremacist and xenophobic social movements prove, collective "grassroots" action is not always virtuous.

CHALLENGES FOR THE FUTURE

Three challenges for the concept of justice in the Catholic social teaching of the future can be briefly indicated.

Decentralization

As a moral and political tradition, Catholic social teaching necessarily looks to specific historical developments and particular contexts to embody, discern, and define what justice means in the concrete. This process begins with the industrial revolution in Europe and reaches to the destruction of the Amazonian rainforest, the habitat of its Indigenous peoples. More explicitly than ever before, Pope Francis, convening the Synod on the Amazon in 2019, held up local wisdom as the source of just solutions for the peoples of the Amazon. For Francis, popular movements generate solidarity and are critical to the fight for social and structural justice.[64]

Moreover, in continental and regional expressions of Catholicism around the globe, pluralism is undoubtedly more in evidence and more vocal than in 1891.[65] What does this attention to regional differences, and synodality in general, mean for the centrality of pontifical social teaching, its relevance, and its authority? On the one hand, newly visible "Catholicisms" usefully and powerfully decenter biased conceptions of justice generated from the Global North. On the other hand, the fact that local churches ignore or do not (theologically) "receive" culturally unpopular teachings (whether on nonviolence, the environment, market capitalism, birth control, women's rights, or legal protections for LGBTQ+ persons) deserves more sustained and consistent analysis.

Limited Success and Recurrent Failure

Laudato Si' is typical of the entire Catholic social teaching tradition in that it is a hopeful encyclical, concluding on a reassuring note: God "does not abandon us, he does not leave us alone, for he has united himself definitively to our earth, and his love constantly impels us to find new ways forward."[66] Yet, given Francis's diagnosis of the power of profit-driven interests and widespread apathy and even complicity regarding climate change, one wonders whether the dire predictions of climate scientists are more likely to be realized than the climate goals held out at UN meetings. Similarly, discouraging observations could be made about the practical effects of Catholic social teaching on world peace, human rights, "integral development," and reform of the world economic order. Can this hopeful justice tradition be sustained? Should justice as a social-structural goal be scaled back, for example, redefined in terms of limited, local, and perhaps short-term successes? What would that mean for a huge, pressing, and highly consequential justice problem like climate change, especially given that so many of us and our communities are most motivated to meet our own near-term needs? And from whose perspective should the determination be made?

Gender Bias

Modern Catholic social teaching has continuously praised women and addressed women's concerns. Yet it purveys a gender-unequal "complementarity" framework, characterizing feminism and other calls for gender justice as "radical feminism" and "gender ideology." Despite the rhetoric of "preferential option for the poor," "empowerment of the poor," popular mobilization, and local wisdom, papal social teaching does not typically prefer women, empower women, mobilize women, or heed women's wisdom. Both Pope Francis and John Paul II identify women's disadvantaged status, women's rights, and women's contributions as real and important. Both John Paul II's 1995 *Letter to Women* and Francis's *Fratelli tutti* make genuine advances in this regard. But the realization of justice for women—whether interpersonal or structural—and for those who do not fit the gender binary needs much improvement in Catholic social teaching, and within the church, as Agnes Brazal emphasizes in her chapter.

CONCLUSION

Global Catholic diversity is having an impact on Catholic social teaching. Pope Francis has advocated a decentralization of authority in crises of justice that have disparate causes and impacts (especially climate change) and has called for empowering popular action. It seems that greater decentralization of the tradition of Catholic social teaching is not so much a trend as a lasting modification. Agnes Brazal's contribution to this volume adds the critical point that participatory diversification will not be sustained unless there are structures that support it, which thus far is not the case for every Catholic constituency, most especially women.

For example, however important local peoples and popular movements may be for the Catholic social teaching of the future, the participation of formerly excluded races, classes, castes, and genders, even within those same peoples and movements, will not be meaningful unless guaranteed by established structures of inclusion upheld by committed participants. Otherwise, exclusionary biases will simply perpetuate unjust, though more localized, structures. As Brazal and Orobator make explicit regarding Asia and Africa, many societies and the Catholic Church are still quite far from having prioritized, much less implemented, participatory structures that include women. This is an area in which the church itself would do well to heed the prophetic message of popular movements for gender equality.

Decentralization presents at least one further challenge regarding Scriptural diversity and authority identified in this volume by Anathea Portier-Young. This is the problem of adjudication among competing worldviews and practices in a church that is becoming ever more diversified.

This challenge was fully displayed in the episcopal debates that went on in, between, and after the 2014 and 2015 sessions of the Synod on the Family. Francis's convening the Synod on Synodality raised similar concerns. It appears, too, in Pope Francis's attempts to regard all respectfully in *Amoris laetitia* (2019) while returning the settlement of the most contentious issues to the local churches. Portier-Young is undoubtedly right that self-criticism is essential, including "accountability, a surrender of interpretive power-over, and a commitment to shared interpretive power and authority."

When we consider the crises of violence, undemocratic government, economic inequality, and environmental destruction that threaten the flourishing of communities and peoples worldwide, the recurrent practical failure of Catholic social teaching's norms and goals makes it evident why even sporadic local successes are cause for gratitude and rejoicing. Solidarity in working for a cause not only engenders community and hope, but it also enhances experience and creative thinking about what will work better in the future or on a larger scale.

Thus, while proponents of Catholic social teaching should be wary of sanguine claims about common humanity, universal good will, and global governance, they must sustain their commitment to large-scale change. Catholic social teaching is a mandate for local churches together to be the body of Christ in the world, building institutions, governance structures, and alliances for political action that are more just. As such, charity-informed justice can lead to the comprehensive social, political, economic, and lifestyle changes required to preserve the common good, the dignity of all persons, and humanity's planetary environment.

BIBLIOGRAPHY

Alexander, Michelle, and Cornel West. *The New Jim Crow: Mass Incarceration in the Age of Colorblindness.* 10th anniversary edition. New Press, 2010.

Aquinas, Thomas. *Summa theologiae.* Complete American ed. in two vols. Translated by Fathers of the English Dominican Province. Benziger Brothers, 1948.

Azetsop, Jacquineau. "The Return to the Common as a Challenge to the 'Eclipse of the Public:' Five Usages of the Common Good," In *Public Theology and the Global Common Good: The Contribution of David Hollenbach, SJ.,* edited by Kevin Ahern, Meghan J. Clark, Kristin E. Heyer, and Laurie Johnston. Orbis Books, 2016.

Cloutier, David. "What Can Social Science Teach Catholic Social Thought About the Common Good?" In *Empirical Foundations of the Common Good,* edited by Daniel Finn. Oxford University Press, 2017.

Francis. "Address to World Meeting of Popular Movements." https://www.vatican.va/content/francesco/en/speeches/2014/october/documents/papa-francesco_20141028_incontro-mondiale-movimenti-popolari.html.

Francis. *Amoris laetitia*. https://www.vatican.va/content/francesco/en/apost_exhortations/documents/papa-francesco_esortazione-ap_20160319_amoris-laetitia.html.

Francis. *Fratelli tutti*. https://www.vatican.va/content/francesco/en/encyclicals/documents/papa-francesco_20201003_enciclica-fratelli-tutti.html.

Francis. *Laudato si'*. https://www.vatican.va/content/francesco/en/encyclicals/documents/papa-francesco_20150524_enciclica-laudato-si.html.

Francis. "Letter to the Popular Movements." Apostolic Journey—Bolivia: Participation at the Second World Meeting of Popular Movements at the Expo Feria Exhibition Centre, Santa Cruz de la Sierra, July 9, 2015. https://www.vatican.va/content/francesco/en/letters/2020/documents/papa-francesco_20200412_lettera-movimentipopolari.html.

Francis. "Participation at the Second World Meeting of Popular Movements." https://www.vatican.va/content/francesco/en/speeches/2015/july/documents/papa-francesco_20150709_bolivia-movimenti-popolari.html.

Gudorf, Christine E. "Commentary on Octogesima Adveniens," In *Modern Catholic Social Teaching*, edited by Kenneth Himes, OFM, et. al., 315–332. 2nd ed. Georgetown University Press, 2018.

Himes, Kenneth R., Lisa Sowle Cahill, Charles Curran, David Hollenbach, and Thomas A. Shannon, eds. *Modern Catholic Social Teaching*, 2nd ed. Georgetown University Press, 2018.

Hinze, Christine. "Commentary on *Gaudium et spes*." In *Modern Catholic Social Teaching*, edited by Kenneth Himes, OFM, et. al., 151–74. 2nd ed. Georgetown University Press, 2018.

Hollenbach, David. "Commentary on *Quadragesimo anno*." In *Modern Catholic Social Teaching*, edited by Kenneth Himes, OFM, et. al., 266–91. 2nd ed. Georgetown University Press, 2018.

Hollenbach, David. *The Common Good and Christian Ethics*. Cambridge University Press, 2002.

Holy See Press Office. "New Revision of Number 2267 of the *Catechism of the Catholic Church* on the Death Penalty." August 2, 2018. https://press.vatican.va/content/salastampa/en/bollettino/pubblico/2018/08/02/180802a.html.

John Paul II. *Evangelium vitae*. https://www.vatican.va/content/john-paul-ii/en/encyclicals/documents/hf_jp-ii_enc_25031995_evangelium-vitae.html.

John Paul II. "Letter to Women." https://www.vatican.va/content/john-paul-ii/en/letters/1995/documents/hf_jp-ii_let_29061995_women.html.

John Paul II. *Sollicitudo rei socialis*. https://www.vatican.va/content/john-paul-ii/en/encyclicals/documents/hf_jp-ii_enc_30121987_sollicitudo-rei-socialis.html.

John XXIII. *Pacem in terris*. https://www.vatican.va/content/john-xxiii/en/encyclicals/documents/hf_j-xxiii_enc_11041963_pacem.html.

Leo XIII. *Rerum novarum*. https://www.vatican.va/content/leo-xiii/en/encyclicals/documents/hf_l-xiii_enc_15051891_rerum-novarum.html.

Miller, David. "Justice." *The Stanford Encyclopedia of Philosophy*. 2021. https://plato.stanford.edu/entries/justice/.

O'Neill, William. *Catholic Social Teaching: A User's Guide*. Orbis, 2021.

Opongo, Elias, and Agbonkhianmeghe Orobator. *Faith Doing Justice: A Manual for Social Analysis, Catholic Social Teachings, and Social Justice.* Pauline Publications, 2008.

Second Vatican Council. *Gaudium et spes.* https://www.vatican.va/archive/hist_councils/ii_vatican_council/documents/vat-ii_const_19651207_gaudium-et-spes_en.html.

Pius XI. *Quadragesimo anno.* https://www.vatican.va/content/pius-xi/en/encyclicals/documents/hf_p-xi_enc_19310515_quadragesimo-anno.html.

Porter, Jean. *Justice as a Virtue: A Thomistic Perspective.* Eerdmans, 2016.

Rawls, John. *A Theory of Justice.* Harvard University Press, 1971.

Rawls, John. *Political Liberalism.* Columbia University Press, 2005.

Ricoeur, Paul. *Oneself as Another.* University of Chicago Press, 1990.

Riordan, Patrick. Review of *Empirical Foundations of the Common Good: What Theology Can Learn from Social Science,* edited by Daniel K. Finn. *The Heythrop Journal* 60, no. 6 (2019): 197.

Second Vatican Council. *Gaudium et spes.* https://www.vatican.va/archive/hist_councils/ii_vatican_council/documents/vat-ii_const_19651207_gaudium-et-spes_en.html.

NOTES

1. Miller, "Justice," 1.1–2.1.
2. Miller, 1.1-2.1.
3. Miller, 1.1-2.1.
4. Rawls, *A Theory of Justice,* 3.
5. Ricoeur, *Oneself as Another,* 197.
6. Miller, "Justice," 1.0.
7. Aquinas, *Summa theologiae* II–II.58.1.
8. Aquinas, I–II.21.4.ad.3: "Man is not ordained to the body politic according to all that he is."
9. Aquinas, II–II.64.2. In article 3, Aquinas places limits on who has the authority to kill, in respect both of social order and of the offender's basic human dignity.
10. Alexander, *The New Jim Crow.*
11. Liberalism is only touched on here, to set justice in Catholic social teaching in context. A more thorough treatment is provided by Francis Fiorenza in his chapter in this volume.
12. Over time, Rawls adapted and changed the ideas in the original book, especially in *Political Liberalism* (1993). This volume considers pluralism of worldviews, the role of democratic government, and the possibility of civic unity in diversity, but these later developments of Rawls's work don't affect the argument here.
13. Rawls, *A Theory of Justice,* 60–62, 75.
14. Opongo and Orobator, *Faith Doing Justice,* 58.
15. John Paul II, *Evangelium vitae,* nos. 27 and 56.
16. Holy See Press Office, "New Revision."
17. Second Vatican Council, *Gaudium et spes,* nos. 30 and 74.
18. *Pacem in terris,* nos. 132–40.
19. The literature on the common good in Catholic social teaching is immense. See Hollenbach, *The Common Good;* and Azetsop, "The Return to the Common as a Challenge," and multiple other chapters in the same book.
20. Cloutier, "What Can Social Science Teach," 178, 183.

21. Himes, *Modern Catholic Social Teaching*.
22. Rawls, *Theory of Justice*, 65.
23. Leo XIII, *Rerum novarum*, no. 27.
24. On the difference between a conservative and a subversive common good concept, see Riordan, "Review of Empirical Foundations," 957. On the processive nature of the common good and the recognition of a constructive character of contention and conflict, see Cloutier, "What Can Social Science Teach?," 178–79, 183–84.
25. His programmatic statement is Pope Francis, *Participation at the Second World Meeting*.
26. Francis, *Laudato si'* (2015), no. 38.
27. Francis, "Letter to the Popular Movements."
28. Francis, "Letter to the Popular Movements."
29. Pius XI, *Quadragesimo anno*, no. 110.
30. Hollenbach, "Commentary," 210.
31. Aquinas, *Summa theologiae* II-II.48. Aquinas also includes an infused moral virtue of justice (I-II.65.3), leading to extensive debates about the relation of nature and grace in morality for Aquinas. Those will not be undertaken here.
32. Jean Porter, *Justice as a Virtue*, 171.
33. A caveat might be that he does address the justice and injustice of institutions or structures such as war, marriage, and forms of government.
34. Aquinas, *Summa theologiae* II-II.58–61. In her chapter in this volume, Jean Porter holds that justice in Aquinas does not refer to the common good. For the ways these types of justice remain but operate in a more dynamic way in Catholic social teaching, see O'Neill, *Catholic Social Teaching*, 31–8.
35. S.T., I-II.94.2.
36. S.T., I.92.3.
37. Pius XI, *Quadragesimo anno*, no. 58.
38. Pius XI, no. 58.
39. Pius XI, no. 110.
40. Pius XI, no. 88.
41. Pius XI, no. 101.
42. Pius XI, no. 88.
43. Pius XI, no. 88
44. John Paul II, *Solicitudo rei socialis*, no. 38.
45. Hollenbach, "Commentry on *Quadragesimo anno*," 160.
46. Hinze, 179.
47. Hollenbach, "Commentary," 289
48. John XXIII, *Pacem in terris*, no. 60.
49. See Cloutier's critique in "What Can Social Science Teach?," 172.
50. *Pacem in terris*, no. 30. *Gaudium et spes*, no. 30, affirms this by saying that justice is only fulfilled if each person contributes to the common good.
51. *Gaudium et spes*, no. 30.
52. See Gudorf, "Commentary on Octogesima," 326–44.
53. *Gaudium et spes*, no. 69.
54. Hollenbach, "Commentary," 296.
55. John Paul II, *Sollicitudo rei socialis*, no. 42. See also no. 47, where "solidarity and love of preference for the poor" are used.
56. John Paul II, 39.

57. John Paul II, nos. 36–38.
58. John Paul II, no. 20.
59. John Paul II, no. 101.
60. Francis, *Laudato si'*, no. 169.
61. Francis, no. 175.
62. Francis, no. 169.
63. Francis, no. 179.
64. Francis, "Address to World Meeting of Popular Movements," 2014.
65. Agnes Brazal (in this volume) shows that more participatory ecclesial governance and decision-making had already begun in earlier pontificates, especially with respect being accorded to the leadership of "native" clergy and bishops. *Caritas in veritate* takes subsidiarity to the "grassroots" level. Francis's emphasis on synodality is a further phase in this trajectory of development.
66. Francis, *Laudato si'*, no. 245. The occurrence five times in this one sentence of male pronouns in reference to God ("God" replaced one of them) is an instance of the gender bias that pervades the Catholic social teaching tradition.

CHAPTER 8

Experience, Social Location, and Justice

Agnes M. Brazal

Any effort to re-think justice in Catholic social thought must attend to more than theory. The intellectual history of debates about justice is important. But so are inquiries into how people experience justice and how the social locations of individuals affect their understanding of it. Whether in positions of public authority, subject to it, or theorizing about justice, one's social location and personal experience of justice and injustice are essential to any adequate understanding of justice itself.

This chapter will address the relation of theories of justice to experience and social location by focusing on the issue of justice for women. Gender inequality has persisted "despite decades (indeed centuries) of social protest, policy initiatives, educational reform, nongovernmental organization activity, national and international legislation."[1] Gender inequality is typically legitimated by the belief that the division of labor between men and women is natural. That is, it is thought to be grounded in biological characteristics and is, as a result, seen by many as divinely ordained.

This chapter focuses on two approaches to justice that provide alternative views of gender inequality—one based on universalizable experience of sameness and another on the recognition of group differences. On the one hand, Martha Nussbaum analyzes gender inequality by employing what she identifies as shared human capabilities. On the other, Iris Marion Young focuses on recognizing (gender) differences among social groups and group-based oppression. These two approaches are complementary, not mutually exclusive. Each has something important to contribute to re-thinking justice in Catholic social thought.

The last part of this chapter extends the discussion of difference by arguing the importance of participative community mediation as a feature of just institutions. The resulting insights from the above discussion help attend to justice obligations related to gender and to justice as a characteristic of the church as a social structure.

THE GENDERED DIVISION OF LABOR IN THE CHURCH AND SOCIETY

As Jean Porter and Lisa Sowle Cahill have made clear in their chapters in this volume, justice has classically been understood as rendering to others what is due to them. But in a hierarchical society, this means equality within particular groups, where some groups (identified, say, by class, race, or gender) are considered superior by others. For instance, all persons of the same class, race, and gender are equal, but this equality often disappears if persons differ in even one of these characteristics.[2]

With the Second Vatican Council, the concept of justice shifted to include the condemnation of all forms of discrimination and the acknowledgment of the equality of all peoples regardless of social status.[3] However, it maintained a view of women and men as possessing different natures that become the ground for their differing roles and vocations in the church and in society.[4] A similar critique appears in chapter 7 by Lisa Cahill and chapter 1 by Agbonkhianmeghe Orobator. Women are primary nurturers and caretakers, while men are primary breadwinners. Women's vocation is motherhood or virginity, and they cannot have the vocation to priesthood. These "complementary" roles are not viewed as unjust to women.

This form of gender complementarity is the ideology used to justify sexism in society and within the church. It leads to unequal wages given to women and men for the same work, since women's salary is considered supplementary. It also results in a double burden on women. They earn income for the family while simultaneously being fully responsible for taking care of the children and managing the household. This leads some parents to invest more in the education of their sons than their daughters, since it is not the primary responsibility of women to earn a living. Consequently, in poverty and without proper education, some women are forced into jobs like prostitution.

The magisterium clearly distinguishes between its support for gender equality in areas of education, employment, and wages, from equal access to the ordained ministry.[5] This is because, as *Inter Insignores* claims, the church is not a simple government.... It is not granted by people's spontaneous choice; even when it involved designation through election...; and it is the Holy Spirit, given by ordination, who grants participation in the ruling power of the Supreme Pastor, Christ (Acts 20:28)....

For this reason one cannot see how it is possible to propose the admission of women to the priesthood in virtue of the equality of rights of the human person, an equality which holds good also for Christians... Moreover, and above all, to consider the ministerial priesthood as a human right would be to misjudge its nature completely:... it is the object of a specific and totally gratuitous vocation: "You did not choose me, no, I chose you; and I commissioned you...." (Jn 15:16; Heb 5:4)[6]

Far from seeing the exclusion of women from the ordained ministry as unjust, the official position of the church regards it instead as a divinely ordained division of labor.

JUSTICE WITHIN A POLITICS OF SAMENESS

For the philosopher Martha Nussbaum, the best way to address the issue of gender inequality is to start with a shared notion of what it means to be and to function as human. On this basis, she identifies capabilities that are more integral to human life than others. Her approach is universalist, focusing on commonalities rather than on differences. Yet unlike the tradition flowing from Thomas Aquinas explored in Jean Porter's chapter, her universalism is based not on metaphysical realism or ahistorical a priori principles but on universalizable concepts drawn from cross-cultural human experiences.[7]

NUSSBAUM'S LIST OF HUMAN CAPABILITIES

Nussbaum's list of the main characteristics that make one "worthy of the dignity of human being" includes: (1) mortality; (2) human body and its need for food and drink, shelter, and its sexual desire and satisfaction; (3) capacity for pain and pleasure; (4) capacity to sense, imagine, think, and reason; (5) emotions; (6) the practical reason; (7) affiliation with other humans; (8) relatedness to nature and other species; (9) humor and play;

(10) separateness or individuality; and (11) strong separateness or need for space or freedom.[8]

These characteristics generate the following central human capabilities, which also can be regarded as freedoms and rights: (1) the ability to live a normal length of life; (2) having access to good nutrition, adequate shelter, opportunities for satisfaction of sexual desire, reproductive choice, and mobility; (3) the capacity to avoid unnecessary pain on the one hand and access to opportunities for pleasure on the other; (4) the ability to sense, imagine, think, and reason, along with access to education that is integral to realizing these capacities; (5) the capability to be attached to persons and things, to feel emotions, and access to forms of human association that foster its development; (6) the capacity to discern what is good and to reflect critically on the world and in the planning of one's life, which today entails being able to work outside the home and to engage in political life; (7) concern for other human beings; (8) concern for other species and nature; (9) the capacity for humor, play, and recreation; (10) the capability to make decisions for one's own life without undue interference, especially with regard to "marriage, childbearing, sexual expression, speech, and employment"; and (11) freedom of association and freedom from unwarranted search and seizure.[9]

The main question a capability approach would ask about a woman is: "What is she actually able to do and to be?"[10] What are her opportunities and liberties? The above list also portrays a "minimal conception of the good." This view of human good is not as robust as in Catholic social teaching, reviewed in chapter 7, by Lisa Cahill, but, for Nussbaum, a lack of any of these capacities prevents full human flourishing or well-being. Everyone must be entitled by the government and other relevant institutions to these capabilities.

CHURCH AS ENABLER OF WOMEN'S CAPABILITIES?

The official teaching of the church has endorsed the fundamental rights of women, including the right of women to an education, and their participation in every aspect of life—socioeconomic, cultural, artistic, and political. It has condemned all forms of violence against women and has taught against male domination.[11] However, as we have noted, its complementary anthropology reinforces inequality in wages and access to education, thereby restricting both the development of women's capacities and their opportunities for work.

In turn, the exclusion of women from ordination has severely limited their official participation in church life. The official roles of sanctifying, teaching, and governing[12] have been entrusted solely to the ordained, and the magisterium has declared this exclusion of women as part of its "deposit of faith."[13]

Theological ethicist Lisa Sowle Cahill notes the similarity between the church's natural law theory and Nussbaum's capabilities approach.[14] Each presupposes moral realism, the insight that ethical positions can be based on a reality that is in some way external to the person or culture making the ethical judgment. Both are convinced of shared characteristics of humans that are grounded in the human body and that can be the basis of universalizable norms. This is in line with what Richard Gula refers to as the church's reading of natural law based on the order of reason, which takes reason as what is most natural for humans. In an inductive approach, it examines human experience taken in all its internal and relational complexity to discern what would promote the well-being of persons.[15] Consequently, both Nussbaum and Catholic social thought reject relativism and are convinced that there are minimum basic conditions for human flourishing.

However, Nussbaum and the Catholic tradition differ in the importance they attribute to sociality (kinship and family) and interdependence in society, which Catholic social teaching and most non-Western cultures view as essential to human flourishing. Here Nussbaum is part of the liberal tradition on justice addressed in Francis Fiorenza's chapter, as Nussbaum emphasizes individual autonomy even as she underscores the importance of structures that would enable the freedom of choice.[16] She does identify "affiliation" as a basic human capability. Still, she does not elaborate on marriage, kinship, or family, which she generally regards through the lens of their oppressive impact on women and not as embodied contexts of sexuality with and for others.[17] While it is essential to be critical of how these structures have been oppressive to women, it is also crucial to see how they are integral to human flourishing.

Another difference between Nussbaum and Catholic social thought on justice is how they view the significance of the body in one's social roles. Cahill remarks:

> Catholic tradition typically has exaggerated the significance of women's sexual and reproductive embodiment in relation to that of men. It has defined women's identity more in terms of sexual and reproductive roles, and has also either given less social importance to these roles, or interpreted functioning in them in a way that limits access

to other roles. It has made an almost absolute link between women's sexual embodiment and reproduction, though it has not done so regarding men. Sex and gender represent areas in which Catholicism has interpreted the significance of embodiment for structural justice for men and women unequally.[18]

This difference is rooted in the church's physicalist reading of natural law in areas of sexuality, which applies a deductive logic that begins with biology and derives the nature and role of women in the church.[19] Gula points out how the magisterium employs natural law based on the order of reason when dealing with social issues but natural law based on the order of nature when addressing sexual issues. This magisterial choice in reading the tradition mirrors a similar issue in how the location of the interpreter affects biblical interpretation, as Anathea Portier-Young argues in her chapter. Here, as head of the Congregation for the Doctrine of Faith, Cardinal Ratzinger decried what he alleged as the tendency in an approach to women's issues to free the concept of human nature from any biological conditioning.

> In order to avoid the domination of one sex or the other, their differences tend to be denied, viewed as mere effects of historical and cultural conditioning. In this perspective, physical difference, termed *sex*, is minimized, while the purely cultural element, termed *gender*, is emphasized to the maximum and held to be primary. . . . Its deeper motivation must be sought in the human attempt to be freed from one's biological conditioning. According to this perspective, human nature in itself does not possess characteristics in an absolute manner: all persons can and ought to constitute themselves as they like, since they are free from every predetermination linked to their essential constitution.[20]

Nussbaum distinguishes her perspective by avoiding the term "human nature." Though taking into account the body and biological factors, she eschews the term's association with a "value-free science" or theological metaphysics.[21] She does not neglect biology; she attends to the body as it plays a role in shaping human experience. But she focuses on the body's needs that we share across cultures. She consistently prioritizes women's autonomy and freedom and the ability to choose and fashion a life, albeit within a liberal mode. She regards women's fundamental rights, including sexual rights, as essential justice concerns that should not be subordinated to women's reproductive roles.

Lisa Cahill suggests that Nussbaum can learn from Catholic social teaching's greater acknowledgment of the social nature of persons and the embeddedness of our bodies and sexuality in society. Catholic social teaching, for its part, can learn from Nussbaum's stress on the primacy of women's basic human needs and rights, which are too often theoretically affirmed but indirectly undermined.[22]

JUSTICE WITHIN A POLITICS OF POSITIONAL DIFFERENCE

While Nussbaum emphasizes sameness, philosopher Iris Marion Young stresses difference. She underlines that just institutions require public support for group-based difference and needs.[23]

YOUNG'S POLITICS OF DIFFERENCE, ROLE EXCLUSION, AND PREFERENTIAL TREATMENT

In her book *Justice and the Politics of Difference*, Young critiques universal or essentialist norms of justice and argues for the recognition of differences among social groups in areas where the suppression of difference can contribute to social group oppression. Out of a similar conviction, Maria Inês de Castro Millen's chapter attends carefully to a variety of civil society groups in Brazil striving for justice. Young's egalitarian politics of difference includes respect for "self-defined groups and identities" and their assertion of their difference to resist assimilation. Examples of such groups today would include minority and Indigenous groups, LGBTQ+ groups, and deaf groups that resist cochlear implants and see themselves as an ethnicity with a shared language.

For Young, social groups are a product of encounter with the other as well as of social processes (e.g., sexual division of labor). As forms of social relations, these collectivities are not fixed; their identities have been "either forced on them or forged by them or both."[24] These social groups are situated structurally along important axes of advantage and disadvantage, such as the "social division of labor, hierarchies of decision-making power, practices of sexuality and body aesthetic, and the arrangement of persons in physical and social space."[25] Young's view of social groups suggests affinities with intersectional perspectives because an individual can occupy multiple positions in structures (gender, class, race, ethnicity, caste, disability, etc.) that vary depending on the institutional setting and how others are therein positioned.[26]

Thus, intersectionality from this perspective can be understood as the overlapping of social structures of disadvantage that limit people's development and the exercise of their capacities.[27] Young points out that policies that are blind to these differences will more likely reinforce the injustices these groups suffer. Temporally granting privilege to some groups or even establishing some forms of role exclusion (reserving some positions for members of historically marginalized groups) may be morally necessary until the disadvantaged groups no longer suffer from these structural disadvantages. An example would be the preferential hiring or admission to universities of qualified women and racial minorities that has been instituted in the United States by employers and educational institutions in the 1960s and 1970s. When the structural disadvantages of these groups no longer exist, such preferential treatment would cease.

Agreeing with Young on the need at times for role exclusion, theological ethicist Christine Gudorf further argues that even some sex-based distribution of roles can be just to maintain group difference, if the role exclusion serves equality rather than domination of one group by another.[28] One example is in the precolonial Philippines, where the *datu* (male) leads raids and trading and heads the *barangay*, the basic socioeconomic unit, while the *babaylan* or *catalonan* (usually a woman but at times a cross-dressing male or transgender female) performs religious rituals, heals, guards, and transmits folk knowledge and tradition.[29] Both of these functions had high prestige within the community.

Gudorf observes that even among feminists in the Global South, there is acceptance of the notion of sex-based difference and of motherhood as a sex-based role. What they demand is liberation from the structures that restrict their ability to respond to the demands of motherhood.

Role exclusion is not necessarily unjust. When it is justified, it must be temporary—until equality is achieved. Gudorf admits, though, that Young herself would not be open to a role exclusion defined by a historically dominant group. For instance, the exclusion of women from priesthood is not a decision of women themselves and thus cannot be taken as a fruit of their self-definition. Gudorf, however, thinks that Young's framework is open enough to a reevaluation of this division of labor depending on whether it undermines the oppression of a group. She quotes Young: "Most historical discriminations have been wrong not because they distinguished people according to group attributes, but because they aimed at or resulted in formally and explicitly restricting the actions and opportunities of group members. They have been wrong, that is, because they have contributed to and helped enforce oppression. If discrimination serves the purpose of undermining the oppression of a group, it may be not only permitted, but morally required."[30]

In this manner, Gudorf shifts the focus from scrutinizing the motives of those advocating role exclusion to examining the process and the results in light of a broader movement toward social justice.

To distinguish whether a role exclusion serves the purpose of equality, Gudorf offers four criteria: balance, proportional cost-benefit, a process of participative decision-making, and narrow scope. First, the exclusion of one sex from a role should be balanced by excluding the other in an equally important role. Second, the benefit of the exclusion for the whole community should be greater than the suffering of those excluded from the role and who are thereby unable to develop their own capabilities. Third, the process by which the role exclusion is decided should be participative and honor the valid interest of minorities. Lastly, the exclusions should be narrowly defined, temporary, and not based on essentialist preconceptions.

Does the exclusion of women from ordination in the Roman Catholic Church satisfy these criteria? Does this sex-specific restriction lead to greater equality? Gudorf argues that it fails to meet the above justice criteria for these reasons: (1) even if canon law is revised so that women would no longer be excluded from positions of governance, there would still be asymmetry in power[31]; (2) women's exclusion from priesthood is deemed permanent; and (3) the logic for the exclusion is essentialist, that is, based on women's supposed incapacity to image Christ.

We can apply the same criteria to the gendered division of labor within the family (woman as primary child-caregiver) that is idealized in church teaching, even if some change is noticeable under Pope Francis.[32] Similarly, this role assignment fails to meet the criteria: (1) It leads to asymmetry in power between man and woman both within the family and in society; (2) it is not a fruit of women's collective self-identification; and (3) the logic for the division of labor is essentialist in the sense that it is deduced from women's biological characteristics.

JUSTICE AND PARTICIPATIVE COMMUNITY MEDIATION

Community participation in processes aiming at justice is a very old idea, as illustrated by the African palaver, described in Agbonkhianmeghe Orobator's chapter. Within a politics of positional difference, Young stresses the importance of participative decision-making structures; democratic deliberation is a means to justice. In her article "Justice, Inclusion, and Deliberative Democracy,"[33] Young affirms three principles of democratic deliberation proposed by Amy Gutmann and Dennis Thompson: reciprocity, publicity, and accountability. These conditions will more likely result in policies and institutional relations that are just.[34] The principle of reciprocity requires appeals to reasons and principles acceptable to others. The principle of publicity requires transparency of political deliberations; those deliberating must put forward claims and reasons that can be made public. The principle of accountability says that the deliberators must be able to justifiably support and explain their stance to others, including future generations.[35]

To these three, Young adds the principle of inclusion, which asks who has the opportunity "to make claims to a deliberative public and who is there to listen and hold claimants accountable."[36] Exclusion preserves the interests of those in power without disturbing the process of formal democracy. Through power, money, stereotyping, and prejudice, dominant groups can weaken the voice of marginalized groups. Therefore, there is a need for a more proactive stance for democracies to become more inclusive. Prohibiting explicit exclusion is not enough. Passive exclusions can be prevented by wisely choosing the timing, location, and structures of deliberative events to maximize the representation of marginalized groups. Unorganized groups should be encouraged to organize themselves. We agree with Young that inclusion is not sufficiently taken into account in the principles of reciprocity, publicity, and accountability.

To synthesize, Young proposes an "enabling conception of justice" that examines the structures needed to exercise and enhance individual capabilities and collective cooperation.[37]

DEMOCRATIC DELIBERATION AND JUSTICE IN CATHOLIC SOCIAL THOUGHT

The church itself has increasingly stressed the importance of participation in decision-making in various areas.[38] In 1919, Pope Benedict XV argued for the inclusion of native clergy who can better understand local peoples and thus may be able to introduce the faith more effectively.[39] Pope Pius XI (1926) countered racist allegations about the intellectual inferiority of the native priest,[40] and Pope Pius XII (1939), in *Summi pontificatus*, extended the rights of various ethnic and racial groups to be headed by a bishop from one of their own.[41] As a social norm, participation in decision-making was endorsed in *Quadragesimo anno*, particularly stressing worker participation in the management or ownership of a company.

Gaudium et spes encourages participation of the largest number of people possible at every level in economic development (no. 65) and in juridico-politico structures (no. 75). In light of the need for greater justice among nations, *Octogesima adveniens* advocates "greater share in responsibility and decision-making" for developing countries.[42] In the same context, the statement by the 1971 Synod of Bishops affirms a responsible nationalism that spurs people to organize politically toward their full development.[43] For Gudorf, the most explicit statement on the need of humans to be self-determined appears in *Laborem exercens*: "as the 'image of God,' he is a person, that is to say, a subjective being capable of acting in a planned and rational way, capable of deciding about himself, and with a tendency to self-realization."[44] All of these show the importance that Catholic social teaching gives to participation in decision-making as integral to the process of identity formation.

More recent teachings have further stressed the importance of participative decision-making in society and within the church. *Caritas in veritate* links participation to the principle of subsidiarity, involving even the grassroots level.[45] *Centessimus annus* reports that "the Church values the democratic system inasmuch as it ensures the participation of citizens in making political choices."[46] *Evangelii gaudium* teaches that "participation in political life is a moral obligation."[47] In his call for societies that are open to everyone, Francis admonishes the church to especially ensure the active participation in civil and ecclesial community of "hidden exiles," such as persons with disabilities and the elderly.[48] He endorses a model of socio-political-economic participation that embraces the participation of popular movements on the local, national, and international levels in their "distinctive ways of acting."[49] Francis likewise calls the church to "develop the means of participation proposed in the Code of Canon Law, and other forms of pastoral dialogue, out of a desire to listen to everyone and not simply to those who would tell him what he would like to hear."[50]

In what Lisa Cahill describes as a movement toward "decentralization" in her chapter, the "re-turn towards synodality" spearheaded by Pope Francis will play a significant role in realizing this broader participation. His notion of synodality is expansive, as implied in *Querida amazonia*: "Base communities, when able to combine the defence of social rights with missionary proclamation and spirituality, have been authentic experiences of synodality in the Church's journey of evangelization in the Amazon region."[51]

Women's participation, however, both in the church and in society, has always been qualified with reference to their particularity: "in accordance with their own nature," "in accordance with woman's proper role," or their "own share of responsibility and participation."[52]

In the opening of the synodal journey, October 9–10, 2021, Pope Francis spoke of the need for structures that foster dialogue and participation beyond mere appearances. He warned against applying old solutions to new problems.[53] It remains to be seen how much structural change will happen under his vision of a synodal church. What is clear is that although he endorses a more incisive participation of women and laity, his interventions so far have been restricted to the gradual incorporation of women into non-ordained roles and ministries.[54] He seems to have expressed, however, an openness to women's ordination to the diaconate. Quite unexpectedly, in April 2020, in response to the Synod of Bishops of the Amazon region, the pope reconvened a second commission to study the ordination of women deacons in the Catholic Church after an earlier commission—though establishing the presence of women deacons—came up with an inconclusive report on the role of women deacons in early Christianity.

The exclusion of women from any official deliberation on the role and vocation of women in the church constitutes a fundamental asymmetry in power relations between women and men that limits women's opportunities and the development of their capacities within both church and society. They did not participate in defining their vocation as a social group; the exclusion of women from priesthood was not the decision of women for themselves and, thus, cannot be taken as a fruit of their self-identification. This is not in line with the democratizing thrust of Catholic social teaching and the increasing importance it has given to participatory decision-making.

TOWARD A PRAXIS OF JUST PARTICIPATIVE DECISION-MAKING WITHIN THE CHURCH

In this final section, we wish to build on the four principles for democratic deliberation affirmed by Young for use within the church by complementing them with our own method of community mediation. This runs parallel to the stress on the community's "taking responsibility for justice" in Agbonkhianmeghe Orobator, in chapter 1.

We have argued in our past writings for the epistemological advantage of considering a multiplicity of perspectives in our theological/ecclesial communities to prevent our theologies from being biased in the interest of a single paradigm.[55] The conditions for effective ideology criticism that we have identified can be correlated with Young's principles of democratic deliberation.

First, the principle of reciprocity prescribes appeals to reasons and principles acceptable to others. Reciprocity allows the faithful to justify their claims to one another. Within the church, this can mean that groups with different theological perspectives should be willing to explain the standards they are using when they read scripture and tradition. One crucial effect of this practice is that those whose interpretations are criticized would understand the criteria by which their works are being assessed. These criteria ideally consist of both the scientific norms and moral ideals of the community, as Anathea Portier-Young illustrates so ably in her chapter on scriptures and justice. The identified criteria, however, can be modified or changed when they no longer prove to be productive.

Second, the principle of publicity necessitates the existence of recognized channels for dialogue and criticism within the church. These venues include regular public forums like journals and symposia, the traditional sites for professional theologians to subject each other's work to critical analysis. In addition, there is also the need to recognize forums on the pastoral and popular levels, such as the base Christian communities and other kinds of associations or sectoral groups in the parish, where scripture is read and interpreted and church issues are discussed.

Third, the principle of accountability obligates decision makers and deliberators to attend to the claims of all those who will be affected by their decisions, including future generations. This requires responsiveness to ongoing critical discussions of various communities that are differently constituted by divergent histories, orientations, and interests, as is so well documented in the chapter by Maria Inês de Castro Millen. A homogeneous all-male group such as the church's official leadership allows the patriarchal paradigm to predominate since it is protected from the critical scrutiny of women. The more heterogeneous is the theological or ecclesial community, the more self-critical people become and the less prone to morally objectionable individual or group biases. It is, thus, crucial that such communities include people from a variety of contexts and cultural perspectives.[56]

Fourth, the principle of inclusion ensures the representation of marginalized groups in the decision-making process. This principle presupposes the equality of intellectual authority of various social groups within a Christian community. This Habermasian criterion[57] means that no set of assumptions should predominate because of the political power of its proponents.

To prevent passive exclusions, partial epistemological privilege can be granted to marginalized groups within the Christian community. Since women, persons with disability, LGBTQ+, and other racial and ethnic groups have been traditionally ignored within ecclesial and theological communities, they can be privileged for a time. This means granting them "first hearing." The church should encourage and support their representation in various councils and the development of theologies from their standpoints.

Granting partial epistemological privilege to oppressed groups also requires that one "reinvents oneself as other." This means considering the perspective of the "others" in all the deliberations. This should be done, however, with the consciousness that one's own horizon will limit a person's perception of how others are marginalized. Thus, this awareness should always go hand in hand with the thrust to organize and give voice to marginalized groups themselves.

The epistemological privilege granted to the "others" is partial in the following senses. First, when a subordinated group has assumed a more dominant position, it should no longer enjoy this privilege. Second, the interpretations from the perspective of marginalized groups still have to be subjected to critical analysis, an evaluation vis-à-vis the publicly shared standards of the larger Christian community. And, of course, such interpretations from the perspective of a particular oppressed group can challenge and be challenged by the interpretations of other marginalized groups within the Christian community.

CONCLUSION

What is the relation of the theories of justice we have discussed to experience and social location? Nussbaum's human capabilities approach has demonstrated the value of an inductive approach in discerning a shared experience of human needs and capabilities that are the basis for judging whether one's condition enables human flourishing. Young has shown the importance of recognizing both sameness and differences in experiences and social location in efforts to make social structures truly just. Preferential treatment and role exclusion should not be viewed as permanent; these should cease once the group has been integrated and attained equal recognition in society. A consequence of recognizing difference is the need for participative decision-making in determining what is just. Following Young, democratic deliberation should be guided by the principles of publicity, reciprocity, and accountability to prevent positions founded on sheer self-interest and to foster more just policies and institutional relations. Lastly, the principle of inclusion allows various social groups to make their claims to a deliberative public.

What do the above discussions contribute to re-thinking gender justice in Catholic social thought? Official Catholic social teaching is strong in its recognition of the social nature of the individual and the value of the common good. It has also increasingly taught the importance of participation in decision-making at different levels of society. It has made great strides in endorsing the rights of women and condemning violence against women. However, it continues to maintain a complementary anthropology that is based on a priori fixed roles and excludes women from official leadership positions in the church.

In dialogue with the theorists we have discussed, the church can be challenged to re-think justice in general and for women in particular along the following lines. First, there is the need for the church to move away from a physicalist and deductive reading of nature (natural law based on the order of nature) and shift to an inductive logic to discern universalizable norms based on our shared experiences (natural law based on the order of reason). Second, just structures will recognize group-based differences and claims. This may result in role exclusion or differential treatment of some social groups for equality and not domination. Lastly, participative deliberative structures in the church are essential not only to ensure decisions that promote the common good but also to prevent or dismantle institutionalized domination. This democratic deliberation should be guided by reciprocity, publicity, accountability, and inclusion.

Catholic social thought has slowly recognized the importance of participation, and church structures have started to be more inclusive of various voices. However, the magisterium continues to limit the participation of women by speaking of their share of responsibility "in accordance with their nature," an ideology that reinforces sexism not only within the church but also in the wider society.

The 1971 Synod of Bishops powerfully declared that "while the Church is bound to give witness to justice, she recognizes that anyone who ventures to speak to people about justice must first be just in their eyes."[58] Fifty years have passed since this proclamation. How much longer must women wait for church structures to be transformed for greater gender justice?

BIBLIOGRAPHY

Barretto-Tesoro, Grace. "Where Are the Datu and Catalonan in Early Philippine Societies? Investigating Status in Calatagan?" *Philippine Quarterly of Culture and Society* 36, no. 3 (2008): 74–102. https://www.jstor.org/stable/29792647.

Benedict XV. *Maximimum illud* in *Acta apostolicae sedis* 11. Typis Polyglottis Vaticanis, 1919. https://www.vatican.va/content/benedict-xv/en/apost_letters/documents/hf_ben-xv_apl_19191130_maximum-illud.html.

Benedict XVI. *Caritas in veritate*. https://www.vatican.va/content/benedict-xvi/en/encyclicals/documents/hf_ben-xvi_enc_20090629_caritas-in-veritate.html.

Brazal, Agnes M. *A Theology of Southeast Asia: Liberation-Postcolonial Ethics in the Philippines.* Orbis, 2019.

Brazal, Agnes M. "Feminist Ideology Criticisms, the Bible, and the Community." *MST Review* 2, no. 2 (1999): 97–117.

Cahill, Lisa Sowle. "Justice for Women: Martha Nussbaum and Catholic Social Teaching." In *Transforming Unjust Structures: The Capability Approach,* edited by Séverine Deneulin, Mathia Nebel, and Nicholas Sagovsky, 83–104. Springer, 2006.

CBCP News. "Pope Francis: Path to 2023 Synod on Synodality Faces Three 'Risks.'" October 9, 2021. https://cbcpnews.net/cbcpnews/pope-francis-path-to-2023-synod-on-synodality-faces-three-risks/?fbclid=IwAR3dx9vXET5oU4VOGJL68lt5SNgEu-F6AmzkNzzziINCGoWAfvMokhSPjTMU.

The Code of Canon Law. Collins Liturgical Publications, 1983.

Congregation for the Doctrine of the Faith. *Inter Insignores: On the Question of Admission of Women to the Ministerial Priesthood,* October 15, 1976. https://www.vatican.va/roman_curia/congregations/cfaith/documents/rc_con_cfaith_doc_19761015_inter-insigniores_en.html.

Congregation for the Doctrine of the Faith. "On the Collaboration of Men and Women in the Church and in the World," May 31, 2004. https://www.vatican.va/roman_curia/congregations/cfaith/documents/rc_con_cfaith_doc_20040731_collaboration_en.html.

Congregation for the Doctrine of the Faith. *Responsum ad Propositum Dubium Concerning the Teaching Contained in "Ordinatio Sacerdotalis,"* October 28, 1995. https://www.vatican.va/roman_curia/congregations/cfaith/documents/rc_con_cfaith_doc_19951028_dubium-ordinatio-sac_en.html.

Francis. *Amoris laetitia,* October 1, 2015. https://www.vatican.va/content/dam/francesco/pdf/apost_exhortations/documents/papa-francesco_esortazione-ap_20160319_amoris-laetitia_en.pdf.

Francis. *Antiquum ministerium*: Instituting the Ministry of Catechist. May 2021. https://www.vatican.va/content/francesco/en/motu_proprio/documents/papa-francesco-motu-proprio-20210510_antiquum-ministerium.html.

Francis. *Evangelii gaudium.* November 24, 2013. https://www.vatican.va/content/francesco/en/apost_exhortations/documents/papa-francesco_esortazione-ap_20131124_evangelii-gaudium.html.

Francis. *Fratelli tutti.* October 3, 2020. https://www.vatican.va/content/francesco/en/encyclicals/documents/papa-francesco_20201003_enciclica-fratelli-tutti.html.

Francis. *Magnum principium.* September 9, 2017. https://press.vatican.va/content/salastampa/en/bollettino/pubblico/2017/09/09/170909a.html.

Francis. *Querida amazonia.* February 2, 2020. https://www.vatican.va/content/francesco/en/apost_exhortations/documents/papa-francesco_esortazione-ap_20200202_querida-amazonia.html.

Francis. *Spiritus domini.* January 15, 2021. https://www.vatican.va/content/francesco/en/motu_proprio/documents/papa-francesco-motu-proprio-20210110_spiritus-domini.html.

Gudorf, Christine E. "Probing the Politics of Difference: What's Wrong with an All-Male Priesthood?" *Journal of Religious Ethics* 27, no. 3 (1999): 377–405. https://www.jstor.org/stable/40015265.

Gula, Richard M. *Reason Informed by Faith: Foundations of Catholic Morality.* Paulist Press, 1989.

Gutmann, Amy, and Dennis Thompson. *Democracy and Disagreement.* Harvard University Press, 1996.

John XXIII. *Pacem in terris.* https://www.vatican.va/content/john-xxiii/en/encyclicals/documents/hf_j-xxiii_enc_11041963_pacem.html.

John Paul II. *Centessimus annus.* May 1, 1991. https://www.vatican.va/content/john-paul-ii/en/encyclicals/documents/hf_jp-ii_enc_01051991_centesimus-annus.html.

John Paul II. *Laborem exercens.* September 14, 1981. https://www.vatican.va/content/john-paul-ii/en/encyclicals/documents/hf_jp-ii_enc_14091981_laborem-exercens.html.

John Paul II. "Letter of Pope John Paul II to Women." June 29, 1995. https://www.vatican.va/content/john-paul-ii/en/letters/1995/documents/hf_jp-ii_let_29061995_women.html.

John Paul II. *Mulieris dignitatem.* https://www.vatican.va/content/john-paul-ii/en/apost_letters/1988/documents/hf_jp-ii_apl_19880815_mulieris-dignitatem.html.

John Paul II. *Ordinatio sacerdotalis.* May 22, 1994. https://www.vatican.va/content/john-paul-ii/en/apost_letters/1994/documents/hf_jp-ii_apl_19940522_ordinatio-sacerdotalis.html.

Kymlicka, Will. *Multicultural Citizenship: A Liberal Theory of Minority Rights.* Clarendon Press, 1996.

Leo XIII. *Rerum novarum,* no. 14. https://www.vatican.va/content/leo-xiii/en/encyclicals/documents/hf_l-xiii_enc_15051891_rerum-novarum.html.

Nussbaum, Martha C. "Human Capabilities, Female Human Beings." In *Women, Culture and Development,* edited by Martha C. Nussbaum and Jonathan Glover, 61–104. Oxford University Press, 1995. https://doi.org/10.1093/0198289642.003.0003.

Paul IV. *Gaudium et spes.* https://www.vatican.va/archive/hist_councils/ii_vatican_council/documents/vat-ii_const_19651207_gaudium-et-spes_en.html.

Paul VI. *Octogesima adveniens.* May 14, 1971. https://www.vatican.va/content/paul-vi/en/apost_letters/documents/hf_p-vi_apl_19710514_octogesima-adveniens.html.

Pius XI. *Rerum ecclesiae* in *Acta apostolicae sedis* 18. Città del Vaticano: Typis Polyglottis Vaticanis, 1926. https://www.vatican.va/content/pius-xi/en/encyclicals/documents/hf_p-xi_enc_28021926_rerum-ecclesiae.html

Pius XII. *Summi pontificatus* in *Acta apostolicae sedis* 31. Città del Vaticano: Typis Polyglottis Vaticanis, 1926. https://www.vatican.va/content/pius-xii/en/encyclicals/documents/hf_p-xii_enc_20101939_summi-pontificatus.html.

Ryan, Maura A. "Justice and Gender in Ministry: Debating Women's Ordination. *Journal of Hindu-Christian Studies* 18 (January 2005): Article 6. https://doi.org/10.7825/2164-6279.1339

Scott, Joan Wallach. "The Persistence of Gender Inequality: How Politics Constructs Gender, and Gender Constructs Politics." *The Institute Letter.* 2018. https://www.ias.edu/ideas/scott-gender-inequality.

Synod of Bishops. "Justice in the World." 1971. https://www.cctwincities.org/wp-content/uploads/2015/10/Justicia-in-Mundo.pdf.

Weldon, S. Laurel. "The Structure of Intersectionality: A Comparative Politics of Gender." *Politics and Gender* 2, no. 2 (2006): 235–48. https://doi.org/10.1017/S1743923X06231040.

Young, Iris Marion. *Justice and the Politics of Difference.* Princeton University Press, 1990.

Young, Iris Marion. "Justice, Inclusion, and Deliberative Democracy." In *Deliberative Politics: Essays on Democracy and Disagreement,* edited by Stephen Macedo, 151–58. Oxford University Press, 1999.

Young, Iris Marion. *On Female Body Experience: "Throwing Like a Girl" and Other Essays.* Oxford University Press, 2005.

Young, Iris Marion. "Structural Injustice and the Politics of Difference." In *Justice, Governance, Cosmopolitanism, and the Politics of Difference: Reconfigurations in a Transnational World,* edited by Engelbert Habekost, 1–38. Forschungsabteilung der Humboldt-Universität zu, 2007. https://d-nb.info/1208196243/34.

NOTES

1. Scott, "The Persistence of Gender Inequality."
2. "Let it be laid down, in the first place, that humanity must remain as it is. It is impossible to reduce society to a level. The Socialists may do their utmost, but all striving against nature is vain. There naturally exists among mankind innumerable differences of the most important kind: people differ in capability, in diligence, in health and in strength: and unequal fortune is necessary result of inequality in condition. Such inequality is far from being disadvantageous either to individuals or to the community" (Leo XIII, *Rerum novarum,* no. 14).
3. *Gaudium et spes,* no. 29.
4. *Gaudium et spes,* no. 60 qualified women's right to participate in the different spheres of life "according to their own particular nature." *Octogesima adveniens,* no. 13 stated, "We do not have in mind that false equality which would deny the distinctions laid down by the Creator himself and which would be in contradiction with woman's proper role, which is of such capital importance, at the heart of the family as well as within society."
5. Ryan, "Justice and Gender in Ministry," Article 6.
6. Congregation for the Doctrine of the Faith (CDF), *Inter Insignores.*
7. Nussbaum, "Human Capabilities."
8. Nussbaum, 76–80.
9. Nussbaum, 83–86.
10. Nussbaum, 230.
11. John Paul II, *Mulieris dignitatem* no. 10; Francis, *Amoris laetitia,* no. 54.
12. Canon Law 1983, no. 129.1 reserves the task of governance to the ordained in the Roman Catholic Church. *The Code of Canon Law.*
13. Congregation for the Doctrine of the Faith, *Responsum.*
14. Cahill, "Justice for Women."
15. Gula, *Reason Informed by Faith.*
16. Nussbaum, "Human Capabilities," 95.
17. Such relations foster the survival of the family and unity through intermarriage and provide a structure for living and care giving arrangements.
18. Cahill, "Justice for Women," 85.
19. Gula, *Reason Informed by Faith.*
20. Congregation for the Doctrine of the Faith, "On the Collaboration of Men and Women in the Church and in the World," #2 and 3.
21. Cahill, "Justice for Women," 83–104.
22. Cahill, 86.
23. Young distinguishes her version of politics of difference from identity politics or politics of cultural difference such as that represented by Will Kymlicka. Kymlicka differentiates

groups defined by "societal culture" (based on ethnicity or nationality) from other marginalized groups. Without regarding politics of difference and politics of identity as two mutually exclusive categories, Young nevertheless sees the risk of underplaying differences and experiences of injustice within a national or ethnic group in a politics of identity. Kymlicka has been criticized for seeing societal culture as overly homogeneous. See Young, "Structural Injustice," 79–116; Kymlicka, *Multicultural Citizenship*. See also Young's critique of the concept of "community" in Francis Schüssler Fiorenza's chapter in this volume.

24. Young, *Justice and the Politics of Difference*, 44.
25. She considers disability as "paradigmatic of structural injustice." Young, "Structural Injustice," 83, 85.
26. Young, *On Female Body Experience*.
27. Weldon, "The Structure of Intersectionality," 239.
28. Gudorf, "Probing the Politics of Difference," 395–99.
29. Barretto-Tesoro, "Where Are the Datu and Catalonan?"
30. Young, *Justice and the Politics of Difference*, 197.
31. Gudorf did not explicitly elaborate on this, but she must be assuming that there should be a separate sacramental role of equal status for women. Ryan, "Justice and Gender in Ministry."
32. See Francis, *Amoris laetitia*, nos. 215–216.
33. Young, "Justice, Inclusion, and Deliberative Democracy," 151–58.
34. See Gutmann and Thompson, *Democracy and Disagreement*.
35. Young regards principles 3–6 in Gutmann and Thompsons's list of principles of democratic deliberation—basic liberty, basic opportunity, and equal opportunity—as requirements of justice but not principles of democratic deliberation. On their reply to Young, see Gutmann and Thompson, *Democracy and Disagreement*, 263–64.
36. Young, "Justice, Inclusion, and Deliberative Democracy," 155.
37. Young, 39.
38. See also Gudorf, "Probing the Politics of Difference," 383.
39. Benedict XV, *Maximum illud*, 14.
40. Pius XI, *Rerum ecclesiae*, 24.
41. Pius XII, *Summi pontificatus*, 413–53.
42. Paul VI, *Octogesima adveniens*, no. 47.
43. Synod of Bishops 1971, no. 17.
44. John Paul II, *Laborem exercens*, no. 6.
45. Benedict XVI, *Caritas in veritate*, nos. 57 and 58.
46. John Paul II, *Centessimus annus*, no. 46.
47. Francis, *Evangelii gaudium*, no. 220.
48. Francis, *Fratelli tutti*, no. 98.
49. Francis, no. 169.
50. Francis, *Evangelii gaudium*, no. 31.
51. Francis, *Querida amazonia*, no. 96.
52. *Gaudium et spes*, no. 60; *Octogesima adveniens*, no. 13; and *Justice in the World*, no. 42.
53. CBCP News, "Pope Francis."
54. See Francis, *Magnum principium*; Francis, "*Spiritus domini*."
55. See Brazal, *A Theology of Southeast Asia*; and Brazal, "Feminist Ideology Criticisms."
56. The view of community here is "fluid"; it recognizes that women, for instance, do not constitute a homogeneous group and their interests can intersect with the concerns of other liberational groups.

57. For Habermas, an ideal speech situation exists when there is freedom and equal access for all the participants in the discourse to put forward their interpretations, justifications, objections, or refutations. Otherwise, the result of any consensus would be less than rational, meaning that it is not the product of the force of the better argument but of hidden or open manipulations.

58. Synod of Bishops, *Justice in the World*, no. 40.

CHAPTER 9

Justice as a Characteristic
of Social Structures

Daniel K. Finn

INTRODUCTION

Over several years beginning in 1905, a French archaeological excavation team at Delphi, Greece, discovered a group of stone fragments bearing a Greek inscription. It contained the words from a letter to the city from Emperor Claudius that confirms that L. Iunius Gallio was proconsul of Achaia in 51–52 CE. According to the Acts of the Apostles (18:12–16), Gallio was the proconsul before whom the Apostle Paul was brought on charges of "persuading people to worship God contrary to the law."[1] As a result of this discovery of "the Gallio inscription," the account in Acts received some extra-biblical confirmation. More importantly, archaeology enabled biblical scholars to precisely date the travels of Paul around the Mediterranean.[2]

Other archaeological evidence[3] has established that there was no collapse of the walls of Jericho in the thirteenth century BCE, requiring a reinterpretation of the "conquest" of Canaan.[4] Biblical scholars have also relied on the sociology of Max Weber and others to understand better the tribal system that constituted Israel, the effects of the centralization of worship and political authority in seventh-century Jerusalem,[5] and the character of sexual control of women by men in Deuteronomy.[6] As these examples illustrate, scripture scholars have long employed insights from other disciplines to enrich their own. This essay proposes that theologians have much to gain in similarly relying on a social-scientific understanding of the social world in articulating what justice is.

Throughout most of the history of Christianity, justice has been defined as a virtue, as a characteristic of persons. It *is* a virtue, of course, but justice and injustice are also characteristics of social structures. Popes since John Paul II have referred to "unjust social structures," even though some neo-conservative Catholics have denied legitimacy to such talk. Samuel Gregg has argued that justice is a virtue for individuals and "structures in themselves cannot be good or bad."[7] Michael Novak rejected the view of social justice articulated in Catholic social thought since Pius XI's *Divini redemptoris*. Novak instead cited libertarian economist Friedrich Hayek to argue that "social justice is a virtue, an attribute of individuals, or it is a fraud."[8]

People like Gregg and Novak, who resist significant changes in economic and political institutions, see an ideological advantage in putting those institutions beyond the reach of accusations of injustice, but more than ideology is involved here. We also don't find Augustine or Aquinas analyzing justice as a characteristic of social structures. So some might cite this as evidence that the extension of the notion of justice to social structures is a philosophical and theological error.

Consider, however, that we also don't find these earlier giants of Christian theology using modern geology to teach that the earth was formed billions of years ago or modern historical critical methods to speak of the different literary traditions in the Hebrew scriptures.

Although some conservatives resist the awareness, the history of theology demonstrates vividly that new knowledge—often from purely secular sources—has brought about a development of doctrine. Although all the popes since John XXIII have stressed the moral importance of human rights, their papal predecessors in the previous century condemned the idea. A similar shift has occurred concerning social structures.[9] Over the past fifty years, popes have highlighted their moral importance. For example, Pope Benedict XVI opened the meeting of the Latin American bishops at Aparecida, Brazil, in 2007, asking two questions about justice as a characteristic of social structures. "In this context, we inevitably speak of the problem of structures, especially those which create injustice. In truth, just structures are a condition without which a just order in society is not possible. But how do they arise? How do they function?"[10] He might have asked a third: What *is* a structure? Unfortunately, Benedict did not look to that field of social science that specializes in studying social structures: sociology.

EMPLOYING SOCIAL SCIENCE WITHIN THEOLOGY

Perhaps one reason Benedict did not was that there are several competing understandings of social structures on offer in sociology. Furthermore, it takes a careful philosophical judgment to choose among them, one that constraints of space in this chapter do not allow for a full explanation here.[11] Yet a few comments can indicate why one particular approach—that of critical realist sociology—is most compatible with the commitments of Christian, particularly Catholic, theology.

Some sociological approaches are holistic, in the sense that they understand the causal forces of social structures as so powerful that they leave little room for the individual freedom that we as Christians know we possess. Others are individualistic, in the sense that everything that occurs in the social world is attributed to the actions of individuals or groups, leaving no room to acknowledge the causal impact of social structures.

Critical realist sociology threads the needle here. It articulates how social structures impact and frequently alter the decisions we make within them, while recognizing that this impact does not cancel our freedom.

THREE INSIGHTS FROM THE PHILOSOPHY OF SCIENCE

But before we can adequately investigate what this means for justice as a characteristic of social structures, we should start with three foundational ideas in the critical realist understanding of science that undergirds the sociological analysis. We will be describing social structures as ontologically real "things" in the world, and these three philosophical insights will show how such descriptions are quite pervasive in both the natural and social worlds.

First, emergence is a fundamental fact of the natural world. Two or more "lower-level" elements combine and a "higher-level" thing emerges that has properties not found in the lower-level elements that together produce it. The most straightforward example is water, which emerges from hydrogen and oxygen but has characteristics different from each of them. Hydrogen and oxygen feed a fire while water puts it out. Such novelty is the essence of emergence.[12]

Within the atom, neutrons and protons emerge from up quarks and down quarks. Three billion years ago, earthly life emerged from a slurry of inert chemicals. The human mind emerges from the electrochemical synapses in the brain.

Because the novel emergent thing is qualitatively different from the elements that combine to produce it, the world is "stratified," distinguishable into different "levels," requiring different methods of investigation. This is why we have physics, chemistry, and biology to study different levels of the natural world. Studying atoms is in important ways different from studying molecules. Studying living cells is different from studying molecules.

Not only is the newly emergent reality something ontologically different from the elements that combine in its creation, but at higher levels of emergence, the new reality can act back on the lower-level elements. This becomes clear as we consider the mind as emerging from the physiological brain, allowing a trained surgeon to operate on the brain itself. (And as we will see, social structures emerge from the actions of individual persons and yet have a causal impact on how persons within those structures make decisions.)

The second insight concerns the character of scientific laws. Consider a simple example. When I open my hand, the book I am holding falls to the floor. The standard explanation for this is Isaac Newton's well-known inverse-square law of gravity.

One of the most influential twentieth-century views of good scientific explanation was developed by the philosopher Carl Hempel.[13] An event is explained if it can be shown to be a logical result of one or more scientific laws in a situation where the conditions present correspond to those when the laws pertain. Thus, for example, because I live in St. Cloud, Minnesota, which is about 1,000 feet above sea level, the conditions are appropriate for Newton's law to apply. When I release the book, it will fall to the floor because of the law of gravity. In accord with Hempel's construal, most of us think of such scientific laws as independently existing forces in the world that cause things to happen. This view of things has entered into everyday language: we all say that "the book hits the floor because of the law of gravity."

The understanding of social structures in critical realist sociology is ultimately rooted in the critical realist philosophy of science developed by British philosopher Roy Bhaskar. Bhaskar was troubled by the dominant view of science provided by empiricism, which, in its various forms since David Hume, insists that the only reliable knowledge comes through our five senses. Bhaskar objects that empiricism does not explain what scientists actually do, and, of course, it does not explain what they think they are doing.

Bhaskar objects that the empiricist approach erroneously treats scientific laws as if they are independently existing forces, which, as Bhaskar explains, they aren't.

The argument is detailed, and explained elsewhere,[14] but the basics can be simply stated. A better explanation is that the book hits the floor because of the relation between the book and the earth, something most of us might readily acknowledge. Moreover, this relation generates the force (not the law) of gravity, something that Bhaskar says we should get used to thinking. If the relation between the book and the earth were different, say if I were standing in the International Space Station, 254 miles above the earth, the book would not fall when I release it. Neither the earth nor the book alone can explain the fall of the book to the floor of my office. It is their relation that generates the force of gravity.

From the critical realist perspective, then, scientific laws are not independent forces causing things to happen in the world. They are instead helpful human statements describing how real forces in the world operate. These human statements that we call scientific laws point beyond themselves to objective "things" in the world that *do* cause things to happen.

This brings us, then, to the third insight we need from the philosophy of science: that we can have reliable knowledge about things that are not sense-perceptible. The reason that an empiricist philosophy of science doesn't admit this insight—doesn't talk about the relation between the book and the earth—is that this relation is not sense-perceptible. Such talk is forbidden, Bhaskar argues, by the faulty epistemological assumption that only sense-perceptible knowledge is real knowledge. But since, based on scientific experiments, we *can* know quite adequately that the underlying cause of the book falling to the floor is its relation to the earth, we should jettison empiricism and begin thinking differently about what qualifies as a "thing" in the world. The relation between the book and the earth is an ontologically real "thing" that generates the force of gravity. This runs parallel to the widely approved acceptance of magnetic fields, themselves not perceptible by our five senses, as real things that science can study and we can know about.

WHAT IS A SOCIAL STRUCTURE?

Social structures are ubiquitous. Throughout the day, we pass into and out of many of them. When we rise each morning, whether we reflect on it or not, some of us are in relation to whatever financial institution holds the mortgage on our house, others in relation to the owners of the apartment that we rent, and all of us are in relation to the various levels of government that have something to say about renting or owning a residence. When we back the car out of the driveway, we take on the position of driver in the traffic system. We similarly take on social positions when we enter our workplace or the grocery store, when we get on the city bus or go to church on Sunday, when we walk to the first tee, enter a restaurant, or hike into the backcountry at Yosemite National Park. In each case, we enter into a social position within a social structure and face both restrictions and opportunities generated by that structure.

Critical realist sociologist Douglas Porpora has provided a simple definition of a social structure: a system of relations among (preexisting) social positions.[15] In each of the examples just mentioned, we enter a social position whose character has been defined long before we arrived. Although social structures evolve over time, they have *emerged* from the decisions of many persons over long periods of time. Leading critical realist sociologist Margaret S. Archer describes this as the "historicity" of structures.[16] The relations between social positions at work or on the first tee have come to be what they are because of the decisions of many people who came before us, usually a long time before us. Archer argues that human interaction over time generates "emergent properties" that have a facticity that endures in time beyond the actions (and often beyond the lifetimes) of the human agents within them, and these properties influence (and often alter) the decisions agents make.[17] She reminds us of Auguste Comte's aphorism that "the majority of actors are the dead."[18]

Nobody invents a social structure, or ever has. Many social structures have obviously emerged (evolved) over a very long time with far more spontaneity than planning. Here we might list the traffic system of Paris, the dating habits of college students, the process for vetting scientific findings in journals, and the market for wheat. But even the founders of organizations—whether the "father" of a nation or the originating patriarch of a family business—didn't "invent" them. In all cases, such founders were constrained by a prior understanding of what a nation or a business "should be." They had more leeway in making adjustments to such expectations than their successors today, but each was altering, not inventing, something. They, too, had taken on a social position that faced restrictions and opportunities. As Archer has argued, "people . . . either reproduce or transform structure, rather than creating it."[19]

Social structures are emergent, ontologically real "things." They cannot continue to exist without the persons within them who sustain them, and thus are not subject to the accusation that they are intellectually irresponsible reifications of rules or patterns. But they do have causal impact on those very persons.

Consider your local parish as a social structure. There are many social positions in a religious congregation, each in relation to other social positions. When you go to church on Sunday, you enter into the position of congregant. This position is in relation to the position of other congregants, as well as to the positions of presider, usher, and lector. Each of these relations existed long before you or any of the other persons in attendance first entered into them, and each generates restrictions and opportunities.

As a member of the congregation, you know well that after you take your seat, you are restricted from shouting out to a friend you see on the other side of the church, not allowed to raise your hand to ask a question at the end of the homily, and forbidden to remove money from the collection basket as it passes by you. Restrictions in social structures always have an enforcement mechanism, which in these examples may be no more than the strange looks you'd get from other congregants if you decided to violate the restriction.

We face restrictions in every social structure as we take on a position within it. Some are enforced by formal legal penalty, as when caught driving over the speed limit on the way home from work. But most rely on less severe but still effective penalties. When you take on the position of golfer, you don't tee off until the foursome in front of you is out of range. When you are a passenger on a city bus, you use earbuds so your music doesn't bother other riders. And when you take on the position of patron at the local library, you don't raise your voice. Even in the social position of backpacker at Yosemite, you are in relation to the positions of park superintendent and park ranger, and, without seeing either of them, you comply with their restrictions concerning campfires.

There is no determinism here. You are still free to speed, stand to ask questions during Mass, hit your golf ball into the foursome ahead of you, play loud music on the bus, and shout in the library. But you'd pay a price for this, and, almost always, the price is sufficient to keep you from doing so. Most of the time most of us "go along" with the structural restrictions we face. We may think the boss's insistence on getting that reimbursement request in duplicate is foolish, but we do as we're told. And every time we do go along, we help to maintain the social structure as it is. This is what sociologists call the reproduction of social structures, and this is why structures are so robust and hard to change.

Opportunities have an analogous causal impact on our decisions. Taking on the role of rider on the city bus means you will face restrictions (you can't alter the route, you must not play loud music, etc.), but it also provides the opportunity of getting somewhere you want to go and allows you to read or daydream while doing it. Our position as congregant on Sunday generates the opportunity to worship in community and, if we're fortunate, to hear an insightful reflection on the readings. When we take on the position of shopper at Best Buy to purchase something on sale, we are responding to an opportunity that has had a causal impact on our decision. The sale isn't the only reason we buy, but it's one of the causes. Taking advantage of the causal power of opportunity is why Facebook is free, why airline tickets are cheaper on weekends, why your agent gets to keep part of your payment to the insurance company, why universities offer to reimburse expenses for faculty attending professional conferences, and why the federal government reimburses your health care provider for vaccinating your kids.

The impact of structural restrictions and opportunities on our decisions occurs, of course, in the context of our goals and values. We typically take on a social position in a structure because we're trying to accomplish a goal we have. That's why we go to work, or the convenience store, or to church. And in many situations, existing restrictions are not a problem. You intend to do the work the boss expects, to pay for that gallon of milk before leaving the store, and to sit without raising your hand during your pastor's sermon. Virtue plays a big role here. We typically do these things because we believe we should do them. It's what virtue requires. A "graceful" social structure is one where the restrictions and opportunities encourage virtuous decisions. But at times social structures can be sinful; they can discourage virtuous decisions. In this situation, a virtuous person will not only resist those restrictions but also will try to change the structure itself.

Although most of us most of the time "go along" with the restrictions and opportunities we face, thereby sustaining the social structures around us, we know that structures do at times change. But to understand how and why they change, it's first necessary to notice that not everyone within a social structure faces the *same* restrictions and opportunities. Of course, those holding positions of formal authority—presidents, CEOs, department heads—have more leeway in resisting or altering restrictions. But patterns of privilege and disadvantage are more pervasive. Seniority is frequently accompanied by privilege, as are credentials, whether that means having an MBA at a global business firm or a reputation for effective violence in a street gang. Similarly, race, ethnicity, and gender have frequently been markers for the line between privilege and disadvantage.

The relevance of disadvantage for the transformation of social structures is clear. Rarely do those with privilege initiate structural change. It's those who feel unjustly disadvantaged who are most apt to be willing to "pay the price" imposed by structures when restrictions are violated, the usual first step in moving toward transformation. Vivid examples include the challenge to apartheid by Blacks in South Africa and to Jim Crow laws by African Americans in the United States.

JUSTICE AND INJUSTICE AS STRUCTURAL CHARACTERISTICS

This essay will set aside important questions in social ethics and fundamental moral theology about the appropriateness of notions of social sin, centering as they do on whether the notion of sin requires a conscious subject committing it. Similar questions exist concerning whether the classic Christian notion of virtue can be applied to an organization or other social structures. John Rawls has referred to justice as "the first virtue of social institutions,"[20] and, in chapter 7, Lisa Cahill endorses Rawls's language. The critical realist understanding of social structures makes such questions unnecessary, as theologians can employ this view to understand justice and injustice as characteristics of organizations or of social structures more broadly.

It should remain clear in what follows that the contributions provided by critical realist sociology to these issues can at no point substitute for the needed moral judgments to distinguish justice from injustice. Its contributions can be summarized in two points.

First, justice can be understood as a characteristic of social structures that penalize unjust activities and encourage just ones. As we have seen, social structures always generate restrictions that penalize certain behaviors and opportunities that encourage others. Most frequently, these restrictions and opportunities help to sustain and reproduce the social structure over time. A sense of being treated justly within a social structure helps solidify the commitment of persons to its ongoing existence. However, every social structure generates differences of privilege and disadvantage, if only that leaders face more opportunities than others. Quite frequently, privilege and disadvantage are more dramatic, and a moral analysis often finds some of those differences unwarranted. Thus, it is rare that a large organization can exist without morally objectionable disadvantage faced by one or another subgroup within it. This, of course, is why Pope Benedict XVI observed that "the Church's wisdom has always pointed to the presence of original sin in social conditions and in the structure of society."[21]

Thus, the first great advantage of this critical realist approach to structural injustice is that it supplements the traditional moral analysis of the personal vices related to injustice—attitudes of malice, prejudice, indifference, and so on. It instead focuses the attention on the objective restrictions and opportunities faced by different subgroups within the group. Injustice is thereby understood as consisting in any restrictions or opportunities that encourage unjust activities or penalize just ones.

The second advantage flows quickly from the first. Any organization that wants self-consciously to investigate whether injustice exists within it can begin not with an examination of conscience concerning personal attitudes but with a face-to-face conversation about objective restrictions and opportunities. The first step is to identify all relevant subgroups—whether based on gender, race, seniority, ethnicity, education, or any other characteristic—that may face restrictions or opportunities different from others. Small organizations can include everyone around the table, while larger groups must rely on representatives of the relevant subgroups.

Each speaker identifies the restrictions and opportunities they face and how those differ from those faced by others. The group listens to each participant and then discusses whether the differences cited can be agreed on. Conversation makes clear how large or small those differences are between the privileged and disadvantaged.

This is as far as critical realist sociology can take the conversation into the arena of justice. At this point, moral assessments have to be made about the appropriateness of privilege and disadvantage. Those with seniority and the benefit of greater experience may deserve the deference they expect in decision-making—or they may not. Unjust disadvantages perceived by one subgroup may turn out to be shared by others, and the dividing line between privilege and disadvantage may be different from what participants initially thought. Moral deliberation will be needed.

Beginning this conversation does not guarantee either ultimate agreement or greater justice. However, it is a fact of organizational life that the privileged are rarely aware of the extent of their advantage or of the problems that their advantage generates for others. Justifications that are well rehearsed among the privileged often appear thin when exposed to even respectful objection from the disadvantaged.

Of course, leaders rarely have the moral courage to initiate this sort of conversation about privilege and disadvantage, for two reasons. First, these differences in status are long-standing characteristics of each organization, and they have helped maintain and reproduce it. Second, leaders are typically chosen for their commitment to sustaining the organization they are to lead. Reinhold Niebuhr famously argued that groups are more susceptible to self-interest than individuals,[22] and confronting injustice, even within organizations formally committed to justice, requires both visionary leaders and a pervasive culture of integrity.

JOSEF PIEPER'S TYPOLOGY

Justice has been a fundamental part of Christian theology from the scriptures and early church to the twenty-first century. Thomas Aquinas, the most influential intellectual force shaping modern Catholic social thought, had much to say about justice, both as a virtue and an obligation, incorporating diverse sources from Greek and Christian traditions. However, his views are difficult to summarize briefly.

In the 1950s, in what one scholarly commentator described as a "beneficent act of eisegesis," German philosopher Josef Pieper proposed a systematization and simplification of the Thomistic view of justice.[23] His construal of three forms of justice has come to be widely accepted within Catholic social thought, particularly in the English-speaking world. It was employed, for example, by the US bishops in their pastoral *Economic Justice for All*.[24]

Pieper asked, "When might justice be said to prevail in a community?" He replied, "St. Thomas's answer might have run like this: . . . whenever the three basic relations [in a community's life] are disposed in their proper order."[25] The three relations, and their corresponding forms of justice, are (1) individuals to one another (commutative justice), (2) the social whole to individuals (distributive justice), and (3) individuals to the social whole (legal or general justice).

This three-part typology remains helpful today, but this current research project, "Re-thinking Justice in Catholic Social Thought," has been undertaken because Pieper's summary suffers from the same shortcomings as does Aquinas's entire work on justice today. Arising at the height of the Middle Ages, Aquinas could not have anticipated the social, cultural, political, and economic changes that have occurred between his day and ours.

Any "updated" account of justice will need to attend to the impact of social structures on the decisions of persons within them. The remainder of this essay does not attempt a survey of structural injustices. Instead, it presents a series of examples to illustrate how a concern for the structural dimensions of justice are among the major reasons for re-thinking justice beyond the tripartite typology of general, distributive, and commutative justice.

GENERAL JUSTICE

In Pieper's account of the Thomistic understanding of justice, general justice is the obligation of each person to the well-being of the social whole, an obligation to the common good. In a democracy, each citizen is called to active participation in political life, from neighborhood efforts to improve the local playground to electing just leaders at local, regional, and national levels.

The provision of structural opportunities for greater participation and the elimination of structural restrictions on that participation are essential dimensions of institutionalizing justice in society. Consider the electoral system. Some nations value such participation so highly that they require all citizens to vote (though enforcement varies).[26] In recent years, efforts to reduce voter participation have become frequent in the United States and represent a critical dimension of injustice facing racial and ethnic minorities. Many state legislatures have passed laws that reduce opportunities to vote and create restrictions on doing so,[27] thereby reducing what might be called "participative justice." In addition to reversing these structural patterns, a straightforward way to generate greater opportunity for electoral participation would be to alter structures to make voter registration automatic any time a citizen has a formal interaction with government at any level: for example, when filing tax returns, applying for a driver's license or license plate renewals, or soliciting help at social service agencies.

A related issue of structural injustice in the electoral process concerns gerrymandering.[28] After each election, we often hear that "the people have spoken," but structural factors are also fundamental causes in the outcome of elections. In the United States, after every decennial census, each state must redraw the boundaries of election districts to reflect population changes. Suppose the state legislature and the governor's office are controlled by the same political party. In that case, that party can "pack" large majorities of voters of "the other" party into a few districts, shaping the rest of the districts in the state to favor their own candidates. As a result, a state with about a 50–50 split between Democrats and Republicans can elect strong majorities of one party or the other to the US House of Representatives and state legislatures. John Rawls called this a violation of "the meaning of political participation" because it gives more weight to the vote of some citizens than others.[29]

Within economic life, many structures influence the participation of different groups differently. Feminists have for decades pointed out the injustices facing women due to structural restrictions against taking time off from work: the presumption that career-minded, "serious" workers do not have significant responsibilities for childcare.[30] African American and Latinx workers have long faced structural restrictions on their economic participation ranging from union seniority rules to straightforward attitudes of discrimination. Environmental injustice in the industrialized world frequently imposes the costs of environmental damage on communities of color.

DISTRIBUTIVE JUSTICE

In the premodern world, the obligations of distributive justice fell on the shoulders of the king or the prince. It was his obligation to promote the good of the people. In a democratic world, all citizens bear this responsibility of the community for the well-being of all.

The Judeo-Christian tradition has a long history of attention to distributive justice even before that phrase was in use. The Hebrew Scriptures employed gleaning laws and the sabbatical and Jubilee years (restrictions on owners) to structurally embed standards of just treatment of the widow, the orphan, and the resident alien. The Fathers of the early church are well known for their strong and often strident denunciation of the wealthy who did not share their surplus with the needy around them.[31] As Jean Porter explains in her chapter, Thomas Aquinas supported the personal ownership of property but only when this was understood to include "common use."[32] Each of these understandings of the obligations of owners of property toward those with unmet needs was rooted in the fundamental insight that God had given the world to humanity to ensure that everyone's needs were met.

In one of the most important transformations in human history, after some 7,000 years when nearly all humans required access to land for their survival, the industrial revolution transformed that majority from farmers to wage laborers. This brought about a dramatic shift in the teaching of the Catholic Church, typically marked from the date of Pope Leo XIII's 1891 encyclical, *Rerum novarum*.[33] From then on, attention to jobs, just wages, working conditions, and labor unions has been central to papal and episcopal concern for distributive justice.

Although shocking to those holding an absolutist view of the rights of property owners, Pope John Paul II articulated this structural link between distributive justice and labor markets when he asserted, "Ownership of the means of production, whether in industry or agriculture, is just and legitimate if it serves useful work."[34] Many European nations have embedded that link structurally in corporate law through codetermination, a requirement, varying by country, that a sizable portion of the board of directors of large corporations be elected by the employees. Law in the United States has favored the rights of stockholders. Structural restrictions continue to face racial and ethnic minorities in the economics of nations around the globe.

As a result, in addition to the various necessary supports for those who are unable to meet needs by their own efforts, distributive justice requires strong support for altering the restrictions and opportunities generated by social structures so that they adequately prepare people for employment (education, even beyond high school), ensure justice in employment (health and safety, wages and benefits, nondiscrimination, support for unions), and overcome cultural biases against women and families in employment (childcare).

In addition to justice issues related to employment, structural injustice occurs in a variety of other ways, including "redlining" of neighborhoods that had had long-term effects on African Americans: reduced home ownership, lower home values, and increased racial segregation—effects that began in the 1930s and continue decades after.[35] Here too, understanding that social structures alter our decisions through restrictions and opportunities helps to illuminate requirements for structurally embedded distributive justice.

COMMUTATIVE JUSTICE

Throughout the history of secular and religious accounts of justice, the relation between two individuals—classically described as commutative justice—has been central. Persons are to treat each other justly, and any violation of commutative justice requires restitution. The laws of every nation on earth incorporate this commitment to commutative justice structurally by a detailed set of prohibitions and procedures for punishment and rectification.

These one-to-one relations are important, but conceiving of this dimension of justice as only an issue between two individuals betrays a dominant individualism. Many traditional cultures have a far more communal understanding of such relations and of the violations of justice between persons. As Father Orobator's chapter makes clear, in Africa the "palaver" represents an alternative that includes the community in the resolution of disputes between individuals.[36] In recent years, many European nations have developed a structured place for restorative justice within their criminal justice systems.[37] Similar efforts in the United States to move from retribution to restoration have been fruitful even if limited in application.[38]

CONCLUSION

Formal Catholic social teaching has for decades spoken about unjust social structures. However, it has not specified how structures have their unjust effects and has not even said what a social structure is. Critical realist sociology, rooted in an underlying philosophy of science, provides an analysis of social structures that avoids pitfalls of both holism—where structures make human freedom impossible—and individualism—where the causal impact of structures is eclipsed. Social structures do not control human decisions, but by generating restrictions and opportunities, they frequently alter what persons within them would otherwise have decided.

These structural forces are most frequently morally positive, as they provide background "software" that allows daily life to boot up. Good moral character that leads individuals to virtuous decisions is supported when social structures present restrictions against morally objectionable activity. A vast array of structures—from traffic systems to corporate codes of business ethics to morality enforced by disapproving stares—support virtuous society.

Nevertheless, structures can and often do generate both restrictions penalizing virtuous behavior and opportunities for destructive action. In these cases, we can rightfully describe structures as unjust, not because the structures themselves "do" something unjust but because they influence decisions within them in the direction of injustice

This essay has not attempted a survey of all the dimensions of justice and injustice in contemporary life. Instead, it has presented examples illustrating how social structures generate causal forces that make justice more or less likely. Re-thinking justice in Catholic social thought can be enriched by employing the critical realist understanding of social structures.

BIBLIOGRAPHY

Aaronson, Daniel, Daniel Hartley, and Bhashkar Mazumder. "The Effects of the 1930s HOLC 'Redlining' Maps." *American Economic Journal: Economic Policy* 13, no. 4 (2021): 355–92. https://doi.org/10.1257/pol.20190414.

Aquinas, Thomas. *Summa theologica*. Benziger, 1947–48.

Archer, Margaret S. *Realist Social Theory: The Morphogenetic Approach*. Cambridge University Press, 1995.

Archer, Margaret S. *Structure, Agency, and the Internal Conversation*. Cambridge University Press, 2003.

Benedict XVI. *Caritas in veritate*, 2009, 34. http://w2.vatican.va/content/benedict-xvi/en /encyclicals/documents/hf_ben-xvi_enc_20090629_caritas-in-veritate.html.

Benedict XVI. "Plenary Address," Inaugural Session of the Fifth General Conference of the Bishops of Latin America and the Caribbean (CELAM), Shrine of Aparecida, May 13, 2007, no. 4. http://www.vatican.va/content/benedict-xvi/en/speeches/2007/may/documents/hf_ben-xvi_spe_20070513_conference-aparecida.html.

Bhaskar, Roy. *A Realist Theory of Science*. Routledge, 2008.

Brennan Center for Justice. "Gerrymandering Explained." https://www.brennancenter.org/our-work/research-reports/gerrymandering-explained.

Brennan Center for Justice. "Voter Suppression." https://www.brennancenter.org/issues/ensure-every-american-can-vote/vote-suppression.

Conway, Trudy. David, Matzko McCarthy, and Vicki Schieber, eds. *Redemption and Restoration: A Catholic Perspective on Restorative Justice*. Liturgical Press, 2017.

Crepaldi, Giampaolo, and Stefano Fontana. *La dimensión interdisciplinar de la doctrina social de la Iglesia: Un estudio sobre el Magisterio*. Instituto Mexicano de Doctrinal Social Cristiana, 2006.

Finn, Daniel K. *Consumer Ethics in a Global Economy*. Georgetown University Press, 2019.

Friedmann, Jonathan L. "The Fall of Jericho as Earthquake Myth." *Jewish Bible Quarterly* 48, no. 3 (July 2020): 171–78. https://search.ebscohost.com/login.aspx?direct=true&db=lsdar&AN=ATLAiACO201116000307&site=ehost-live&scope=site.

Gregg, Samuel. *Challenging the Modern World*. Lexington Books, 1999.

Hempel, Carl. *Aspects of Scientific Explanation*. Macmillan, 1965.

John Paul II. *Centesimus annus*, 43. https://www.vatican.va/content/john-paul-ii/en/encyclicals/documents/hf_jp-ii_enc_01051991_centesimus-annus.html.

Leo XIII. *Rerum novarum*, May 15, 1891. https://www.vatican.va/content/leo-xiii/en/encyclicals/documents/hf_l-xiii_enc_15051891_rerum-novarum.html.

Long, Burke O. "The Social World of Ancient Israel." *Interpretation* 36, no. 3 (July 1982): 243–55. https://doi.org/10.1177/002096438203600303.

Marder, Ian D. "Restorative Justice and the Council of Europe: An Opportunity for Progress." *Penal Reform International*. July 4, 2018. https://www.penalreform.org/blog/restorative-justice-and-the-council-of-europe/.

Niebuhr, Reinhold. *Moral Man and Immoral Society: A Study in Ethics and Politics* (1932). Scribner, 1960.

Novak, Michael. "Defining Social Justice." *First Things* 108 (December 2000): 11–13. https://www.firstthings.com/article/2000/12/defining-social-justice.

Okin, Susan Moller. *Justice, Gender, and the Family*. Basic Books, 1989.

Orobator, Agbonkhianmeghe E. *Reconciliation, Justice, and Peace: The Second African Synod*. Orbis Books, 2011.

Phan, Peter C. *Social Thought: Message of the Fathers of the Church*. Vol. 20. Michael Glazier, 1984.

Pieper, Josef. *Justice*. Pantheon Books, 1955.

Porpora, Douglas. "Four Concepts of Social Structure." *Journal for the Theory of Social Behavior* 19, no. 2 (1989): 195. https://doi.org/10.1111/j.1468-5914.1989.tb00144.x.

Rawls, John. *A Theory of Justice* (Revised). Belknap Press, 1999.

Reeder, Caryn A. "Sex and Execution: Deuteronomy 22:20–24." *The Expository Times* 124, no. 6 (March 2013): 272–81. https://doi.org/10.1177/0014524612465382.

Singh, Shane. "How Compelling Is Compulsory Voting? A Multilevel Analysis of Turnout." *Political Behavior* 33, no. 1 (2011): 95–111. https://www.jstor.org/stable/41488276.

Slingerland, H Dixon. "Acts 18:1–18, the Gallio Inscription, and Absolute Pauline Chronology." *Journal of Biblical Literature* 110, no. 3 (1991): 439–49. https://www.jstor.org/stable/3267781.

Smith, Christian. *What Is a Person: Rethinking Humanity, Social Life, and the Moral Good from the Person Up*. University of Chicago Press, 2010.

United States Catholic Bishops. *Economic Justice for All: Pastoral Letter on Catholic Social Teaching and the U.S. Economy*, 1986, para. 69–71. https://www.usccb.org/upload/economic_justice_for_all.pdf.

NOTES

1. Slingerland, "Acts 18:1–18," 439–49.
2. I am indebted to my friend and colleague Michael Patella, OSB, for this example.
3. I am indebted to my friend and colleague Dale Launderville, OSB, for these examples.
4. Friedmann, "The Fall of Jericho as Earthquake Myth," 171–78.
5. Long, "The Social World of Ancient Israel," 243–55.
6. Reeder, "Sex and Execution," 272–81.
7. Gregg, *Challenging the Modern World*, 197.
8. Novak, "Defining Social Justice," 11–13.
9. See, for example, Crepaldi and Fontana, *La dimensión interdisciplinar*.
10. Benedict XVI, "Plenary Address," no. 4.
11. For a more complete discussion of how theology should and should not make this decision, see Finn, *Consumer Ethics*, chapter 5.
12. For a helpful discussion of emergence, see Smith, *What Is a Person?* 25–42.
13. Hempel, *Aspects of Scientific Explanation*.
14. See Bhaskar, *A Realist Theory of Science*, chapter 4.
15. Porpora, "Four Concepts of Social Structure," 195.
16. Archer, *Realist Social Theory*, 66–79.
17. Archer, *Structure, Agency, and the Internal Conversation*, 165–83.
18. Archer, *Realist Social Theory*, 73.
19. Archer, 71.
20. Rawls, *A Theory of Justice*, 3.
21. Benedict XVI, *Caritas in veritate*, 34.
22. Niebuhr, *Moral Man and Immoral Society*.
23. Pieper, *Justice*.
24. United States Catholic Bishops, *Economic Justice for All*, no. 69–71.
25. Pieper, *Justice*, 50.
26. Singh, "How Compelling Is Compulsory Voting?" 95–111. As of 2019, these nations had mandatory voting: Australia, Belgium, Costa Rica, Luxembourg, and Uruguay.
27. See, for example, Brennan Center for Justice, "Voter Suppression."
28. Brennan Center for Justice, "Gerrymandering Explained."
29. Rawls, *A Theory of Justice*, 196.
30. Moller Okin, *Justice, Gender, and the Family*, chapter 1.
31. Phan, *Social Thought*.
32. Aquinas, ST, II–II, 66.2.

33. Leo XIII, *Rerum novarum*.
34. John Paul II, *Centesimus annus*, 43.
35. Aaronson, Hartley, and Mazumder, "The Effects of the 1930s HOLC 'Redlining' Maps," 355–92.
36. Orobator, *Reconciliation, Justice, and Peace*, 49–50.
37. Marder, "Restorative Justice."
38. Conway, Matzko McCarthy, and Schieber, *Redemption and Restoration*.

PART II

Three Constructive Accounts of Justice

CHAPTER 10

A Synthetic Statement of What Justice Might Be Understood to Entail in Catholic Social Thought Today

Agbonkhianmeghe E. Orobator, SJ

In theory and practice, the concept of justice is vastly explored yet critically contested in a wide range of philosophical, theological, and political traditions of intellectual inquiry. There are numerous ways we can try to make sense of justice. This variety suggests that justice is multidimensional and renders any attempt to subsume it under a single article pretentious, futile, and impracticable. From earliest conceptualisations of justice in antiquity to present time, religious beliefs, narratives, and institutions have played an important role in the articulation of what justice is about, at times resulting in clearly enumerated divine commandments and moral imperatives. One particular articulation of the understanding, knowledge, and practice of justice is contained in Catholic social thought. With the passage of time and the evolution of context, changes or developments have taken place, revealing diverse ways of understanding the theoretical foundations of justice and applying its principles to lived reality and refining overall the concept of justice within Catholic social thought.

In our era, "justice" continues to evolve from how it was understood in the time of Plato and Aristotle, and Augustine and Aquinas, and Hobbes and Rawls after them. The concept of justice is no longer confined to the regulation of relationships among individuals within closed social and political constructs. There has emerged a broadening of the scope and a more inclusive conceptualisation of justice. One discernible trajectory moves from a less atomistic and individualistic conception of justice to a greater attention to communal and social contexts that shape the understanding and practice of justice. And the spheres of analysis have expanded and developed significantly in recent times. Justice can be conceived of in global (spatial), integrative (open-ended), or multivalent (extensive) terms, depending on the context, the issue, and the objective.

To situate what justice might be understood to entail in Catholic social thought today, the following brief examples may highlight instances of how the concept of justice has developed more consistently within Catholic social thought relative to the typologies of justice characteristic of antiquity, the Middle Ages, and modern times.

First is ecological or environmental justice. It is an acceptable belief within Catholic social thought that beyond the relationship of self to other humans, justice imposes a moral value on the relationship of humans to their environment. The distributive quality of justice no longer pertains only to individuals or groups in society but is inclusive of nature, where the latter represents an open-ended "environment" of the society that inhabits and depends on it. Viewed from this perspective, the conceptualisation of justice shows that human beings are neither exceptional nor separate from the natural world. The actions of the former have severe implications for the survival of the latter. In this sense, how we construct or conceive of the self is inclusive of what society morally owes nature.

What justice might be understood to entail in its ecological expression in Catholic social thought today benefits greatly from the pioneering, consistent, and critical vision of Pope Francis articulated in his letter on ecology, *Laudato si'*. In this letter, perhaps Francis's most innovative contribution to what justice is about in Catholic social teaching, is the intrinsic connection he makes between "the cry of the earth and the cry of the poor" (LS, 49). He notes: "We are faced not with two separate crises, one environmental and the other social, but rather with one complex crisis which is both social and environmental" (LS, 139). It is two sides of the same coin. The ecological situations we are in as humans bear direct and indirect relationship to how we relate to one another in our world and together with the nonhuman world. One can infer from this understanding that the constituents of nature live and operate within a common moral landscape.

Recent developments have shown that those who bear the burden of climate change are not those who cause it. Hence, elements like sustainability, transition, and loss and damage have shifted to the fore as concrete expressions of justice in its ecological expression that is not limited to individuals but extends to and includes whole peoples and geopolitical entities and ecosystems.

The second example relates to how gender legitimately features in the conceptualisation of justice as a criterion for critiquing and remedying the domination of one gender by another on the basis of a conscious or unconscious assimilation of utilitarian, exploitative, and discriminatory attitudes, chief among them being patriarchy. On the basis of its expansive nature, it becomes possible to see that justice is at the heart of contemporary social action from the #MeToo movement to advocacy for women's rights in bastions of patriarchy in geographical spaces like Saudi Arabia, Afghanistan, and Iran; and in institutional spaces like the church; and in a variety of industries (e.g., entertainment, media, and sports).

The third and final illustration of expansiveness is how justice today relates to generational justice of which the historical institution and practice of slavery offers a relevant example. The conceptualisation of justice in this context prioritises the ongoing need for accountability for historical acts committed institutionally, moral responsibility for which extends to generations to come. Considered as a duty to honour the memory of victims and address the material needs and moral claims of descendants, the concept of justice in this context takes the form of reparation, restitution, forgiveness, and reconciliation. A comparable way of conceiving of justice in this context is racial justice, examples of which are global, multidimensional, and particularly recalcitrant, including caste systems that reduce minority groups to misery and servitude, institutionalised discrimination against non-whites, and anthropological and cultural dispossession of Indigenous communities. In all these instances, the value system is the same in the ways it ascribes privilege based on racialized criteria and the construction of narratives of superiority to justify, rationalise, permit, propagate, and promote discrimination, segregation, exploitation, and oppression.

All of these instances offer useful elements for reconceptualising justice within Catholic social thought in our era. On the basis of the foregoing, justice might be understood within Catholic social thought in the following terms: Justice is a transcendent good that bears a quality of wholeness in its conceptualisation and application because it performs an integrative function and is capable of accounting for many issues and concerns in everyday life of individuals and communities. In sum, justice represents an expansive reality. This quality of expansiveness—characteristic of how justice might be conceived of in our era is important—not least because it offers the basis for confronting instances of injustice.

What justice is or how it should be understood within Catholic social thought in the twenty-first century requires an intellectually open, mutually respectful, and constructive dialogue among cultures, with the belief that the knowledge, understanding, and practice of justice is enriched in the fuller perspective made possible by this open approach. Whether the outcome is a synthesis among the constitutive elements of each culture or not, the important aim would be to avoid a static or monolithic concept. Stated differently, it would be dangerous to reduce the vibrant cultural attributes that inform and shape our perception of justice to a dominant and convenient narrative of particular intellectual influences. Celebrated Nigerian author Chimamanda Ngozi Adichie has cautioned against the danger of the "single story."

In reality, if justice were conceived of as a "story," it would be a story with many sides or layers told from multiple perspectives, by diverse narrators, and valid for varied contexts, without succumbing to the hegemony of the powerful. In this sense, there is a distinct contribution from the viewpoint of the Global South to the way justice is understood in a coherent and comprehensive manner that welcomes the perspectives of vulnerable, oppressed, impoverished, and marginalised communities, no matter how different and disturbing their perspectives may be.

Embedded in the conceptualisation of justice as an expansive reality is the ideal of inclusiveness. The idea of a story captures this conceptualisation. Perhaps a more apt idea would be Pope Francis's image of a polyhedron, to which he refers in two important documents: *Fratelli tutti* and *Querida Amazonia*. As Francis describes it, "our model must be that of a polyhedron, in which the value of each individual is respected, where 'the whole is greater than the part, but it is also greater than the sum of its parts'" (FT, 145). He continues:

> This means working to create a many-faceted polyhedron whose different sides form a variegated unity, in which "the whole is greater than the part." The image of a polyhedron can represent a society where differences coexist, complementing, enriching and reciprocally illuminating one another, even amid disagreements and reservations. Each of us can learn something from others. No one is useless and no one is expendable. This also means finding ways to include those on the peripheries of life. For they have another way of looking at things; they see aspects of reality that are invisible to the centres of power where weighty decisions are made. (FT, 215)

In borrowing this imagery from Pope Francis, it is important to bear in mind that he speaks primarily of resolving the tension between hegemonic cultural tendencies that produce the colonialisation of the rights, dignity, identity, and cultural assets of a people—and how to resolve this tension through a proper intersection of the global or universal with the local or particular. Importantly, it serves an analogical purpose to describe how justice might be perceived in Catholic social thought in today's highly networked and globalised world. However, there is a limit to the extent that this imagery can be applied to the purposes of this statement.

What insight could we derive from this imagery, or rather how does it advance our cause of developing a creative account of how justice within Catholic social thought might best be conceived in our era? The first thing to note is the polyvalent quality of the reality called justice. However we conceive it, justice is not one thing. To speak of justice as a polyvalent reality is to recognise its historical rootedness and contemporary dynamism. While there are enduring and venerable traditions that illustrate the former, there are equally distinct and valuable innovations that demonstrate the latter. The examples above are a case in point. It is important to preserve both trajectories of history and foundations and change and development, and Francis's imagery underlines this dimension. Stated differently, the understanding, knowledge, and practice of justice derive from a diversity that yields a vital synthesis and a unique form of wisdom that can be applied in a variety of circumstances.

The second insight is a caution against the imposition of notions of justice that are essentially bounded by the biases, stereotypes, or mindsets of its proponents. More positively, though, it is an invitation—at least from a methodological standpoint—to develop a dialogical model. Such a model or conceptualisation is characterised by openness and receptivity to the unfamiliar qualities, disturbing perspectives, and unique paths of other cultures that ultimately generate an enriched understanding, knowledge, and practice of justice.

Taking the foregoing into account, it is not a complicated task to perceive how a polyhedron of many complementary approaches would produce a richly textured understanding, knowledge, and practice of justice. Each element of the conceptualisation of justice has a value and makes a valid contribution to the sum of all the elements. These elements can be articulated to highlight various aspects or ideas in Catholic social teaching in view of producing a coherent and comprehensive response to social life. The outcome presents a concept of justice "in which the value of each individual is respected, where 'the whole is greater than the part, but it is also greater than the sum of its parts'" (FT, 145). The diversity of voices, the multiplicity of elements, and the polyvalence of perspectives strengthen rather than weaken how justice within Catholic social thought is conceived in our era.

To illustrate this idea of diversity, we may consider an example from the Global South. In this context, there is widespread belief that justice is founded on relationality or mutual interdependence and the advancement of humanity in practical ways that oppose social inequality, promote the dismantling of dehumanising structures, and support the flourishing of individuals in their communities. Such an approach would prioritise a preferential option for the weakest and most vulnerable. Also, within this context or from this perspective, justice would assume a certain mystical quality, not in a quasi-religious sense but based on understanding it as a virtue that connects the various constituents of nature or the created world—that is, the totality of cosmos—and regulates their relationship in a manner that aims to guarantee ecological balance, social cohesion, and shared progress. Yet none of these would be inimical to or contradict that long-established political conceptualisation of justice—favoured in the Global North—that emphasises individual rights within a free society of reasonable citizens cooperating for the purposes of attaining mutual advantage.

Accordingly, a threefold shift is required in the enterprise of re-thinking justice in Catholic social thought. Its understanding ought to be hermeneutically variegated, contextually relevant, and culturally critical. Such diversity of understanding, knowledge, and practice of justice underlines aspects, dimensions, and perspectives of a complex reality that can be held together within a wider Catholic and global framework that is not manifestly individualistic, purely sectarian, or totally generalising, albeit subject to ongoing debate and renewal. This kind of shift guards against purely theoretical understanding that risks making an abstraction of the lived reality of justice.

FOUR CHARACTERISTICS

From the foregoing, the following considerations appear key in the project of formulating or characterising what justice might be understood to entail in Catholic social thought today.

Justice Inculturated

As a transcendent good, justice lends itself to a process of inculturation in the way the core or constitutive elements are understood, discovered, and practiced in the religious, cultural, and social context of the lived reality of people for whom it remains a value, a virtue, a criterion, and a solution. It can no longer be plausibly maintained that classical theories have exhausted the understanding, knowledge, and practice of justice.

Applied to justice, this idea of inculturation does not amount to a conceptual decline or dilution of universally held principles, norms, or values (such as human dignity, common good, and preferential option for the poor), but holds that their understanding, knowledge, and practice are interpreted and applied in the context of individuals, their histories, their communities, and their societies. The particular condition, the nature of the issue at stake, and the specific circumstance have a bearing on how justice is conceptualised. The same applies to the processes for delivering the goods of justice, be it *Gacaca, Mato Oput*, or *Ubushingantahe/bashingantahe.*

Thus, inculturation facilitates a deepening of what justice might be understood to entail in Catholic social thought today. By implication, justice appears as a cultural phenomenon, that is, a means of humanising people and their institutions in ways that restore dignity, prioritise respect, and strengthen cooperation.

Justice sans Frontier

Justice is an expansive reality. Whether considered in distributive or commutative terms, understanding, knowledge, and practice of justice extend to a range of dimensions and are inclusive of many layers of religious, social, cultural, and political interests and structures. The issues, conditions, areas, and situations that justice covers are not limited to the conceptual preferences of its proponents. It is open-ended. Inclusivity trumps exclusivity. Justice may be likened to a large tent where participation of minorities—however they are defined or identified—and attention to their concerns are values. In this sense, justice is a global good that relates to world issues, such as poverty, forced migration, war, pandemics, democracy, racism, Indigenous rights, extractive industry, and climate change, and the creation of social conditions to fulfil the basic needs and guarantee the flourishing of individuals and their communities.

One of the advantages of this way of conceptualising justice is that is allows us to redefine the liberal conception of justice that effectively separated human beings and the nonhuman world (creation largely) on account of the generally accepted idea that not only are we exceptional in relation to the latter, we are also superior (as taught by the principle of karma). Thus, the sphere of application of justice goes beyond the behaviour of human beings and the conduct of their civil, economic, political, and religious institutions.

It concerns how these relate to and affect other constituents of nature. Justice means justice to people and justice to nature and all that the latter represents or encompasses. In this sense it is easy to conceive of justice as generative of an inclusive community of being—human and nonhuman.

Justice as Praxis

Although an abundance of academic literature focuses on analysing and critiquing theories and concepts of justice, re-thinking justice within Catholic social thought warrants a complementary approach that places the emphasis on praxis. Justice has practical consequences for personal, communal, and corporate life. The practice of justice is not exhausted in analytic or academic philosophical discourses; it applies to everyday life of people and the institutions or structures that regulate their manner of interaction. Justice is a practical reality that responds to and seeks to remedy injustices, whether embedded in structures or associated with the moral agency of individuals. How individuals behave (e.g., corruption), how states conduct themselves (e.g., unjustified war of aggression against an independent and sovereign nation), and how institutions or social systems function (e.g., abuse of minors and vulnerable people within religious organisations) are matters of justice. These levels of justice are interconnected and are not conceived hierarchically but function interdependently. What justice is about is not dissociable from how it is practiced.

To conceive of justice as a form of praxis with concrete impact on the world of humans in relationship with others and together in relationship with the world of nonhumans prevents its meaning from being dissolved in purely theoretical, abstract, and speculative debates, no matter how compelling or sophisticated. The understanding, knowledge, and practice of justice is not limited to realms of academic analysis and discourse; it also integrates strategies adopted by activists, advocacy groups, and civil society organisations to influence public policy to transform situations of injustice as a matter of preference in favour of the weakest and most vulnerable members of our societies. The concept of justice is both an ideal to be discoursed and a practice to be lived. The end result is transformational.

Dialogical Justice

Re-thinking justice opens a path of dialogue that acknowledges differences among religious traditions. The understanding, knowledge, and practice of justice draw inspiration from explicit religious warrants, such as those contained in the Gospel, developed in Christian theology, and embedded in Catholic social thought. The catholicity of Catholic social thought recognises other explicitly religious traditions that provide warrants, criteria, and rationale for how justice is understood and practiced. Faith-inspired approaches show that justice lends itself to constructive mutual enlightening between religious and secular pluralistic conceptualisations and is related to the most fundamental beliefs, concerns, commitments, and values held by people and their communities. Universality and uniformity do not exhaust the understanding, knowledge, and practice of justice. The preference is for a relative and contextualised understanding of what constitutes justice. Only in a dialogue open to robust debate, critical re-thinking, and divergent perspectives does this understanding become manifest.

CONCLUSION

This attempt to develop a synthetic statement of what justice might be understood to entail in Catholic social thought today leaves some unanswered questions and opens up areas for further research. The expression "Catholic social thought" suggests that whatever we might understand justice to mean is anchored in the traditions of Catholicism. Also, its ongoing development is of particular interest to this community called the Catholic Church. In this regard, two questions are worth considering.

First, to what extent does Catholic social thought embrace the contribution of other religious traditions to the development of a richer understanding, knowledge, and practice of justice? And how does it resolve tensions between divergent and opposing conceptualisations of justice? Similarly, second, how does Catholic social thought consider the contribution of other Christian and ecclesial traditions? This project demonstrates in part that in this era the understanding, knowledge, and practice of justice intersect with and are enriched by the goals, objectives, and practices of interreligious dialogue and ecumenical relations. For the former, the idea of the dialogue of theological exchange, "where specialists seek to deepen their understanding of their respective religious heritages, and to appreciate each other's spiritual values," would be particularly important.[1] For the latter, the idea of receptive ecumenism as an experience of mutual "Catholic learning" would be of interest.[2]

In the final analysis, justice in Catholic social thought appears as an integral part of a wider conceptual field where inclusive Catholicity rather than exclusive Catholicism is the operative term, because the re-thinking of justice is not confined to Roman Catholic theology. Further analysis and sustained critical dialogue are essential to the goal of re-thinking justice within Catholic social thought and learning better how to say, live, and interpret "justice" within the diversity of cultures, multiplicity of social situations, and plurality of religious traditions. The resultant meaning of justice is not immune to critical tensions, nor does it obviate an unrelenting search for compatibility of purposes among various constitutive and complementary ideas in Catholic social thought. Accordingly, drawing on traditional African cultural and religious notions, what justice might be understood to entail in Catholic social thought today, could be summarised as follows: "Justice is a lived virtue and a transcendent good characterised by and practiced in relationality and mutual interdependence as a communal commitment to uphold, humanise, and respect the dignity, well-being, and flourishing of the human person and creation, and to promote the virtuous action, disposition, or behaviour of individuals, groups, institutions, and structures in pursuit of the common good."

BIBLIOGRAPHY

Francis. *Fratelli tutti.* https://www.vatican.va/content/francesco/en/encyclicals/documents/papa-francesco_20201003_enciclica-fratelli-tutti.html.
Francis. *Laudato si'.* https://www.vatican.va/content/francesco/en/encyclicals.index.html.
Francis. *Querida amazonia.* https://www.vatican.va/content/francesco/en/apost_exhortations/documents/papa-francesco_esortazione-ap_20200202_querida-amazonia.html.
The Pontifical Council for Inter-Religious Dialogue and Congregation for the Evangelization of Peoples. "Dialogue and Proclamation: Reflections and Orientations on Interreligious Dialogue and the Proclamation of the Gospel of Jesus Christ." 1991, no. 42. https://www.vatican.va/roman_curia/pontifical_councils/interelg/documents/rc_pc_interelg_doc_19051991_dialogue-and-proclamatio_en.html.
Ryan, Gregory. "Preface." In *Receptive Ecumenism as Transformative Ecclesial Learning,* edited by Paul D. Murray, Gregory A. Ryan, and Paul Lakeland. Oxford University Press, 2022.

NOTES

1. Pontifical Council for Interreligious Dialogue. "Dialogue and Proclamation."
2. "The fundamental principle within Receptive Ecumenism and Catholic Learning is that each tradition should focus first on the self-critical question: 'What can we learn, or receive, with integrity, from our various others in order to facilitate our own growth together into deepened communion in Christ and the Spirit?'" Ryan, "Preface," ix.

CHAPTER 11

Justice

A Three-Dimensional Account from Catholic Social Teaching

David Cloutier

A full account of justice requires three dimensions. I will unfold these three dimensions from simplest to most complicated.

THE FIRST DIMENSION: SUBJECTIVE JUSTICE— INTENDING DESERT AND EQUALITY

The first and simplest dimension is justice as a virtue of agents, of persons making decisions. The virtue of justice is a disposition to give people what they are due. It is classically the "relational" virtue, indicating that right relationship for human beings involves reason and will—that is, some kind of correct, truthful seeing and some kind of rational desire. While it makes sense to speak of human duties to care properly for animals[1] and to condemn a "tyrannical anthropocentrism"—that fails to recognize that "other living beings have a value of their own in God's eyes"[2]—these injustices are analogical to the primary understanding of justice as a virtue of agents who are in reciprocal relationships, governed by each agent's reason and will. The account of God's agency in Hebrew and Christian scriptures attributes justice to God in this sense of reason and will. God gives people their due, though God also makes the sun rise and the rain fall on the just and unjust alike (Mt 5:45), inviting humans to recognize how God's justice is compatible with mercy.[3]

In addition to a notion of desert, justice involves some idea of equality. To lack the virtue of justice is to make *unwarranted* distinctions in one's relations with others, for example, to give some more than they deserve and others less. The motto over the US Supreme Court, "equal justice under law," could be seen as redundant: justice is necessarily equal justice, for if it were unequal, it would not be justice.

THE SECOND DIMENSION: OBJECTIVE JUSTICE—
RIGHTS, DIGNITY, AND THE COMMON GOOD

Desert and equality are formal terms. They don't answer the question of what is deserved or what counts as equality.[4] I take it as evident in many human relations that what is deserved is not some kind of "strict" equality; nearly all accounts of justice assume that equality is a matter of proportion, of "treating like cases alike." Put another way, exercising justice is necessarily contextual; its exercise as a subjective virtue of agents depends on an account of the context, which influences what is due to whom—an account of "right," which Aquinas describes as "those norms which define the relationship of each person to others."[5] But to say it is "contextual" is not to say it is relativistic. Rather, any account of justice will necessarily have an objective dimension that involves truth claims about social order. This says what Alasdair MacIntyre claims when he says every morality "presupposes a sociology"— that is, an account of right social relations—and what critical realists claim when emphasizing that moral agency always occurs within existing structures, which are "real" (i.e., objective).[6] Justice is always contextual, but what is just and unjust in a given context necessarily depends on appeals to some objective account of "*ius*," or "right."

Clearly, this second, "objective" dimension of justice is complicated. The subjective virtue of justice, the first dimension, can be understood today much as Aquinas did, but the content of the objective norms of *ius* that define the context of proper social relationships most certainly cannot! Most importantly, the historical emergence of modern political orders based on a notion of "subjective rights"—rights that are inherent in persons— differs in fundamental ways from almost all premodern orders of "right," in which complex patterns of rights and duties arise out of larger social hierarchies and/or cosmologies.[7] As Joan Lockwood O'Donovan articulates it, "in earlier patristic and medieval political theology, God's right established a matrix of divine, natural, and human rights or objective obligations that determined the ordering justice of political community. Justice (*iustitia*) was synonymous with objective right (*ius*)."[8] Instead of these existing social networks of ordered relations and/or cosmological claims, most modern accounts of justice rely for their objective content on a list of personal rights that are understood to be "inherent" in or "possessed by" individuals.[9] In addition, various forms of political liberalism seek to complement subjective rights claims with constitutional procedures that aim at fairness in exercising and protecting such rights. "Equal justice under law" indicates that the court system—and above all the justices—administer the law impartially (i.e., equally, with no one above the law). And they do so in accord with laws legitimately passed by legislators, who are themselves selected by just (i.e., fair and equal, one-person–one-vote) procedures by the people. Thus, at least in the United States, the paradigmatic cases of ("objective") injustice are cases in which people are denied what are deemed to be subjective rights and/or denied fair (i.e., equal) participation in constitutional processes of lawmaking.

The Catholic tradition has come to accommodate this broadly defining rights-based context for justice. In particular, rights language has been very effective for people resisting unjust rule, as well as using state power to overcome injustices in traditional cultural customs. As Jean Porter's essay notes, numerous commentators (including herself) have seen notions of subjective rights as at least implicitly present in Aquinas. It is not tenable to set the Catholic social tradition at odds with modern subjective rights.[10]

That said, this Catholic acceptance of individual rights is qualified in a number of ways. Most importantly, the tradition's premodern roots resist the individualism (or "libertarianism") toward which the modern conception tends.[11] The social nature of the person cannot be reduced to atomistic, contract-like individual relations within a fairness-based political order and its typical economic complement, the protection and support of private property and market exchange rights. One way to explain this is that the tradition resists an account of justice that is reduced to commutative (one-to-one) justice. All human relations must not be understood as market exchange relations or even to a "one-person-one-vote" voting procedure. There is more to be said about human social ontology than that.

But what more is to be said? From the French Revolution to Vatican II, the tradition struggled to explain this "something more" in the objective dimension of justice. Attempts were often nostalgic. Some reactionaries sought to restore Catholic monarchy, and popes like Leo and Pius sometimes wistfully looked back to medieval guilds. And while this history is richer and more complex than often depicted,[12] one can see both before and after Vatican II a gradual resolution based on two concepts of Catholic social thought that are essential to the objective dimension of justice: the dignity of the person and the common good. Both entail an objective dimension of justice that is more substantive than a libertarian conception—particularly by identifying relationships with others as part of the essence of the person. The two concepts, at bottom, protect the Catholic conception of justice from being reduced to the rights claims of atomized individuals.

Dignity

The notion of dignity of the human person is crucial to Catholic receptivity to guaranteeing universal subjective rights. But the Catholic notion of dignity goes further than the more deist claims of rights in the Declaration of Independence, or the individual liberties against government of the Bill of Rights. Dignity is not the mere exercise of rights. Human dignity is rooted first in the "vertical" dimension—everyone deserves respect because every person is, to put it simply, loved by God. Not only are we created by God, but we are created in God's image and "called to a fullness of life which far exceeds the dimensions of [our] earthly existence, because it consists in sharing the very life of God. The loftiness of this supernatural vocation reveals the greatness and the inestimable value of human life even in its temporal phase."[13] The importance of orienting this dignity toward an openness to vocation is made even clearer in *Populorum progressio*'s insistence that "every life is a vocation" that requires "the fullness of authentic development, a development which is for each and all the transition from less human conditions to more human conditions," the highest of which is human "unity in the charity of Christ."[14]

This "thicker" sense of dignity is not simply about relation to God but relation to others as well. In the classic text from *Gaudium et spes*, dignity is articulated in terms of the goodness of our nature as bodily, rational, possessed of a conscience, and free. This nature can be seen fulfilled by the person of Christ, the true "*imago Dei*."[15] Further, the document goes on to link dignity to the *social* nature of the person, as I will address in a moment. The other classic magisterial text on dignity, *Pacem in terris,* contains a lengthy set of "rights and obligations flowing directly and simultaneously from his very nature."[16] However, these rights are not merely individual protections against government and others, but rights like "food, clothing, shelter, rest, medical care . . . security in cases of sickness," to list only a few.[17] John XXIII insists on the importance of understanding the duties related to the rights, such that our obligation to others cannot merely be to stay out of their way.[18]

Both texts assume that the dignity rooted in relation to God has substantial implications for our social lives.

In these documents, a non-individualist, non-libertarian understanding of the dignity of the person rests on substantive "objective" notions of universal human nature and human flourishing, and not merely on subjective rights-claims. This tradition faces the confusion generated when some voices today appeal to a notion of human dignity but deny any notion of universal human nature or a universal account of flourishing. A universal account need not and should not try to define human flourishing too narrowly or down to the last detail, but without some general account of human flourishing, justice can have no objective referent in terms of *ius*—at least, none beyond the libertarian claims about the right of the atomized individual to self-determination.[19] It is a great danger—indeed, a fatal error for well-intentioned people—to think that by denying human nature, they are defending human dignity.

This confusion is rooted in two good intentions of inclusivity, one oriented to global diversity and the other to sexual diversity. An account of universal human rights need not be "colonialist" (although, of course, it has been); in fact, respect for much cultural particularity (but not every cultural practice) is actually intrinsic to universal human rights. Yet this *general* compatibility simply opens us to questions of particular conflicts over the substantive universal account in relation to any *particular* culture and its structures. For example, a claim about the dignity of women and their equal rights evidently suggests that some cultures have unjust norms denying and controlling women in certain ways.[20] But if such a claim is not rooted in some account of universal human flourishing (i.e., dignity), then the critique of patriarchy is rooted simply in individual autonomy (as a libertarian account of justice would be).

This same point of *general* compatibility can be made in regard to sexual diversity that in no way should a universal account of human sexual flourishing enshrine a single, time-bound family *structure*. But to say this is not to go to the other extreme, in which there is *no* universal account of sexual flourishing. Quite the contrary, it is evident that the horror of sexual violence against women or minors is related to an account of what human dignity universally requires of sexuality.[21] But once again, the problem is that if you stop at consent, your account of dignity is simply that of the libertarian. It is beyond the scope of this paper to adjudicate the particulars of these cultural and sexual conflicts, but appeals to justice rooted in dignity must *necessarily* engage some more substantive account of the *content* of such dignity if they are to be more than a libertarian defense of individual autonomy and self-determination.[22]

The Common Good

As already noted, among the most important aspects of our dignity is our social nature, which is often spoken of in Catholic social thought in terms of "participation."[23] But participation in what? Ultimately, the importance of participation is rooted in the fact that our very humanity is fulfilled by sharing life with others—in acting together for the common good.[24] Thus, as *Gaudium et spes* identified, the dignity of persons is *intrinsically* linked to the common good: "the goal of all social institutions is and must be the human person, which for its part and by its very nature stands completely in need of social life," which "is not something added on to man."[25] The achievement of dignity and the pursuit of the common good are not rivals, as they necessarily are when we are faced with a utilitarian-style trade-off account of the good of a society as merely an aggregate of individual good.[26]

For a number of reasons, modern political orders have had great difficulty integrating the common good into a rights-based scheme without slipping into a totalitarianism that seeks a collective good while (and by means of) violating individual rights.[27] At best, modern states have tried to maintain an always-shifting "balance," sometimes (as typically in the United States) allowing individual rights to override the pursuit of some shared goods, sometimes (as typically in postwar Western Europe) constraining the scope of rights in order to pursue some shared goods more thoroughly. And at various times, Catholic social thought documents have seemed to endorse (though never fully) one or the other balance.[28]

What is often missed in such a discussion is that the primary referent of "common good" (on which notions of desert and equality depend in defining justice) is not the nation-state. The well-known definition of the common good given by John XXIII and reiterated by *Gaudium et spes* is "the sum of those conditions of social life by which individuals, families, and groups can achieve their own fulfillment in a relatively thorough and ready way."[29] A politics of the common good is not one that simply maximizes individual benefits, nor one that defines an overarching shared good (a "general will") for the whole society. Rather, it *facilitates* flourishing by creating conditions for persons to "achieve their own fulfillment," and importantly it facilitates the fulfillment of groups, not simply individuals. "Common good," understood in its primary referent, names the common ends and common action of group-persons (teams, families, businesses, schools, etc.), and the "political common good" is a secondary (though not any less essential) aim meant to be in service of the primary common goods.

Perhaps the most overlooked aspect of Catholic social thought in many discussions of justice is that the objective dimension of justice depends on what might be termed a "pluralist social ontology,"[30] in which the social nature of the person is instantiated first in communities other than the nation-state.[31] In such communities—households, schools, businesses, community-action groups, choirs, sports teams, and many others—persons not only find their dignity but do so by learning and practicing the pursuit of genuinely shared goods with others. In the course of doing so, the person must develop the virtue of justice, giving to others what they are due—not only for the shared ends of the activity but by recognizing the "due" that is required by the "different gifts" or roles or positions that necessarily make up these groups. The unity and the differentiations in the structures of such groups, which determine the details of justice, depend on the particular common good. For example, choirs may divide men and women in ways that businesses would not. In professional baseball, a pitcher gets four days off between games in a way that a starting outfielder would not.

Is such a pluralist social ontology "timeless"? No. We cannot join Pope Leo XIII pining for the guilds or Americans today who yearn for the 1950s. Given the twin tendencies of modern nation-states toward individualism and totalitarianism, this pluralist social ontology requires that justice be understood in terms of the dignity of all persons and their participation in common goods. Catholic social thought developed the principle of subsidiarity in light of those tendencies, insisting that states have an obligation to "help" such common-good-oriented communities but not to replace their proper internal ordering and shared activity. Subsidiarity is not "small is beautiful" but rather "particularity is beautiful" or "pluralism is beautiful." Larger structures, most especially the modern nation-state, ought to help rather than replace the particularities of the groups within which we pursue goods in common with others, whether sports, musical ensembles, workplaces, schools, or dozens of others. To be sure, Catholic social thought clearly does think that at least two aspects of this social ontology—the family and the church—are "timeless" and in some sense universal (at least prior to the eschaton), but they are not "timeless" in the sense that the structures of just parenting or just parishes are fixed.[32]

It is also in this context of a pluralist social ontology that the question of distributive justice must be addressed.[33] Such questions are uniquely difficult in our individualistic context, dominated by subjective rights understood as possessions of individuals. From this perspective, people assume that the primary moral responsibility of being just is simply not violating individual rights:

persons have first and foremost a negative responsibility toward others—don't interfere, don't harm—and political authority has the primary task of protecting individuals against such interference and harm. The very language of "possessing" rights prejudices discussions toward the ownership of property as the paradigmatic case of a right to be protected. While such an approach to protecting the liberty of individuals to exercise rights is essential for resisting tyrannies—including a tyranny of a majority—the approach makes it difficult to handle the more "positive" duties involved in distributive justice. Some of the key disputes about justice in contemporary political philosophy, such as that between John Rawls and Robert Nozick, hinge on sharply different conceptions of distributive justice.[34] As an extreme example, Friedrich Hayek claims that the idea of distributive justice (which he confusingly renames as "social justice") is a fiction, even suggesting that people shouldn't describe market outcomes themselves as distributionally just since in markets people receive not what they deserve but what others choose to transfer to them.[35]

The root of the individualistic problem with distributive justice is the inability to adopt a *truly* social account of the human person, in which human sociality is intrinsic to individual flourishing. Perhaps understandably concerned about the inability of the state (or any centralized authority) to engage in just distribution, they ignore the fact that such distribution must in fact occur within sub-political contexts, such as families and businesses. As Taylor explains, "the structure of society provides the essential background for any principles of distributive justice,"[36] which is to say that arguments about just and unjust distribution (a distribution that serves the common good) presumes a particular ordering of group activity and group aims. For example, while Hayek criticizes medieval efforts to determine "just" prices and wages as impossible, he overlooks the fact that a just wage is not a number but concerns a particular relation of persons—of employers to workers—which, in a firm oriented to shared activity toward a shared end, necessarily involves distributive judgments.

The key is to recognize that such distributive judgments must be made in the particular contexts of different groups devoted to differing common goods. Michael Walzer offers the most comprehensive argument in political philosophy along these lines, suggesting that there are distinct "spheres" of justice, each with its own rules for just distribution. The most important task for the larger society is to protect these differences and not allow particular spheres (such as the market or the state) to "dominate" others, and so in essence control their distributions from without.[37]

Such an approach to distributive justice is analogous to the effort of modern Catholic social thought to avoid a market-state binary, in which social relations are sorted either as mere exchange relations between individuals or as assigned and managed by the state. In essence, the teaching requires us to recognize that various particular relationships of justice (e.g., parent-child, employer-employee, teacher-student, etc.) are neither market exchanges nor assigned by the state. Of course, such relations do involve both (1) individual transactions and (2) some oversight by the state. For example, most would accept that the employer-employee relationship (1) has a voluntary aspect to it and also that (2) laws should exist to prevent significant abuses. Yet we fail to understand the fullness of the possibility of reciprocity in this relationship if we reduce it to something contractual or attempt to regulate it from above in too great a detail. A purely voluntaristic or purely state-defined relation may in fact be unjust.

THE THIRD DIMENSION: ESCHATOLOGICAL JUSTICE— SIN, MERCY, AND THE PREFERENTIAL OPTION

A pluralist social ontology—the context for the second, objective dimension of justice—suggests an inherently social account of the dignity of persons engaged in various groups that work together to achieve common goods, including just distribution. But this account alone is flawed. Even in contexts with a relatively effective authority protecting against grave injustices, this account omits something crucial: the history of the abuse by authorities within such groups, to the detriment of weaker parties. Any analysis of such social groups, past and present, will turn up abuses of power, both within the primary groups where people seek flourishing and between groups vying for advantage over each other.

Put another way, we need a better account of sin, both at a personal level (bad parents, employers, etc.) and at a structural level (customary family or work cultures that perpetuate injustice, social groups that seek unjust power and advantage over other groups, etc.). Thus, a full picture of Catholic social thought's teaching on justice requires a third dimension, a preferential love for the poor and marginalized, manifested especially in solidarity. A succinct set of paragraphs in *Laudato si'* summarize Catholic social thought principles under the heading of the common good. After treating dignity and distributive justice as general principles of "social ethics," Pope Francis places these further principles in precisely this context of the world of sin: "In the present condition of global society, where injustices abound and growing numbers of people are deprived of basic human rights and considered expendable, the principle of the common good immediately becomes, logically and inevitably, a summons to solidarity and a preferential option for the poorest of our brothers and sisters."[38] Elsewhere, Francis confirms that "the option for the poor is primarily a theological category rather than a cultural, sociological, political, or philosophical one,"[39] rooting it in God's exercise of mercy and a direct imitation of the self-emptying of Christ. Such an approach might be even better characterized as taking on the perspective of the poor. The roots of liberation theology are found in the biblical interpretation of base communities, reflecting on the scriptural narratives from the perspective of the poor.[40] Francis has been relentless in advocating for such a closeness to the poor. It is significant that Jorge Bergoglio clashed with some liberationists early in his career not because he did not share their commitment to the praxis of justice but because he viewed their approach as a form of elite ideology, as opposed to his "theology of the people." His insistence on direct contact with the poor led one of his Marxist-liberationist opponents to critique his whole approach as "sacramentalist, a-critical, and assistentialist."[41]

The scriptural basis of this dimension is found in the paradigmatic acts of compassion (such as the Good Samaritan, Luke 10) and the works of mercy (Matt 25). However, it is incorrect to suggest that such matters represent a "new law of love." Instead, they build on the Hebrew scriptures' consistent teachings of special concern for the poor, hospitality to strangers and migrants, generosity to neighbors and workers, and the like—all of which are, of course, written into God's Law.[42] This special concern has always sprung from a sense of the sinfulness of the world, especially Israel's own self-understanding as an oppressed people in Egypt—and a concomitant rejection of the assumption that the poor and the outcast are such because of their own sinfulness.[43] Such an emphasis is fundamentally a reconciling justice, one that insists on love even of enemies and that, in Francis's words, "unity prevails over conflict."[44]

But is this dimension really a dimension of *justice*? As a response to sin, aren't these teachings of compassion and mercy really a matter of *gift*, of supererogatory actions that go beyond "what is deserved"? The short answer is no: The Good Samaritan is not to be understood as a story of something supererogatory. It is the proper specification of the basic commandment to love neighbor, which Jesus draws from Leviticus. Yet the discomfort we might feel about making it mandatory—how many of us stop to help in such situations, especially when they are dangerous?—does speak to a complexity present in the call of the Gospel.

This complexity, which must never be an excuse for inaction, can be captured by the central image of the Kingdom of God. God's reign is evidently present in Christ; it is "at hand" (Mark 1:15), it is "among you" (Luke 17:21); it must be sought "on earth as in heaven" (Matt 6:10). Yet the kingdom is also "to come." It is a kingdom of full justice and peace, in which every tear is wiped away and in which all are united. Jesus, and by extension the Body of Christ that is the People of God, is called to make this future kingdom present, as the sacramental sign of the unity of the human race.[45] The Reign of God is eschatological, focused on the promised destiny of human relationships.

What does this mean? Concretely, it means that in our time, between the Pentecost and Christ's return, the already and the not-yet are mixed together. On the one hand, teachings like the universal destination of goods—from the Church Fathers, like St. John Chrysostom, into modern Catholic social thought—are seen as matters of justice. Chrysostom is clear that the "alms" given to the poor are exactly what they deserve, what is in fact already theirs. To deny such giving is an injustice. When John Paul II defines solidarity in terms of "we are all really responsible for all,"[46] he means to suggest that such universal mutual responsibility is a matter of justice.

Yet in another way, the teaching recognizes that "desert" is not an entirely satisfactory category for these matters. Benedict XVI's *Caritas in veritate* most explicitly tries to make this connection, by rooting its teaching in "the astonishing experience of gift." The experience of gift is prior to any claim of justice, not least because the experience of gift rejects any notion that humans are "self-sufficient"—most especially, they are not self-created. Benedict connects this mistaken sense of self-creation and entitlement to original sin.[47] Even more importantly, humans are made for gift, such that the "earthly city" is not simply about rights and duties but about "relationships of gratuitousness, mercy, and communion" that can be a "prefiguration of the undivided city of God."[48] John Paul suggests an alienated society is one in which "forms of social organization, production, and consumption" hinder this vocation to self-gift.[49] *Gaudium et spes* describes the social nature of the person as an image of the Trinity itself insofar as the person "cannot fully find himself except through a sincere gift of himself."[50] In every one of the preceding cases, an eschatological kingdom-image of "unity of the human race" or humanity as ultimately "one family" is invoked. Note that this is also a social ontology but one that clearly exceeds the pluralist conception laid out in the prior section. This dimension is the ultimate eschatological social ontology: the truth of the destiny of the unity of the human race in Christ. Solidarity and the universal destination of goods are the key Catholic social thought principles that manifest this eschatological dimension of justice.[51]

This third dimension of justice requires us to guard against two misunderstandings. The first mistake is to forget how intertwined this dimension of justice is with the experience of gift, of God's grace, of the activity of the Holy Spirit. Forgetting this, one imagines that these aspirations can be made a matter of "mere" justice—that is, justice in the sense of the first two dimensions. This is an overreach. Attempts to realize total solidarity or the universal destination of goods completely via earthly means will end up violating dignity and the common good. Such overreach tends to do this not least because the "solidarity" that it claims to realize—for example, the party, the "will of the people"—is actually a claim of some in the society over against others, and hence not true solidarity. It also conveniently tends to neglect a most important existing solidarity: our solidarity in sin.

But if this dimension can involve overreach, we can certainly underreach, too.[52] The second misunderstanding is to make this dimension of justice wholly personal or spiritual, imagining that such gratuitousness might be present in one-to-one relations but not in wider social structures. *Caritas in veritate* contains many warnings against this, particularly in economic life, such as Benedict's insistence that "without internal forms of solidarity and mutual trust, the market itself cannot completely fulfill its proper economic function" and his further claim that "friendship, solidarity, and reciprocity can also be conducted within economic activity, and not only outside or 'after' it."[53]

There is a corrective to both underreach and overreach: the eschatological, in-between character of the overcoming of brokenness imposed on human relations by sin. Again, to use the universal destination of goods as an example, it is important to see how Catholic social thought on property differs not just from a simple right-to-property model but even from a common good model in which resources are distributed to best accomplish the shared good of the group. We might ask the question at the root of the principle of solidarity, "what is the shared good of the whole human race?" And the answer to that will be theological and eschatological—and will help us see why a preference for the poor is not contrary to justice so long as this theological cosmology is kept in view.

It is particularly important to view issues such as incarceration/punishment, migration, and war/international peace in this eschatological dimension.[54] They (and perhaps others like them) present unique difficulties because of their inherent relation to sin; in the Reign of God, we believe there are no borders, no prisons, and no wars. Such issues can tempt us both to overreaching (e.g., imagining a borderless world) and to underreaching (e.g., simply accepting "borders are the way it is" and building walls and ruthlessly enforcing laws). Appeals to dignity are, of course, extremely important, but various conventions (e.g., of warfare) assume that one can accept the basic dignity of an enemy (or a migrant or a prisoner) while also treating them in ways that would be deemed unjust if applied to an ordinary citizen. Moreover, the justification for war, incarceration, and exclusion is almost always a defense of the common good—the obvious example being a just war, such as the struggle of Ukraine against Russian invasion. Nevertheless, the activity of the church as a distinct body—as the sacrament of the unity of the human race[55]—keeps the kingdom view as central. And while recognizing that this view is a matter of hope, the church must act as an effective sign of the universal common good in the midst of a world that is not yet ruled by Christ. Hence, the church will view issues of this sort not only as crucially important for its mission to the world but also as needing unique mediations through the institutions and networks of the church itself.

CONCLUSION

In summary, an adequate understanding of justice in Catholic thought includes three dimensions: the subjective, the objective, and the eschatological. Indeed, one could equally say that all accounts of justice depend on the moral psychology of agency, social structures, and an account of history. Offering a single, if three-dimensional, framework for understanding justice should not obscure the conceptual work that remains to be done to understand particular situations—to use the terms of my education as a chemist, any framework of justice cannot be a "plug-and-chug" formula to solve problems by inputting variables! With that understood, the framework yields the following definition:

> Justice is a disposition to give what is due to others within a pluralist social ontology that upholds human dignity, enables participation in common goods, and envisions the overcoming of sin in the eschatological unity of the human race.

BIBLIOGRAPHY

Barbieri, William A. *Constitutive Justice*. Macmillan, 2015.
Benedict XVI. *Caritas in veritate*. https://www.vatican.va/content/benedict-xvi/en/encyclicals/documents/hf_ben-xvi_enc_20090629_caritas-in-veritate.html.
Catechism of the Catholic Church. Penguin, 2003, #2418.

Cloutier, David. *Walking God's Earth: The Environment and Catholic Faith.* Liturgical Press, 2014.

Dupré, Louis. "The Common Good and the Open Society." *The Review of Politics* 55, no. 4 (1993): 687–712. https://www.jstor.org/stable/1407612.

Elsbernd, Mary. "Papal Statements on Rights: A Historical Contextual Study of Encyclical Teaching from Pius VI -Pius XI (1791–1939)." PhD diss., Catholic University of Louvain (1985): 38.

Finn, Daniel K, ed. *Moral Agency Within Social Structures and Culture: A Primer on Critical Realism for Christian Ethics.* Georgetown University Press, 2020.

Finnis, John. *Natural Law and Natural Rights.* Oxford University Press, 2011.

Firer Hinze, Christine. "The Drama of Social Sin and the (Im)Possibility of Solidarity: Reinhold Niebuhr and Modern Catholic Social Teaching." *Studies in Christian Ethics* 22, no. 4 (2009): 442–60. https://doi.org/10.1177/0953946809340947.

Francis. *Evangelii gaudium.* https://www.vatican.va/content/francesco/en/apost_exhortations/documents/papa-francesco_esortazione-ap_20131124_evangelii-gaudium.html.

Francis. *Fratelli tutti*, October 3, 2020. https://www.vatican.va/content/francesco/en/encyclicals/documents/papa-francesco_20201003_enciclica-fratelli-tutti.html.

Francis. *Laudato si'.* https://www.vatican.va/content/francesco/en/encyclicals.index.html.

Hittinger, Russell. "Sites of Human Joy: The True Purpose of Intermediate Societies," *Church Life Journal* (December 17, 2021). https://churchlifejournal.nd.edu/articles/sites-of-human-joy-the-true-purpose-of-intermediate-societies/.

Hittinger, Russell. "The Coherence of the Four Basic Principles of Catholic Social Doctrine: An Interpretation." *Nova et Vetera*, English Edition 7, no. 4 (2009): 791–838.

Hogan, Linda. *Keeping Faith with Human Rights.* Georgetown University Press, 2015.

Ivereigh, Austen. *The Great Reformer: Francis and the Making of a Radical Pope.* Picador, 2014.

John XXIII. *Mater et magistra.* https://www.vatican.va/content/john-xxiii/en/encyclicals/documents/hf_j-xxiii_enc_15051961_mater.html.

John XXIII. *Pacem in terris.* https://www.vatican.va/content/john-xxiii/en/encyclicals/documents/hf_j-xxiii_enc_11041963_pacem.html.

John Paul II. *Centesimus annus.* https://www.vatican.va/content/john-paul-ii/en/encyclicals/documents/hf_jp-ii_enc_01051991_centesimus-annus.html.

John Paul II. *Evangelium vitae.* https://www.vatican.va/content/john-paul-ii/en/encyclicals/documents/hf_jp-ii_enc_25031995_evangelium-vitae.html.

John Paul II. *Sollicitudo rei socialis.* https://www.vatican.va/content/john-paul-ii/en/encyclicals/documents/hf_jp-ii_enc_30121987_sollicitudo-rei-socialis.html.

MacIntyre, Alasdair. *After Virtue: A Study in Moral Theory*, 2nd ed. University of Notre Dame Press, 1984.

MacIntyre, Alasdair. *Whose Justice? Which Rationality?* University of Notre Dame Press, 1988.

O'Donovan, Joan Lockwood. "Rights, Law, and Political Community: A Theological and Historical Perspective." *Transformation* 20, no. 1 (2003): 30–38. https://doi.org/10.1177/026537880302000103.

O'Neill, William. *Reimagining Human Rights: Religion and the Common Good.* Georgetown University Press, 2021.

Second Vatican Council. *Lumen gentium.* https://www.vatican.va/archive/hist_councils/ii_vatican_council/documents/vat-ii_const_19641121_lumen-gentium_en.html.

Paul VI. *Populorum progressio.* https://www.vatican.va/content/paul-vi/en/encyclicals/documents/hf_p-vi_enc_26031967_populorum.html.

Perreau-Saussine, Emile. *Catholicism and Democracy: An Essay in the History of Political Thought.* Princeton University Press, 2012.

Ratzinger. "Freedom and Liberation." In *Church, Ecumenism, and Politics.* Ignatius Press, 2008.

Ryan, Alan, ed. *Justice.* Oxford, 1993.

Second Vatican Council. *Gaudium et spes.* https://www.vatican.va/archive/hist_councils/ii_vatican_council/documents/vat-ii_const_19651207_gaudium-et-spes_en.html.

Second Vatican Council. *Lumen gentium.* https://www.vatican.va/archive/hist_councils/ii_vatican_council/documents/vat-ii_const_19641121_lumen-gentium_en.html.

Smith, Christian. *To Flourish or Destruct.* University of Chicago Press, 2015.

Taylor, Charles. "The Nature and Scope of Distributive Justice." In *Philosophy and the Human Sciences: Philosophical Papers 2*, 289–317. Cambridge University Press, 1985.

Thornton, John, and Susan Varenne, eds. "Liberation Theology." In *The Essential Pope Benedict XVI.* HarperOne, 2007.

Tierney, Brian. *The Idea of Natural Rights.* Eerdmans, 1997.

USCCB's Economic Justice for All, no. 68. https://www.usccb.org/upload/economic_justice_for_all.pdf

Walzer, Michael. *Spheres of Justice: A Defense of Pluralism and Equality.* Basic Books, 1983.

NOTES

1. *Catechism of the Catholic Church*, no. 2418.
2. *Laudato si'*, 68–69. I have previously written extensively about ecological matters in *Walking God's Earth*, and space limitations preclude a great deal of attention to them here.
3. It is particularly important, as I explain further on, to avoid contrasting attributes like love or mercy *against* justice, as if God has numerous "sides" that appear erratically. For example, Anathea Portier-Young's chapter rightly highlights Micah 6:8, in which *mispat* and *hesed*—*doing* justice and desiring loving-kindness or steadfast love—are what the Lord requires of the people; and she goes on to point out numerous passages in which both "are fundamental to God's own character and actions."
4. In chapter 7, Lisa Cahill also points this out.
5. MacIntyre, *Whose Justice?* 198–99.
6. See MacIntyre, *After Virtue*, 23, and Finn, *Moral Agency Within Social Structures.*
7. Thus, the African accounts of justice rooted in *Ubuntu*, an identity with community (Orobator in chapter 1 of this volume), and the Asian concepts rooted in rita, grounding dharma as "the obligation to follow the rita, the cosmic moral principle of order" (Kodithottam) are versions of this (premodern) objective dimension that do not have their foundations in individual claims of rights. George Kodithottam's chapter on Asian tradition makes particularly clear the connection between a *cosmic* order and a specific *social* order, one that is especially reinforced by an understanding of karma as a cosmic justice that determines one's status in the social order.
8. O'Donovan, "Rights, Law, and Political Community," 30–38.
9. Mary Elsbernd notes that a key juncture is the shift of a notion of "dominion" to something one possesses: "It was this most important shift which moved right out of the realm of justice and equality in a communal setting to that of an individual power possessed." Elsbernd, "Papal Statements on Rights," 38.

10. Brian Tierney's study *The Idea of Natural Rights* argues cogently against a "semantic revolution" in Ockham and early modernity in favor of "a more gradual evolutionary approach" (18). However, the discontinuities must also be stressed. Tierney affirms that premodern justice and right involved "a whole structure of language built around a set of concepts different from" ours, emphasizing that premodern jurists did not view the legal order "as essentially a structure of individual rights" (18). He says that the contrast between modern doctrines and Aquinas is "true enough so far as it goes" but that the contrast has led to "radical error in periodization" that his study ameliorates. John Finnis says a subjective sense of rights can accord with medieval usage "from one point of view" but tends to obscure the way any such claim of right is always embedded in "the ensemble of juridical relationships" that make clear that, contrary to an atomistic view, "due looks both ways." Finnis, *Natural Law and Natural Rights*, 208–9. Porter also notes that "Aquinas does not generally refer to someone's right in possessive terms" (with one exception). A correct view of subjective rights of persons is not foundational apart from a richer social ontology within which such claims might make better sense.

11. Significantly, in chapter 1, Orobator notes the counter-Cartesian resonance of Ubuntu, but such a contrast would not apply to Plato, Aristotle, Augustine, or Aquinas, all of whom develop a (counter-Cartesian!) account of persons essentially embedded in social orders.

12. See especially Perreau-Saussine, *Catholicism and Democracy*.

13. John Paul II, *Evangelium vitae*, no. 2.

14. Paul VI, *Populorum progressio*, no. 15, 20, and 21.

15. Second Vatican Council, *Gaudium et spes*, no. 12–22.

16. John XXIII, *Pacem in terris*, no. 9, emphasis added.

17. John XXIII, no. 11.

18. The importance of duties in relation to rights is also highlighted in Benedict XVI. *Caritas in veritate*, no. 43: "rights presuppose duties, if they are not to become mere license." In his chapter, George Kodithottam also points out the importance of *obligations* in Asian formulations of justice, over against ones rooted in "rights" (i.e., subjective rights).

19. This debate frequently goes off the rails when the contrast between a "static" view and a "historically conscious" view is overdrawn, such that one seems forced to choose *either* a totally fixed account of human nature *or* an entirely contingent one. The right choice is both/and: The Catholic tradition at its best has always incorporated both cultural diversity and universality; human nature is neither entirely determined nor entirely plastic.

20. For example, in chapter 1, Orobator points out how strongly communal and reconciling notions of justice are nevertheless afflicted by patriarchy in the African context.

21. To clarify, nearly any form of sexual violence involves injustices about power willed by perpetrators. But the degree of seriousness with which we take sexual violence—compared to other ways people exercise potentially unjust power over others—indicates the significance of its harm to the nature and development of sexuality.

22. To use just two examples, consider Christian Smith's account of human goods in *To Flourish or Destruct* and the frequent use of Amartya Sen and Martha Nussbaum's "capabilities" approach. Recent Catholic defenses of human rights (notably Hogan, *Keeping Faith with Human Rights* and O'Neill, *Reimagining Human Rights*) have acknowledged the criticisms of the Enlightenment tradition and have sought to ground a more substantive account of rights in a dialogical view of human experience in community that is "situated somewhere between foundationalism and pragmatism" (Hogan, 4). I think

JUSTICE: A THREE-DIMENSIONAL ACCOUNT   223

their accounts do include an implied account of the goods of the human person and human flourishing; the fact that this account emerges from cross-traditional dialogue and liberatory practice, rather than being given from some universal point of view, need not be at odds with the account of "substantive content" given here.

23. As noted in chapter 7 by Cahill, a primary difficulty is not so much the defining of human dignity as much as ensuring "access" to what she calls "requisites of flourishing." I agree.

24. This emphasis on shared practice strongly resonates with Orobator's discussion of the African notion of palaver.

25. Second Vatican Council, *Gaudium et spes*, no. 25.

26. For a very important essay from which I came to understand this crucial point, see Dupré, "The Common Good and the Open Society," 687–712.

27. As Francis Schüssler-Fiorenza's chapter notes, while modern liberal systems are often criticized for individualism, it is nationalism and other collectivist movements that have been responsible for some of the greatest injustices of the twentieth century.

28. For example, John XXIII, *Mater et magistra*, no. 51–67 endorses (though not without qualification) "the growing intervention of public authorities," whereas his *Centesimus annus*, no. 31–48, endorses (though not without qualification) a "market economy" and warns against the "vastly expanded" intervention of the "welfare state."

29. Second Vatican Council, *Gaudium et spes*, no. 74. Note that *Mater et magistra*, no. 65, from which this quote originates, further specifies that in a "correct" understanding of the common good, "various intermediate bodies" should "be ruled by their own laws" and coexist in "a spirit of sincere concord among themselves."

30. For a thorough description of this notion of "social ontology," see Hittinger, "The Coherence of the Four Basic Principles," 791–838.

31. Schüssler-Fiorenza's chapter notes that Luke Bretherton has made a very similar case from a Protestant perspective. Chapter 7, by Cahill, suggests that key themes like dignity, common good, and preferential option often appear "in tension, if not mutually exclusive," but I think this is a problem generated when (1) this pluralist social ontology is not explicitly identified as the social imaginary, and (2) the eschatological dimension (which I will discuss in the next section) is neglected.

32. The extent to which there are somewhat fixed forms for either of these two communities is, of course, a source of ongoing debate within Catholicism. Such debates do connect to substantive claims about dignity and common good—and thus are, in part, about justice—but both also and (I think) inevitably involve metaphysical claims of reason and interpretive claims about God's will as revealed in scripture and tradition. For a wonderful outline of this pluralist social ontology, including its "necessary societies," see Hittinger, "Sites of Human Joy."

33. As Francis explains in *Laudato si'*, no. 157.

34. See the competing essays in many anthologies on justice, including the helpful selections in Ryan, *Justice*, 73–116. Schüssler-Fiorenza's chapter navigates this terrain and helpfully displays how difficult it is to resolve these questions on purely liberal approaches.

35. Hayek, "Social or Distributive Justice," also in Ryan, *Justice*, 117–58. The term "social justice" is used in incompatible ways by different authors. To use just three examples, the way it is used by nineteenth and early-twentieth-century CST (as a new term for Aquinas's "general justice"), by Rawls (to point specifically to institutional arrangements of

political liberalism, ones oriented to distribution), and by current common speech (a use that applies broadly to a range of social ills and their overcoming, not simply via institutional rearrangement but by large-scale action) is inconsistent. The USCCB's *Economic Justice for All*, no. 68, defines social justice as the "duty to organize economic and social institutions so that people can contribute." But this definition is virtually identical to the way *Gaudium et spes* has described the "political common good"; thus, *social* justice really means properly pursuing the political common good.

36. Cited in Barbieri, *Constitutive Justice*, 114, referring to Taylor, "The Nature and Scope of Distributive Justice," 289–317. Taylor is particularly effective in making this point from an "anti-atomism" perspective; a truly social account of the person assumes that one's life and judgments are *already* embedded in normatively defined relations. There is no starting from scratch. An atomistic view of the person may well critique present arrangements (on grounds of autonomy or strict equality), but the anti-atomist view must work harder to explain how existing social bonds can be critiqued, since they form the backdrop for arguments about what is just in the first place.

37. Walzer, *Spheres of Justice*.

38. Francis, *Laudato si'*, no. 158.

39. Francis, *Evangelii gaudium*, no. 198.

40. Maria Inês de Castro Millen's chapter not only highlights the importance of base communities but throughout displays the Latin American approach of starting with the perspective of the poor. For example, her engagement with the crisis of the Amazon starts with the perspective of the Indigenous peoples whose whole way of life has been under constant assault by economic and political exploitation of their homeland.

41. Ivereigh, *The Great Reformer*, 192.

42. For numerous examples and details, see Portier-Young's chapter on biblical justice.

43. The insistence on the work of reconciliation is well represented in chapter 1, by Orobator, identifying the importance of restorative justice.

44. Francis, *Evangelii gaudium*, no. 226–30. In this section, Francis insists that "the unity brought by the Spirit can harmonize every diversity," thus indicating (1) the refusal of a social ontology of fundamental conflict (between ethnic groups, classes, nations, etc.), and (2) the theological and eschatological character of such unity ("brought by the Spirit").

45. See especially Second Vatican Council, *Lumen gentium*, no. 1.

46. John Paul II, *Sollicitudo rei socialis*, no. 38.

47. Benedict XVI, *Caritas in veritate*, no. 34.

48. Benedict XVI, no. 6–7.

49. John Paul II, *Centesimus annus*, no. 41.

50. Second Vatican Council, *Gaudium et spes*, no. 24.

51. For an excellent, illuminating discussion about how CST develops language of "social sin" and language of "solidarity" in tandem, see Firer Hinze, "The Drama of Social Sin," 442–60. In this article, Hinze rightly argues that the Niebuhrian tradition and post-Vatican II CST need each other to "better connect social ethics and spirituality, and more systematically account for the social-theoretical assumptions their moral discourse depends upon or implies" (442). My account of the historical context of the drama of sin and salvation as a distinct dimension is meant to do that.

52. Ratzinger himself accuses Christians of having "insufficiently formulated" their own political alternative because "Christians have no confidence in their own vision of

reality. They hold fast to their faith in private devotion, but they do not dare to presume that it has something to say to mankind as such or that it contains a vision of man's future and his history." See Ratzinger, "Freedom and Liberation," 241. In another essay, Ratzinger makes clear that the problems he saw with certain forms of liberation theology only happened because its real truth had not "been adequately lived and witnessed to in its proper place (in the faith of the church.)" See Thornton and Varenne, "Liberation Theology," 217–25, at 217.

53. Benedict XVI, *Caritas in veritate*, no. 35–36.

54. In this sense, Francis's *Fratelli tutti*, in which these issues are treated at length, might be understood as the most eschatological of the social encyclicals, in its fundamental "dream" about the universal fraternity of the human race.

55. Second Vatican Council, *Lumen gentium*, no. 1.

CHAPTER 12

Justice as a Virtue in Catholic Social Thought

Lisa Sowle Cahill

This chapter proposes that a renewed understanding of justice as a virtue can help address a central dilemma of twenty-first-century Catholic social thought: how to move from magisterial diagnoses of social evils and moral mandates for justice to social-structural changes that make existence more just and participatory in reality—for more people in more social contexts. If we have a better understanding of the nature of structural justice and injustice, it might be easier to imagine what would be needed for change to occur, and to strategize how to bring it about.

I begin with the traditional definition of justice as the will to give each what is their due and as, therefore, a virtuous habit. It will connect this definition with some familiar and important concepts of Catholic social thought (basic equality, common good, dignity of the person, preferential option for the poor, participation and solidarity, and connections among all beings), showing how they relate both to justice as a virtue and to the reality of structural sin. Then it will develop the significance for Catholic thought of John Rawls's definition of justice as a virtue of social institutions. I understand justice to be a social habit of persons acting collectively in and through institutions. Although justice is a virtue of persons, justice regards right relations among all things that exist, human and nonhuman.

The basic thesis is twofold. First, justice, as an ongoing disposition, habit, and virtue, is embedded in social practices and organized patterns of structural-cultural action that give social agency its "character." Second, understanding this will enable social justice advocates to take better advantage of available points of intervention and begin to transform structural injustices that are so deeply entrenched as to seem impersonal, impenetrable, and immovable.

DEFINING JUSTICE

The modern Catholic tradition of social thought begins in 1891 with Leo XIII's denunciation in *Rerum novarum* of the social inequities of European industrialization. This encyclical provides a formal definition of justice from classical thought, as mediated by Aristotle and Thomas Aquinas: justice is giving to each their "due."[1] Aquinas specifies that "justice is a habit whereby a man renders to each one his due by a constant and perpetual will."[2] This definition, regularly cited in church documents,[3] goes back to the sixth-century codification of Roman law, the *Institutes of Justinian*: "the constant and perpetual will to render to each his due."[4] For Aquinas, a habit is a disposition to act so as to accomplish the agent's ends, whether good or bad; a virtue is a good habit, a disposition to act for good ends, in the right order of priority.[5]

What is "due" can be specified by a number of different ranking criteria among recipients, such as strict equality, merit, need, and entitlement. In premodern societies—and in many societies today—it was and is assumed that human beings are hierarchically ordered in accord with higher and lower statuses and associated roles and that higher-status individuals and groups have authority over lower, as well as more access to human goods and social prerogatives. In a fundamentally hierarchical worldview, justice is understood as the conformity of each social member or group to an assigned role and the respect of all for the order of the whole. Societies worldwide began to challenge these enforced hierarchies with the seventeenth-century European Enlightenment and ensuing global movements for decolonization, human rights, and democracy. A premise of modern Catholic discussions of justice is basic human equality and respect, entailing that all deserve to have essential needs met.

Today, Catholic social thought claims that all persons are equal in dignity, no matter their race, ethnicity, gender, or social class. In *Rerum novarum*, national governments must take the welfare of the poor into consideration equally with the rich "or else that law of justice will be violated which ordains that each shall have his due." "Justice, therefore demands that the interests of the poorer population be carefully watched over by the administration."[6] The concern for basic human equality, social rights, and material rights becomes a definitive trajectory of the tradition, exemplified in recent years by Pope Francis: "no human individual or group" is "entitled to bypass the dignity and the rights of other individuals or their social groupings."[7] Further, those whose dignity is denied or undermined by existing social arrangements are owed preferential treatment that will "level the playing field," a dimension of justice that can be called "equity."[8] In sum, Catholic social thought adjudicates what is due persons and communities primarily according to basic equality and to need, with merit (e.g., economic success or professional reputation) as a legitimate secondary criterion of access to nonessential goods. In *Laudato si'*, Pope Francis expands the sense of justice to include the integrity, natural ends, and well-being of nonhuman creatures, reminding readers that "everything is connected."[9]

Three Fundamental Concepts

The three concepts most prominently associated with justice in this tradition, especially since Vatican II, are the common good, dignity of the person, and preferential option for the poor. What is the relation of these goods to justice as a habit of rendering each their due? Aquinas explains that "it is customary among most writers to define habits by their acts."[10] In other words, we can know whether the virtue of justice is present by considering the practical results of socially formative dispositions. Common good, dignity, and proactive inclusion of the excluded characterize just societies and institutions and can serve as criteria of whether a society is more or less just.

Gaudium et spes defines the common good as "the sum of those conditions of social life which allow social groups and their individual members relatively thorough and ready access to their own fulfillment," adding that this good must today be understood as "universal" and as involving "rights and duties with respect to the whole human race." "Every social group must take account of the needs and legitimate aspirations of other groups, and even of the general welfare of the entire human family."[11] *Pacem in terris* introduces the term "universal common good,"[12] while Francis includes the entire planet, with "everything is connected" the recurring refrain of *Laudato si'*.

The dignity of the person is a second criterion of justice, equally essential to that of the common good and interdependent with the common good, if not derivative from it. Some expressions and interpretations of Catholic social thought portray the common good as primarily a vehicle for serving the goods of individuals. *Pacem in terris*, for example, proclaims, "in our time the common good is chiefly guaranteed when personal rights and duties are maintained."[13] But the tradition does not subordinate the common good to individual worth and rights. As John XXIII grants, human beings are "social by nature."[14] Individuals are born and formed within communities; identities are dependent on relationships and social contexts. Although premodern thinkers like Aquinas sometimes erred on the side of subordinating the individual to the common good,[15] the common good is foundational to personal existence, identity, and flourishing. This reality has more resonance in cultures of Latin America, Asia, and Africa; whereas North Atlantic, "Western" cultures prioritize individual freedom and rights.[16] The common good is not an aggregation of individual goods, nor simply the social attainment and provision of goods to individuals.[17] The common good and participation in it are good in themselves and constitutive of flourishing for humans as social and political beings.

Finally, concern for the poor has been the motivating factor behind Catholic social thought from its inception; after Vatican II and *Gaudium et spes,* it becomes increasingly central and is redefined in terms of the empowerment and self-empowerment of the poor themselves. Justice requires more than philanthropy or the redistribution of goods; it demands that individuals, communities, and nations have "the means necessary to helping and developing themselves."[18] John Paul II recognizes, commends, and encourages the agency of the socially disadvantaged who take responsibility for their own futures, which the church should support.[19] He recognizes, moreover, the growing solidarity among the poor.[20] Immediately after his election, Pope Francis named his aspirational Catholic Church not only a "a poor Church for the poor" but "a Church of the poor."[21] The preferential option for the poor is neither authentic nor complete until the poor in their own right are agents of universal dignity and the common good.

Participation and Solidarity

If common good, equal dignity of all persons, and preferential option for the poor are the keynotes of Catholic social thought, then among the most important derivative concepts are participation and solidarity. Participation requires that a just society be structured so that all members can be active, equally respected participants. Solidarity names the ethos of care, compassion, fellowship, and commitment that enable participants to serve the common good, respect the dignity of all, and make inclusion of all stakeholders a priority.

Participation derives from the idea that the common good involves every member of society in basic material, social, and political goods, both as a contributor and as a beneficiary. Dynamic, participatory, and mutually supportive community relationships are essential to a just society; they are already realizations of the common good.[22] Conversely, individuals, individual freedom or agency, and individual rights come to exist and are recognized only as participating in the web of social relations that is their condition of possibility and mode of fulfillment. Vatican II–era encyclicals, especially *Octogesima adveniens*, emphasize that the common good and equity demand the voices, participation, and empowerment of those still on the periphery of social power.

Pope Francis in particular has turned to participation "from below" as a more promising path to social change than appeals to political and economic elites who are vested in the status quo.[23] He proposes a teaching model that includes ecclesial-political interventions on behalf of participation across all levels of society, accentuating those currently furthest from the centers of power. There are many examples of this commitment of his: the annual World Meeting of Popular Movements that Pope Francis initiated in 2014; the Synods on the Family, with their parish-level diagnostic questionnaires and publicized episcopal debates; the Synod on the Amazon, with its consultation of Indigenous peoples; and his 2019 invitation to Sr. Veronica Openibo to address assembled bishops regarding the plight of African women sex abuse victims; as well as his outreach to LGBTQ+ Catholics.

Full participation, seen through the lens of the "preferential option for the poor," depends on a justice-driven process that is necessarily disruptive of the status quo. Such a process creates momentum toward inclusive benefits and access through subversive relations and confrontational actions that follow from compassionate attention to those who have been minimized or excluded.

Initiating or engaging such a process brings us to the motivational side of justice. Motivation goes beyond epistemology as knowing what justice requires. As Aquinas puts it, "we are not said to be just through knowing something aright" but through "doing" it.[24] Motivation to do in a reliable way what we know to be just entails compassionate identification with the situations and needs of others. It requires a sense that in some way "we are all in this together," the intention to engage in a practical way for change, and the expectation that engagement can produce results. In other words, a transformative process that leads to social transformation requires what Pius XI called "a mutual bond of minds and hearts"[25] and what later encyclicals call "solidarity." As defined by John Paul II, solidarity is "a firm and persevering determination to commit oneself to the common good; that is to say to the good of all and of each individual, because we are all really responsible for all."[26] Francis finds that "solidarity finds concrete expression in service" and "an effort to care for others."[27] Both popes see solidarity as a virtue,[28] a Christian virtue,[29] and as essential to defeat what John Paul II calls the "structures of sin."[30]

To appreciate the nature of solidarity not only as a motivating force for justice but as a factor in how structures of sin take hold, it is important to take a step back from solidarity as a virtue and stress that it is more basically a *habit*. Specifically, solidarity is the imaginative-intentional side of a collective organization of relationships and action. Solidarity is interdependent with and sustains the practical-active side of social structures. The *Cambridge Dictionary* defines solidarity as "agreement between and support for the members of group, especially a political group,"[31] disposing the members to act in unity or on one another's behalf for a shared goal or goals.

But solidaristic goals can be nefarious or unjust, as is visible in some identity politics and in populisms and nationalisms that are repressive, racist, or xenophobic. Augustine is getting at this point when he says that a "band of robbers" is like a little kingdom, in that it operates "under the rule of a leader, bound together by a pact of friendship, [whose] booty is divided among them by an agreed rule."[32] The *Oxford Research Encyclopedia of Politics* warns that, although solidarity as a "we-perspective" is necessary for struggles against wrong, "the dark side of solidarity raises suspicion: An internally solidary group may be repressive of the individuality of the members, it may be parochial and sometimes even lead to a dehumanization of outsiders, and it may be exercised in pursuit of unjustifiable ends."[33] Solidarity is a virtue only when the "we-perspective" motivates for just practical outcomes, such as "combatting the structural causes of poverty, inequality, the lack of work, land and housing, the denial of social and labour rights," and "confronting the destructive effects of the empire of money."[34]

An important qualification or caveat for Catholic social thought is that while solidarity is necessary to sustain justice as a social disposition, every society will and should incorporate variety, difference, and divergent interests. The reality of finite social resources, as well as differing evaluations of goods and goals, will inevitably result in barriers to and limits on the realization of the virtue's "acts" in specific cases. Justice in negotiating conflicts means good faith engagement and commitment to constructive outcomes. Building on the work of David Hollenbach, Kristin Heyer uses the term "conflictual solidarity," commenting that conflict lacks the attention it deserves in Catholic social thought,[35] a lacuna that is partly closed by *Fratelli tutti*.[36]

BACK TO JUSTICE AS A SOCIAL VIRTUE

As we have seen, Aquinas defines justice as "a habit [a disposition] whereby a man renders to each one his due by a constant and perpetual will." Justice is a habit that disposes the agent to "constantly and perpetually" desire and thus to act toward good ends in right relationships. Justice is, therefore, a *virtue*, directing the agent toward rightly ordered ends. Justice is properly understood as this agential disposition, not—as is more commonly the case—the resulting state of affairs in which social goods are realized. Yet, after defining justice as an act-producing disposition or habit, Aquinas adds that writers customarily refer to the "acts" to which habits lead when defining the habit itself.[37] This is why justice in Catholic social thought is so often measured by or even equated with social realizations of the common good, dignity of the person, and option for the poor, as premised on equal respect and as sustained within participatory social structures. The common good as structured by participation and motivated by solidarity is, on the one hand, a good to which the virtue of justice leads; it is, at the same time, an embodiment of the virtue of justice (and hence a good in itself) that also fosters justice as a continuing, solidaristic, participatory social disposition.

The phrasing of both Justinian and Aquinas implies that the agent is a justly willing individual and that the virtue of justice regards treatment of individual persons. Yet in specifying that justice takes distributive, commutative, and "general" forms, Aquinas extends the habit and actions of justice to include the agent's social responsibilities. "The virtue of a good citizen is general justice, whereby a man is directed to the common good."[38] Aquinas's definition of justice is nuanced and expanded in Catholic social thought in terms of the concept of "social justice" appearing prominently as early as the second modern social encyclical, *Quadragesimo anno* (1931).[39] The concept of social justice is highly significant as an indicator of what the tradition means by "justice" as a collective and not only individual virtue. Justice is concerned with a complex field of ethical-political agency, comprising social institutions and structures, cultures, and responsibilities of agents within a dynamic, differentiated social body. Justice is more than programmatic statements and criteria. It is not just an ideal, nor is it a fully realized or permanent reality. It is a society's ongoing commitment and tendency to embody just relations, actions, and outcomes.

As mentioned above, the virtue of justice is a disposition to realize, through action, right relationships not only among humans and human societies but among humans and nonhuman creatures and ecosystems. Aquinas recognizes this when he states that moral rectitude consists in "using a thing for the purpose for which it is," according to "the order of things."[40] The basic criterion of just relations among created beings is "the divine ordinance,"[41] for human justice is conformed to divine justice. Humans "imitate" the divine wisdom, according to human powers.[42] But what according to Aquinas are the purposes of nonhuman creatures; what is God's wisdom and ordinance for them? In his view, since "dumb animals and plants" lack reason, they are "naturally enslaved and accommodated to the uses of others."[43] This fact defines their just treatment.

One can agree with Aquinas that "a beast is by nature distinct from man"[44] without agreeing it exists only to serve the purposes of humans, much less that it is "enslaved." He is right that human justice consists in respect for the divine ordering of creation, though contemporary readers would see the natural order as more dynamic and less hierarchical than he. It is important to stress a point that Aquinas himself endorses, which is that the nature of each created being has its own integrity and natural ends. Respect for the fulfillment of the distinctive integrity and ends of other beings is a prima facie obligation of the human virtue of justice. Similarly to humans, the ends and flourishing of animals and plants consist in their self-preservation and growth, their formation of societies (in the case of animals), and their reproduction and (for animals) nurturing of offspring. In violation of justice are wanton destruction, rapacious use, disproportionate consumption, cruel treatment of sentient beings, and waste of other beings and their natural habitats by humans. Justice requires that humans foster the well-being of other creatures, to the degree permitted by respect for the balance of habitats, as well as human proximity, resources, and legitimate needs. A genuinely "common" good involves not only humanity but all beings with, around, and sustaining humanity in a diverse and dispersed yet interconnected web of life and being.

Social Justice and Structures

The philosopher John Rawls makes the social dimension of justice central to the definition of the virtue, showing how the classic definition should be adapted when addressing societal justice and injustice. According to Rawls, justice is a virtue primarily of social institutions or structures: "Justice is the first virtue of social institutions, as truth is of systems of thought."[45] Rawls does not mean only that justice is social because just individuals intend the common good. Rather, justice is a virtue of personal agency as organized collectively in institutions. Just institutions are structured forms of human agency that organize, encourage, and incentivize participants to seek common ends and goods for all members and stakeholders. Structures and institutions are to social "character" what a "constant and perpetual will" is to an individual agent; they constitute the reliable "dispositions" or "habits" of a society that support consistent collective behavior, including the behavior of individual participants in forms of organization such as schools, businesses, government, churches, civic associations, sports clubs, and so on. Thus Rawls rightly names justice as the first and most important virtue of social institutions.

In the social sciences, the term "institutions" is used in a broad, sometimes ambiguous, way. First, it can denote stable patterns of interaction among a set of agents and the social mechanisms generating outcomes, as in "business firms, political parties, schools, and public administrations." Second, it can denote the rules and social norms (both formal and informal) that specify roles and relationships within those patterns.[46] The meaning of the term "structures" overlaps with "institutions." For example, "Social structure refers to patternings in social relations that have some sort of obduracy."[47] Sometimes structures are seen as large-scale organizations of social life, such as the economy, religion, education, or government; whereas "institutions" are more specific and clearly bounded entities that structures comprise, such as markets, churches, universities, and legislatures. Often the two terms are used interchangeably; both indicate the collective, patterned organization of individual social behavior over time, in relationships that are embodied, enabled, and sometimes reformed via participant cooperation. This opens opportunities both for sin and for justice.

Cultures and Justice

An integral aspect of structural formation and reform is the worldview, ethos, shared meaning, or "culture" that validates and guides participant behavior. Cultures are about ideas and attitudes, as well as the customs and ordinary behaviors that express and reinforce values and expectations but are mostly taken for granted. Broadly conceived, culture is "the way of life, especially the general customs and beliefs, of a particular group of people at a particular time."[48] If structures constitute societal "dispositions" at the level of persistent, continuous action in the world, cultures are the symbolic and imaginative flip side of the same dispositions, operating at the level of agents' self-understanding, motivations, intentions, and solidarity. Cultures, structures, material environments, worldviews, and histories of individuals and groups emerge and function interdependently, with a good deal of mutual co-construction.[49] Nevertheless, the concept of culture is a useful way to speak more directly to the intellectual, volitional, emotional, spiritual, and psychological factors within structural justice and injustice.

Cultures are neither monolithic nor static. Like structures, they involve greater and lesser degrees of internal pluralism, stress, and mobility; any particular society, structure, or institution involves more than one culture, of varying levels of dominance, as well as varieties within each culture. Participants in a given cultural-structural formation are participating in, formed by, and reciprocally influencing many others simultaneously. This interpenetration, flexibility, and temporal fluidity provide openings for cultural-structural change. Cultural systems condition agents through the ideas made available; conversely, agents, especially as participating and interacting in multiple material-political forms of life, can generate new ideas and shape particular cultures so that they better embody justice.[50]

While always entailing basic and universal values (common good, equal dignity, affirmative inclusion of the least powerful), justice requires different practical forms in specific contexts. Discernment of what fulfills "due" treatment of persons and communities in any given case must rely on familiarity with the realities under consideration, practical reason, and practical wisdom (prudence). In *Amoris laetitia*, Francis turns to Aquinas to make this point. The pope cites Aquinas's conclusion from his commentary on Aristotle's *Ethics*. Of general knowledge of a rule and "the particular knowledge of the practical discernment," "Aquinas states that 'if only one of the two is present, it is preferable that it be the knowledge of the particular reality, which is closer to the act.'"[51]

The realization that justice is a social disposition, taking shape through social processes and redirecting aspects of complex structures and cultures, means that while Catholic social "thought" may reference an intellectual tradition, it also entails a practical dimension that must be both theorized and engaged. Catholic social thought should intellectually support and actively sponsor an approach to structural change that is contextual, multidimensional, collaborative, and networked across societies. As a "tradition," it already embodies an approach to justice that is not and has never been top-down only. Today, justice is called to become more bottom-up and outside-in, as well as more horizontally interactive among different peoples, geographies, religions, and political traditions. On the cultural side of social dispositions, justice must include symbolic gestures, rituals, the visual and performing arts and music, and imaginative literature. To be transformative, the disposition of justice must lead participants in unjust structures-cultures into worldview-expanding and identity-forming narratives and practices from overlapping but more just structures and cultures. Yet the virtue of justice and the goods to which justice disposes (common good, dignity, proactive inclusion) have always to be "realized each day," which is constantly a "struggle," as Pope Francis puts it.[52]

SUMMARY DEFINITION

The considerations above lead to the following definition of justice:

> Justice is an inherently social virtue, that commits persons and societies to regard one another as equals; to respect the integrity of and connections among all beings in our planetary environment and its diverse habitats; to foster cultures of solidarity, solicitude, and constructive conflict; and to structure social relationships toward the embodiment of the common good, the dignity of all, and the preferential empowerment of those whose participation is at risk.

BIBLIOGRAPHY

Aquinas, Thomas. *Summa theologica: Complete American Edition in Two Volumes*, translated by Fathers of the English Dominican Province. Vol. 2. Benziger Brothers, 1948.

Augustine of Hippo. *City of God*. Penguin, 2004.

Cambridge Dictionary. "Solidarity." https://dictionary.cambridge.org/us/dictionary/english/solidarity.

Cloutier, David. "What Can Social Science Teach Catholic Social Thought About the Common Good?" In *Empirical Foundations of the Common Good: What Theology Can Learn from Social Science*, edited by Daniel K. Finn. Oxford University Press, 2017.

De Schutter, Helder, and Ronald Tinnevelt. "David Miller's Theory of Global Justice: A Brief Overview." *Critical Review of International Social and Political Philosophy* 11, no. 4 (2008): 369–381. https://doi.org/10.1080/13698230802415854.

Francis. *Amoris laetitia*, 2016. https://www.vatican.va/content/dam/francesco/pdf/apost_exhortations/documents/papa-francesco_esortazione-ap_20160319_amoris-laetitia_en.pdf.

Francis. *Fratelli tutti*, October 3, 2020. https://www.vatican.va/content/francesco/en/encyclicals/documents/papa-francesco_20201003_enciclica-fratelli-tutti.html.

Francis. *Laudato si'*, 2015. https://www.vatican.va/content/francesco/en/encyclicals/documents/papa-francesco_20150524_enciclica-laudato-si.html.

Francis. "Letter to the Popular Movements." Apostolic Journey—Bolivia: Participation at the Second World Meeting of Popular Movements at the Expo Feria Exhibition Centre, Santa Cruz de la Sierra, July 9, 2015. https://www.vatican.va/content/francesco

/en/letters/2020/documents/papa-francesco_20200412_lettera-movimentipopolari.html.

Heyer, Kristin E. *Kinship Across Borders: A Christian Ethic of Immigration.* Georgetown University Press, 2012.

John XXIII. *Pacem in terris.* https://www.vatican.va/content/john-xxiii/en/encyclicals/documents/hf_j-xxiii_enc_11041963_pacem.html.

John Paul II. *Sollicitudo-rei-socialis.* https://www.vatican.va/content/john-paul-ii/en/encyclicals/documents/hf_jp-ii_enc_30121987_sollicitudo-rei-socialis.html.

Laitinen, Arto. "Solidarity." *Oxford Research Encyclopedia of Politics,* 2022. https://doi.org/10.1093/acrefore/9780190228637.013.2013.

Leo XIII. *Rerum novarum,* no. 33. https://www.vatican.va/content/leo-xiii/en/encyclicals/documents/hf_l-xiii_enc_15051891_rerum-novarum.html.

Martin, John L., and Monica Lee. "Social Structure." In *International Encyclopedia of the Social and Behavioral Sciences, edited by James W. Wright,* 2nd ed., vol. 22, 713V8. Elsevier, 2015.

Miller, David. "Justice." In *Stanford Encyclopedia of Philosophy* (2017, rev. 2021), 1.1V2.1. https://plato.stanford.edu/entries/justice/.

Paul VI. *Octogesima adveniens.* https://www.vatican.va/archive/hist_councils/ii_vatican_council/documents/vat-ii_const_19641121_lumen-gentium_en.html.

Pius XI. *Quadragesimo anno.* https://www.vatican.va/content/pius-xi/en/encyclicals/documents/hf_p-xi_enc_19310515_quadragesimo-anno.html.

Rawls, John. *A Theory of Justice.* Harvard University Press, 1971.

Second Vatican Council. *Gaudium et spes* (1965), no. 26. https://www.vatican.va/archive/hist_councils/ii_vatican_council/documents/vat-ii_const_19651207_gaudium-et-spes_en.html.

Second World Meeting of Popular Movements: Address of the Holy Father (Bolivia, July 9, 2015). https://www.vatican.va/content/francesco/en/speeches/2015/july/documents/papa-francesco_20150709_bolivia-movimenti-popolari.html.

Shadle, Matthew A. "Culture." In *Moral Agency Within Social Structures and Culture,* edited by Daniel K. Finn. Georgetown University Press, 2020.

Smith-Spark Laura, and Hada Messia. "Pope Francis Explains Name, Calls for Church 'for the Poor.'" https://www.cnn.com/2013/03/16/world/europe/vatican-new-pope/index.html.

Sugimura, Miki. "Equity as a Key Enabler for Inclusive Solidarity," *More Women's Leadership for a Better World: Care as Driver for Our Common Home,* edited by Anna Maria Tarantola. Vita e Pensiero, 2022.

Voss, T.R. "Institutions." In *International Encyclopedia of the Natural and Social Sciences,* edited by Neil J. Smelser and Paul B. Baltes, 7561–7566, 2001. https://doi.org/10.1016/B0-08-043076-7/01901-X.

NOTES

1. Leo XIII, *Rerum novarum,* no. 33.
2. Aquinas, *Summa theologica,* II–II 58 a.1. Aquinas cites Aristotle and Justinian.
3. A recent example is Pope Francis, *Fratelli tutti,* no. 171.
4. Miller, "Justice," 1.1–2.1, see also De Schutter and Tinnevelt, "David Miller's "Theory of Global Justice," 369–81.

5. On a habit as a disposition to act, see Aquinas, ST I–II, 49.3; for a virtue as a good habit, see 55.1 and 3.
6. Leo XIII, *Rerum novarum*, no. 27.
7. Francis, *Fratelli tutti*, no. 171.
8. Consider the difference between equality and equity. "In the context of social policy, equality is the right of different groups of people, such as those of different genders or races, to enjoy the benefits of similar social status and receive the same treatment. Equity, on the other hand, defines the provision of varying levels of support based on individual-specific needs or abilities to achieve greater fairness in treatment and outcomes," Sugimura, "Equity as a Key Enabler for Inclusive Solidarity," 71.
9. Francis, *Laudato si'*, nos. 16, 42, 91.
10. Aquinas, ST II–I, 58.1 ad.1.
11. Second Vatican Council, *Gaudium et spes* (1965), no. 26.
12. See John XXIII, *Pacem in terris*, nos. 132–40.
13. John XXIII, no. 60.
14. John XXIII, no. 30.
15. Aquinas, ST II–II, 6.2, where the individual is to the community as part to whole, with the latter having precedence. Yet, in a. 3, Aquinas places limits on who has the authority to kill, in respect both of social order and of the offender's basic human dignity.
16. See Kodithottam's chapter characterizing Buddhism as holding that "everyone has responsibility for the well-being of others, making this notion the basis of justice," and as emphasizing "compassion and responsibility toward others."
17. See David Cloutier's critique of instrumental concepts of the common good in "What Can Social Science Teach?" 172.
18. Second Vatican Council, *Gaudium et spes*, no. 69.
19. Second Vatican Council, 39.
20. Second Vatican Council, 39.
21. Smith-Spark and Messia, "Pope Francis Explains Name."
22. Cloutier, "What Can Social Science Teach?" 178, 183.
23. See Francis, *Laudato si'*, nos. 169 and 179. Pope Francis's programmatic statement on the essential relation of popular action to equity and the common good is "Letter to the Popular Movements."
24. Aquinas, ST I–II, 58.4.
25. According to Pope Pius XI's *Quadragesimo anno,* justice alone may be able to "remove the causes of social conflict but can never bring about union of minds and hearts" and "solicitous and active love," "whereby the members are united with one another," no. 137.
26. John Paul II, *Sollicitudo rei socialis*, no. 38.
27. Francis, *Fratelli tutti*, no. 115.
28. John Paul II, *Sollicitudo rei socialis*, no. 38; Francis, *Fratelli tutti*, no. 114.
29. John Paul II, nos. 38 and 39.
30. John Paul II, nos. 36–40.
31. Cambridge Dictionary.
32. Augustine, *City of God*. He says similarly that the fact that "a people" is "united by consent of law and common interest" does not necessarily make it just (XIX.21).
33. Laitinen, "Solidarity."
34. Francis, *Fratelli tutti*, no. 116.

35. Heyer, *Kinship Across Borders*, 114, 119. On the processive nature of the common good and the need to recognize and incorporate constructive contention and conflict, see also Cloutier, "What Can Social Science Teach?" 178–79, 183–84; and Shadle, "Culture," 46.
36. Francis, *Fratelli tutti*, nos., 240, 244–45.
37. Aquinas, ST II–II, 58.1.
38. Aquinas, ST II–II, 58.6.
39. Pius XI, *Quadragesimo anno*, nos. 58 and 110.
40. Aquinas, ST. II–II, 64.1.
41. Aquinas, r. ad 1.
42. Aquinas, a 2. r ad 3.
43. Aquinas, r ad 2.
44. Aquinas, a 3. r ad 2.
45. Rawls, A *Theory of Justice*, 3.
46. Voss, "Institutions."
47. Martin and Lee, "Social Structure," 713–8.
48. "Culture," *Cambridge Dictionary*.
49. On this point, as well as on the relation of cultures, structures, and agency in general, see Shadle, "Culture," 43–57.
50. Shadle, 48–50.
51. Francis, *Amoris laetitia*.
52. Francis, *Fratelli tutti*, nos. 11 and 14.

PART III

A Rough Consensus

CHAPTER 13

Toward a Definition of Justice in Catholic Social Thought

Daniel K. Finn

The journal *New Scientist* recently articulated a surprising claim: "Every academic discipline has at its core a 'word of power' that everyone has given up trying to define."[1] It's not fair to say that Catholic theology doesn't have a definition of justice. For centuries, it has turned to Thomas Aquinas, who endorsed Justinian's definition of justice as "a constant and perpetual will rendering to each that which is his right."[2] But we all recognize this definition's shortcomings, documented throughout this volume, and few scholars have attempted a more adequate definition in recent decades. There are hundreds of articles and books on "Justice and X," where X is a particular group or issue of justice, and these are deeply helpful. But they don't attempt a comprehensive account of justice as a whole.

From its inception, the scholarly project that has resulted in this volume has aimed to re-think justice in Catholic social thought. We have aimed for a conception of justice that, as far as possible, is coherent, comprehensive, faithful to the tradition, responsive to the best of contemporary insight, adequate for confronting pressing injustices, and stated simply enough to be accessible to nonexperts.

FOUR INSIGHTS

This final chapter briefly summarizes four of the many issues that earlier chapters investigated in this effort. It concludes with a definition of justice. No one person can speak for a group of scholars as diverse as this one. Thus, there is no claim that the definition would win the hearty endorsement of everyone involved. Nonetheless, the definition arose out of our efforts to reach a consensus at our second conference.

Catholic Social Thought Is Symphonic

One of the most basic intellectual challenges in defining justice is its relation to the many other fundamental moral commitments of the Catholic tradition: the common good, the dignity of the person, the preferential option for the poor, solidarity, subsidiarity, human rights, the rule of law, mercy, love of neighbor, and others. Helpful here is a metaphor proposed by Hans Urs van Balthasar: Catholic theology as symphonic.[3] Just as the music of the philharmonic depends on the subtle interplay of sounds from diverse instruments, so too, Catholic social thought has an integrity based on the interplay of deeply interdependent notions. In the language of software programming today, this is not a bug but a feature of the Catholic tradition.

For example, justice keeps the common good from provincialism, and mercy from favoritism, while in turn, the common good and mercy together help justice avoid rigidity. Where some intellectual systems attempt to begin with a single major premise that has logical priority over all other convictions, Catholic social thought has consistently recognized a more organic relation among its moral commitments. As a result, any adequate definition of justice in Catholic social thought requires references to several of these terms, each of which also needs a definition.[4]

Justice Is a Virtue and a Characteristic of Social Structures and Culture

Papal documents have discussed "social sin" and "sinful social structures" for decades now, but this was not a complete novelty. In 1931, Pope Pius XI extended the Catholic conversation to include "social justice," an early recognition that understanding justice only as a virtue of persons is not adequate. As chapters by Anathea Portier-Young and Jean Porter have indicated, even the ancient scriptures and Thomas Aquinas leaned in this direction. Lisa Cahill suggests taking up a suggestion of John Rawls (whose contributions to this conversation are detailed by Francis Fiorenza). Rawls describes justice as "the first virtue of social institutions." Cahill proposes we understand that while a good moral character leads individuals to make better decisions, so, too, just social institutions make just outcomes more likely.

The result is that any definition of justice in Catholic social thought today must consider it to be not only a virtue of persons but also a characteristic of social structures and culture. This complicates the definition. We'll never again have the simplicity of Justinian's constant and perpetual will—nor of Joseph Pieper's three forms of justice noted in the introduction—but we will have a more adequate and comprehensive understanding of the various dimensions of justice in the world today.

Catholic Social Thought Is Global

The Catholic Church has always been universal, but only in the last seventy-five years has its global nature been so fully acknowledged. Its growth in Europe and North America in prior centuries has given way to growth in the Global South, particularly Africa. As a result, this project to re-think justice has deeply engaged the work of scholars from the South, including careful reports of what Catholic thinking can learn about justice from traditional African religion (Agbonkhianmeghe Orobator) and from Hinduism and Buddhism (George Kodithottam). It has been aided by accounts from Brazil of postcolonial analysis (Maria Inês de Castro Millen) and by accounts from the Philippines of the influence of context and social location (Agnes Brazal).

Catholic social thought can no longer be a monopoly of Western culture. In recent decades, Catholic theologians across the globe have worked to develop dialogue across continental boundaries.[5] Latin American liberation theology has had a significant impact on the magisterial teaching of the popes and bishops worldwide. "St. Thomas Catholics" in India trace their Catholic heritage to the apostle Thomas in 52 CE, developing amid cultural influences quite different from those of ancient Greece and Rome. Even liturgy is part of this reaching out. On three occasions in 2023, the Vatican invited Christian churches not in communion with the pope to celebrate Mass in a major basilica in Rome.[6] The gospel of Jesus and the creeds of the one, holy, catholic, and apostolic church require this intercultural dialogue within a truly Catholic Church.

Experience Is Fundamental

The most challenging proposal arising from scholars in the Global South in this project is the importance of human experience as fundamental to understanding justice. Roman Catholic theology, developed amid the brilliant intellectual insights of the ancient Greek traditions, has prized thinking that is precise, clear, logical, and persuasive. All seven of the first ecumenical councils of the church occurred in Greek cities; the debates among the bishops—and their declarations and creeds—were articulated in Greek. Thomas Aquinas reinvigorated Catholic thought on natural law by bringing the orderly thought of Aristotle to bear on the Christian conviction that God created the world. In turn, the work of Aquinas enabled Popes Leo XIII and Pius XI to engage the sinful economic structures of their day in novel ways.

Nonetheless, the consistent advice we scholars from the North heard from our colleagues from Africa, Latin America, and Asia was that an adequate view of justice must begin with experience, the experience of ordinary people, particularly their experience of injustice. As the reader has already seen, George Kodithottam emphasizes the critical difference between the Hindu notions of *nīti* (an abstract conceptualization of just rules and institutions) and *nyāya* (the realization of justice in the actual life of people). He observes that both Hinduism and Buddhism would suggest that in the Catholic tradition, "more importance needs to be given to the *nyāya* perspective of justice." African traditional religion has not developed the philosophical distinctions of Western thought on justice, but it lives out a lively sense of what justice requires in daily experience. Maria Inês de Castro Millen avoids generalizations about the South American continent out of respect for the variety of experiences there. Agnes Brazal urges attention to context and experience in any consideration of justice.

As a result, the consensus definition of justice to which we came begins not with the traditional "justice is an ideal to be instantiated" but with justice as an experience of a just community. Similarly basic, injustice is the experience of the oppressed and marginalized in an unjust society. Traditional Catholic notions of justice have always aimed for the *implementation* of justice, what we today would call the lived experience of justice by all persons. But that experience was the *goal* of definitions of justice. The call we heard from the Global South was for the experience to be the starting point of our articulation of justice, built on the prior experience of injustice by so many millions of people around the globe.

TOWARD A CONSENSUS DEFINITION IN CATHOLIC SOCIAL THOUGHT

Conversations at the second conference asked whether a consensus definition would be possible in this group of scholars. The eventual answer was "yes." For grammatical simplicity, there are two parts to this definition of justice: an account of its causes and a description of its characteristics.

Justice is a lived experience of communal life animated by both a personal disposition embodied in action and by social structures and culture that encourage that action and sustain the context for that communal life.

A just communal life is characterized by the freedom and equal dignity of all people and by equitable relationships of exchange and access to the common goods of the community. It fosters cultures of solidarity, solicitude, care for nature, and constructive conflict, and it structures social relationships to embody the common good, the dignity of all, ecological integrity, and the preferential empowerment of those whose participation is at risk.

BIBLIOGRAPHY

Ford, Josie. "When the Scientific Publishing Industry Goes Rogue." *New Scientist*, June 1, 2022. https://www.newscientist.com/article/mg25433893-100-when-the-scientific-publishing-industry-goes-rogue/.

Finn, Daniel K., ed. *Empirical Foundations of the Common Good: What Theology Can Learn from Social Science.* Oxford University Press, 2017.

International Network of Societies for Catholic Theology (INSECT). https://www.insecttheology.org/.

"Syro-Malankara Orthodox Celebrate Mass in One of Rome's Four Main Basilicas." *Zenit, September 12, 2023.* https://zenit.org/2023/09/12/syro-malankara-orthodox-celebrate-mass-in-one-of-romes-four-main-basilicas/?eti=11310.

van Balthasar, Hans Urs. *Truth Is Symphonic: Aspects of Christian Pluralism.* Ignatius Press, 1987.

NOTES

1. Quoted in Josie Ford, "When the Scientific Publishing Industry Goes Rogue."
2. Aquinas, ST, II–II 58.1. See the chapter by Jean Porter.
3. Hans Urs van Balthasar, *Truth Is Symphonic.*
4. For example, an earlier project of the Institute for Advanced Catholic Studies asked how the meaning of the common good should change in light of social scientific insight. See Finn, *Empirical Foundations of the Common Good.*
5. See, for example, the International Network of Societies for Catholic Theology (INSECT).
6. First, it was the Anglicans; subsequently, it was the Coptic Orthodox, both at St. John Lateran. Later it was the Syro-Malabar Orthodox, at St. Paul Outside the Walls. "Syro-Malankara Orthodox Celebrate Mass in One of Rome's Four Main Basilicas."

ABOUT THE PARTICIPANTS

AUTHORS

AGNES M. BRAZAL is full professor and research fellow of theology and 2024 nominee for the Miguel Febres Cordero Pillar of Lasallian Excellence in Research award at the De la Salle University, Manila. She is the author of two books, *A Theology of Southeast-Asia: Liberation-Postcolonial Ethics in the Philippines* (Orbis, 2019) and *Toward an Intercultural Church: Bridge of Solidarity in the Migration Context* (Borderless Press, 2015), and is coeditor of ten anthologies that include *500 Years of Christianity and the Global Filipino/a: Postcolonial Perspectives* (Palgrave Macmillan, 2024) and *Toward a Bai Theology: Catholic Feminism in the Philippines* (Claretian, 2023). She was Asian regional coordinator of the Vatican project on "Doing Theology from Existential Peripheries" (October 2021–2022) organized by the Dicastery in Promoting Integral Human Development and the Migrants and Refugees Section. She is a founding member and past president of the Catholic Theological Society of the Philippines (DaKaTeo) and past coordinator of the Ecclesia of Women in Asia. She obtained her STL/MA and STD/PhD in Theology at the Katholieke Universiteit Leuven.

LISA SOWLE CAHILL, PhD (University of Chicago 1976), is the J. Donald Monan, SJ, professor, theology department, Boston College. Dr. Cahill is a past president of the Catholic Theological Society of America (1992–93) and of the Society of Christian Ethics (1997–98) and is a fellow of the American Academy of Arts and Sciences. Her works include *Blessed Are the Peacemakers: Pacifism, Just War and Peacebuilding* (Fortress, 2019), *A Theology and Praxis of Gender Equality* (Dharmaram Publications, 2019), and *Global Justice, Christology and Christian Ethics* (Cambridge University Press, 2013). Her most recent book, coedited with Nicolete Burbach, is *Trans Life and the Catholic Church Today* (Bloomsbury, 2024).

MARIA INÊS DE CASTRO MILLEN is a lay Catholic moral theologian in Brazil, married, with two daughters and two grandsons. She is a physician, graduated in 1971 from the Universidade Federal de Juiz de Fora. She received her bachelor's degree in theology in 1994 from Pontifícia Universidade Católica–Rio de Janeiro and a master's in religious studies from Universidade Federal de Juiz de Fora. In 2004, she successfully concluded her PhD in theology at Pontifícia Universidade Católica–Rio de Janeiro. She served as the first woman president of the Brazilian Society of Moral Theology (2016–2021). She is an active member of Rede Brasileira de Teólogas (Network of Women Theologians in Brazil), SOTER (Brazilian Society of Theology and Religious Studies), and CTEWC (Catholic Theological Ethics in the World Church). Among her publications are *Introdução à ética teológica* and *Formação: Desafios morais*, volumes I and II.

DAVID CLOUTIER (BA, Carleton; PhD, Duke) is professor of moral theology at the University of Notre Dame, teaching primarily social ethics. He is the author of a number of books, including *The Vice of Luxury: Economic Excess in a Consumer Age* (Georgetown University Press) *Walking God's Earth: The Environment and Catholic Theology, Reading Praying Living Pope Francis' Laudato Si'* (both from Liturgical Press), and *Love, Reason, and God's Story: An Introduction to Catholic Sexual Ethics* (Anselm/St. Mary's). His writing has appeared in *Commonweal, America*, and *US Catholic*, among other venues. His current writing project aims at correcting partisan misunderstandings of Catholic social teaching in order to articulate more fully a Catholic social imaginary for contemporary society. When not writing, he spends time running, singing in church choirs, following baseball, and contributing to local food economies.

DANIEL K. FINN is professor emeritus of theology and Clemens Professor Emeritus of Economics at St. John's University and the College of St. Benedict. His books include *Christian Economic Ethics* (Fortress), *Consumer Ethics in a Global Economy* (Georgetown), and *The Moral Ecology of Markets* (Cambridge). He has received lifetime achievement awards from the Catholic Theological Society of America and the Association for Social Economics. He is a former president of those two professional societies and of the Society of Christian Ethics. For twenty-five years, he has been the director of the True Wealth of Nations project at the Institute for Advanced Catholic Studies. He has lectured in more than twenty nations in Latin America, Europe, and Asia and has led a successful affordable housing campaign among five cities in central Minnesota.

DR. GEORGE KODITHOTTAM, SJ, professor (emeritus) of moral theology, was a staff member at Gujarat Vidya Deep Regional Seminary, Vadodara, affiliated with Jnana-Deepa Vidyapeeth (JDV), Pontifical Athenaeum of Philosophy and Theology, Pune, India. He also taught at JDV, Pune and Dharmaram Vidya Kshetram (DVK), Bengaluru. He is a registered civil lawyer and also holds master's degrees in sociology and theology. He did his PhD in moral theology at the University of Innsbruck, Austria. He is a member of the Gujarat Province of the Society of Jesus. While a theology professor, he also worked in the mission parishes in rural Gujarat for over twenty-five years as assistant parish priest and as parish priest.

AGBONKHIANMEGHE E. OROBATOR, SJ, is dean of the Jesuit School of Theology of Santa Clara University, California. He was raised in traditional African religious practice and converted to Catholicism as a teen. He has taught theology and religious studies at Hekima University College in Nairobi, St. Augustine College of South Africa in Johannesburg, and Marquette University. He has served as superior of the Jesuits of the Eastern Africa Province. He is the author of *Theology Brewed in an African Pot* (Orbis Books, 2008), *Religion and Faith in Africa: Confessions of an Animist* (Orbis Books, 2018), and *The Pope and the Pandemic: Lessons in Leadership in a Time of Crisis* (Orbis Books, 2021).

JEAN PORTER is the John A. O'Brien Professor of Moral Theology at the University of Notre Dame, where she has taught since 1990. She received her doctorate from Yale University in 1984. Before coming to Notre Dame, she taught at Vanderbilt Divinity School. She is a member of the American Academy of Arts and Sciences and is a past president of the Society of Christian Ethics. She is the author of numerous articles and books on medieval moral thought. Her books include *Justice as a Virtue: A Thomistic Perspective* (Eerdmans 2016), *Nature as Reason: A Thomistic Theory of the Natural Law* (Eerdmans, 2005), and *Ministers of the Law: A Natural Law Theory of Legal Authority* (Eerdmans 2010).

ANATHEA PORTIER-YOUNG is associate professor of Old Testament at Duke Divinity School. Her recent book *The Prophetic Body: Embodiment and Mediation in Biblical Prophetic Literature* (Oxford, 2024) is part of a larger project on the theme of embodiment in biblical prophetic literature. Her monograph *Apocalypse Against Empire: Theologies of Resistance in Early Judaism* (Eerdmans, 2011) won the Manfred Lautenschläger Award for Theological Promise. She coedited with Gregory Sterling *Scripture and Social Justice: Catholic and Ecumenical Essays* (Fortress, 2018). Her research focuses on prophetic literature, apocalypticism, early Jewish literature, embodiment, violence and nonviolence, and justice. She also teaches and writes in the area of Christian preaching and is a frequent contributor to workingpreacher.org. She holds degrees from Yale University, Jesuit School of Theology/Graduate Theological Union, and Duke University. She is also a runner, dancer, quilter, gardener, and mom.

STEERING COMMITTEE

The steering committee responsible for oversight of this project includes the scholars listed below and three of the authors listed above: David Cloutier, Francis Schüssler Fiorenza, and Daniel Finn (chair).

JULIE CLAGUE is lecturer in Catholic theology at the University of Glasgow, UK, where she is a member of the Gifford Committee. Prior to moving to Scotland, Julie lectured at St. Mary's University, Twickenham, and studied theology at London and Cambridge Universities. Julie currently edits the European writers' forum of Catholic Theological Ethics in the World Church and serves on various editorial boards for journals, including *Ecclesial Practices: Journal of Ecclesiology and Ethnography, Theology in Scotland*, and *Acta Universitatis Carolinae Theologica*. She was editor of the journals *Political Theology* and *Feminist Theology* for over a decade. She has authored numerous articles in moral theology and Catholic social thought. She is a theological advisor to the Catholic Agency for Overseas Development (CAFOD) and the Scottish Catholic International Aid Fund. She has spoken on Catholic approaches to development at a number of UN-organized events, including at the UN General Assembly. Julie is currently working on understandings of structural injustice and health inequity.

FRANCIS SCHÜSSLER FIORENZA is Charles Chancey Stillman Research Professor of Roman Catholic Theological Studies at Harvard Divinity School. His primary interests are in the field of fundamental theology, in which he explores the significance of contemporary hermeneutical theories as well as neo-pragmatic criticisms of foundationalism. His writings on political theology engage recent theories of justice, especially those of John Rawls and Jürgen Habermas, and have dealt with issues of work and welfare. He has also written on the history of nineteenth- and twentieth-century theology, focusing on both Roman Catholic and Protestant theologians. He has published widely, with more than 150 essays in the areas of fundamental theology, hermeneutics, and political theology. His books include *Foundational*

Theology: Jesus and the Church (Crossroads, 1984) and *Rights at Risk: Confronting the Cultural, Ethical, and Religious Challenges* (Continuum, 2012).

JAMES HEFT, SM, is a priest in the Society of Mary (Marianist) and leader for over thirty years in Catholic higher education. He spent many years at the University of Dayton, serving as chair of the Theology Department for six years, Provost of the University for eight years, and then Chancellor for ten years. He left the University of Dayton in 2006 to found the Institute for Advanced Catholic Studies at the University of Southern California in Los Angeles, where until 2023 he served as the Alton Brooks Professor of Religion. He has written and edited fourteen books and published over 200 articles and book chapters. His most recent book, *The Future of Catholic Higher Education: The Open Circle*, was published by Oxford in 2021. He now serves as scholar in residence at the University of Dayton.

CHRISTINE FIRER HINZE is professor and chair of the Department of Theology, and previously, director of the Francis and Ann Curran Center for American Catholic Studies at Fordham University, New York. She holds a BA in religion and an MA in theology from the Catholic University of America and a PhD in Christian social ethics from the University of Chicago. Her teaching and research focus on Christian social ethics with special emphasis on the dynamics of social transformation, Catholic social thought, and economic and work justice for vulnerable women, families and groups. She is a former president of the Catholic Theological Society of America, and her books include *Radical Sufficiency: Work, Livelihood and a U.S. Catholic Economic Ethic* (Georgetown, 2021), *Comprehending Power in Christian Social Ethics* (Oxford, 1995), and *Glass Ceilings, Dirt Floors: Women, Work, and the Global Economy* (Paulist Press, 2015). She has authored scores of scholarly essays in books and journals, including *Theological Studies, The Journal of the Society of Christian Ethics, The Journal of Catholic Social Thought*, and *Studies in Christian Ethics*.

ALEXANDRE A. MARTINS is a theologian and bioethicist from Brazil and an associate professor in the College of Nursing and Department of Theology at Marquette University. His research focuses on bioethics and global health from a liberation approach. He specializes in health care ethics and social ethics, especially in the areas of public health, global health, community-based approach, and Catholic social teaching. His scholarship has been broad. Widely published, he has lectured in various countries. His latest books include *Christology and Global Health: Christology and Global*

Ethics: Encountering the Poor in a Pluralist Reality (Paulist Press, 2023) and *A Prophet to the People: Paul Farmer's Witness and Theological Ethics* (Pickwick Press, 2023), coedited with Jannie W. Block and M. Thesere Lysaught. Currently, he serves as vice president of the Brazilian Society of Moral Theology.

STEPHEN J. POPE is a professor of theological ethics at Boston College. He works in the areas of virtue ethics, justice and reconciliation, and the intersection of science and theological ethics. His essays have addressed cosmic evolution, integral human development, and the use of psychology in ethics. He regularly takes student groups for immersion experiences in the Global South, and he has volunteered at a medium-security prison in Massachusetts for the last fifteen years. His books include *Human Evolution and Christian Ethics* (Cambridge, 2007) and *A Step Along the Way: Models of Christian Service* (Orbis, 2025). He is completing a manuscript entitled *God's Love and Ours: A Christian Ethic of Forgiveness* (Georgetown, forthcoming).

INDEX

1994 Genocide, 23
Acampamento Terra Livre, 58
accountability, 23, 79, 82, 166, 199;
    mutual, 79
Acts of the Apostles, 177
ADC (Citizen Action), 65
affirmative action, 139
African religion, traditional, 13–28
Agenda 21, 69
Albert, Bruce, 70
Amazon, and the environment, 68–73
Amoris laetitia, 235
ancestors, spirits of, 21, 23
androcentrism, in Africa, 27
Aparecida Conference, 61, 64
APIB, 58
Aquinas, Thomas, 42, 100–14, 135–37,
    142, 187, 227–28, 232, 235;
    and justice, 100–115
Archer, Margaret S., 182
Aristotle, 40, 106, 134, 135, 197, 235
Augustine, 134, 178, 197, 231
authority, 79, 104, 109, 138, 227

balance, natural in Hinduism, 37
Baraza, 21
Barna Group, 122
bashingantahe, 24
basic ecclesial communities, 61–64
Benedict XV, 166
Benedict XVI, 178, 185, 217, 218
Beozzo, José Oscar, 61
Bergoglio, Jorge, 216
Berlin, Isaiah, 127

Best Buy, 184
Betto, Frei, 61, 63
Bhaskar, Roy, 180
bias, gender, 150
bible, and justice, 78–96
biblical interpretation, 78
Bill of Rights, 210
Boff, Leonardo, 61, 69
Brazil, 54–74
Brum, Eliane, 71
Buddhism, and justice, 41–47
Buddhist ethics, 41
Burundi, 24

capital punishment, 122, 136–37
Caritas in veritate, 167, 217, 218
castes, 38
catalonan, 164
Catechism of the Catholic Church, 137
Catholic Action, 145
Catholic Theological Ethics in the
    World Church, 68
Catholicism, as a world church, 33
Caxias, 63
CELAM, 61, 139
Centessimus annus, 167
Christianity in sub-Saharan Africa, 14
Christus Health, 86
Chrysostom, John, 217
church and state, 65
civic good, 120
CNPD (the Black Coalition for
    Rights), 58
co-determination, 189

collectives, and the Bible, 82
colonization, 55–60, 200
Comblin, José, 61
common good, 136–38, 212–15, 229; in Aquinas, 104–6; and life preferences, 123; problems with, 120–25; for Rawls, 128; universal, 138
communication, ethics of, 20
communitarianism, 124
commutative justice. *See* justice, commutative
compassion, 28, 42, 43, 44, 46, 216, 229
Comte, Auguste, 182
comunidades eclesiais de base, 62
confidentiality, 24
consciousness, historical, 60, 68
consensus, 20, 136–37, 127, 246; overlapping, in John Rawls, 117
consultation, 20
cosmic order, 37, 42, 43
Covid pandemic, 122
creation and justice, 92

da Silva, Luis Inácio Lula, 66
DaMatta, Robert, 54
daṇḍa, 39
Daniel, Biblical critique of empire, 84
datu, 164
de Souza, Herbert, 65
de Souza, Jessé, 67
death penalty, 136; in Catholic social thought, 137
decentralization of the church, 149–50
Declaration of Independence, 210
decolonization, 227
deforestation, 71, 73
deliberation, democratic, 165–68
democracy, 83–88, 138, 188, 227; pre-figured in the Bible, 83–88
dependent origination, 42

development, integral human, 19
dharma, 35–36, 38, 42
Dharmasūtra, 39
difference principle in Rawls, 139
dignity, of the person, 62, 138–40, 210–11, 228–29; in Aquinas, 102, 112; of power, 138–39; in Rawls, 125
discrimination, 56, 59, 60
disposition, 135
dispositional problem of justice, 140
distributive justice. *See* justice, distributive
diversity, ethic, 60
Divini redemptoris, 178
domination, two kinds in Aquinas, 105
dominion, just, 92
Dominus Iesus, 145
Domitila, 60
Dworkin, Ronald, 114

Earth Bible Team, 92
Earth Charter, 69, 70
Ebola, 122
ecology, 68–73, 149, 198; in the Bible, 91–95; participatory, 72
"Economic Justice for All," 187
economic life, and the Bible, 88–91
economics, Buddhist, 45
Edo, 14
EDUCAFRO (Education to Africans), 59
elders, in the Bible, 83
Elijah, 81
emancipation, spiritual, 37
emergence, 179
empiricism, 180
employment, 40, 129, 158, 160; importance in Catholic social thought, 189
enlightenment, 45, 227
environmental justice, in Buddhism, 46
epistemological privilege, 169
equal dignity, 113, 140

equality, 113, 136; in exchange, 110; as a matter of proportion, 208; among persons in Aquinas, 102; of status, 111
ethnicity, 227
Evangelii gaudium, 66, 167
Evangelii nuntiandi, 63
evangelization, 62, 71
evolution, ladder of, 38
exclusions, passive, 166
extinction, 71

fair equality of opportunity, 129
Ferdinand I, Roman Emperor, 34
food insecurity, 68
forgiveness, 20
Fourth World Meeting of Popular Movements, 141
Francis, 46, 54, 66–67, 68, 71–72, 73, 137, 138, 141, 146, 148–49, 151, 165, 167, 200, 215, 216, 227–28, 229–30, 235
Francis of Assisi Education, Citizenship, Inclusion and Human Rights, 59
Frankfurt school, 121
Fraser, Nancy, 125, 126
Fratelli tutti, 151, 200, 231
freedom, 101, 108–11, 127, 159–62; of religion, 138
Freire, Paulo, 65
FZ, *Fome Zero*, 66

Gacaca, 23, 203
Gadotti, Moacir, 69
Gallio inscription, 177
Gaudium et spes, 147, 166, 210, 212, 217, 228, 229
gender, 199, 227
complementarity, 150, 158
division of labor, 157
generalization avoided, 54
genocide, 59

geography and justice, 21
gerrymandering, 188
gift, and justice, 217
Gilchrist, Luverta, 80, 87
gleaning laws, 189
global public authority, 138
Golden Age, 38
good, the; and inevitably conflicting values, 127; civic/public/common, 120
good Samaritan, 216
Gregg, Samuel, 178
Gudorf, Christine, 164, 167
guilds, medieval, 209
Gula, Richard, 161
Gutiérrez, Gustavo, 61
Gutmann, Amy, 165

Habermas, Jürgen, 126
harmony, normative in Hinduism, 37
Hayek, Friedrich, 178, 214
Hempel, Carl, 180
hermeneutic of humility and justice, 79
ḥesed, 85
Heyer, Kristin, 231
hierarchy, natural in Hinduism, 40
Hinduism, justice in, 34–41
Hinze, Christine, 145
historicity, 182
Hobbes, Thomas, 197
holism, 179
Hollenbach, David, 124, 142, 146, 231
homelessness, 91
hope, 63, 87
human capabilities, 159–63
human dignity. *See* dignity, human
human life as objective of ethics, 16
human nature, universal, 211
human rights, 18, 138, 146–47, 227
Hume, David, 180
humility, 79, 85
hunger, 68, 91
Hutus, 23

Ibanga, 24
ideology criticism, 168
incarceration, 218
inclusion, 59, 166, 169, 228
Indaba, 21
indifference, 69
indigenous people, 56, 57–58, 71
individual accountability, 25
individualism, 116, 147, 179, 209
industrial revolution, 189
inequality; as just in Hinduism, 38; of wealth, 144; for women, 160
Ingando, 21
injustice, 55, 78, 121, 178, 246; in Africa, 25; environmental, 189; as structural characteristic, 56, 81, 141, 185–87
Insaka, 21
Institutes of Justinian, 134, 227
Instituto Conhecimento Liberta, 67
integral development, 27, 150
Interfaith Prison Ministry for Women, 85
Inter-insignores, 158
interpretation, biblical, 78–83
Islam in Africa, 14

jātīs (castes), 36
Jim Crow, 136, 185
Jobe, Sarah, 85, 86
John Paul II, 137, 145, 151, 178, 189, 217, 230
John XXIII, 138, 178, 210, 212, 228
jubilee year, 89, 189
juridical order, in Pius XI, 144
jurisprudence; African, 22, 24; European colonial, 21
justice; administration of, in Hinduism, 38–40; in Aquinas, 100–14; in Buddhism, 41–47; and culture, 234; and gender, 27; and geography, 21; and liberalism, 116–30; as a virtue, 226–37; as communal, 17; as dialogical, 204; as experience,

245; commutative, 103, 105, 209; commutative, distributive, and general, 102, 142-43, 187, 232; criminal, 113; definition, 134, 206, 227, 237, 243, 246; distributive, 102, 113, 189, 198, 213, 214–15; environmental, 198; equal, 208; eschatological, 212–15; founded in world order, 40; general, 102, 104, 188, 232; generational, 199; Hebrew terms, 85; Igbo system, 21; in Hinduism, 34–41; inculturated, 202; karmic, 44; and mercy, 86, 207; mystical quality, 202; and the natural world, 233; as praxis, 204; participative, 188; restorative, 13, 21–22, 25, 190; sans frontier, 203; social, 141–45, 178, 232–33; as structural characteristic, 185–87, 233; subjective, 207; two principles in John Rawls, 118; as virtue of social institutions, 185; and wisdom, 85
Justice and the Politics of Difference, 163
Justice as Fairness: A Restatement, 118
Justinian, 101, 106
Justitia in mundo, 146

Kali Yuga, 39
karma, 203
karmic retribution, 36–37, 38, 39
Kenya, 14
Keown, Damien, 43
Kollman, Paul, 16
Kopenawa, Davi, 70
Krenak, Ailton, 70

Laborem exercens, 167
Latin America, 54–74
Laudato si', 138, 141, 146, 148, 150, 198, 215, 228
Laws of Manu, 39
The Laws of People, 119

laws, scientific, 180
leadership, in the Bible, 83
Lederach, John Paul, 21
legal systems, Islamic and Christian, 14
Lekgotla, 21
Leo XIII, 133, 141, 143, 189, 209, 213, 227, 246
Letter to Women, 151
Libanio, João Batista, 61
liberalism, 116–31, 138, 209; and Catholic social thought, 139; and the good, 127; and justice, 116–30
liberation, 63, 164; in Hinduism, 36; in the bible, 89
liberation theology, 38, 61, 139, 216
libertarianism, 209
liberty. *See* freedom
literacy, 20
literacy projects, 65
Locke, John, 114, 138
Lockwood O'Donovan, Joan, 208
Lorscheider, Aloísio, 62

MacDonald, Angela, 86, 94
MacIntyre, Alasdair, 124, 208
Magesa, Laurenti, 16
Mahabharata, 35
Manu, 36, 39
Manusmṛti., 36
Marley, Tiffney, 86
marriage, as communal in Africa, 13
Mato Oput, 23, 203
MEB, the Basic Education Movement, 64
Medellín Conference, 61, 63–64
Mesters, Carlos, 61
migration, 218
Miller, David, 133
mining, 73
ministry, social, 66
Minow, Martha, 25
Missionary Indigenous Council, 57–60
Moral Monday Movement, 87
moral realism, 161

Moreira, Eduardo, 67
Moses, 81
movements, social, 57–60, 62, 65

NAACP, 87
National Community Action Partnership, 86
National Conference of Bishops of Brazil, 57, 64
National Council for Indigenous Policy, 58
National Literacy Plan, 65
natural rights. *See* rights, natural
nature; and covenant, 92; of humans, Hinduism, 36; and justice, 93; and neoliberalism, 67
Ngozi Adichie, Chimamanda, 200
Niebuhr, Reinhold, 144, 186
Nigeria, 14, 21
Nindorera, Agnes, 24
nīti, 33–34, 142, 246
The Noble Eightfold Path, 45
nonviolence, 43
Nostra Aetate, 145
Novak, Michael, 178
Nozick, Robert, 214
Nussbaum, Martha, 114, 159–63
nyāya, 33–34, 142, 246
nyāya and *nīti*, in Africa, 15

Octogesima adveniens, 167, 230
ontology, social, 213
Openibo, Veronica, 148, 230
Opongo, Elias, 23, 136
opportunities, in social structures, 183
option for the poor, 62, 90,126, 135, 139, 147–48, 216, 230
orality, 20
order of nature/order of reason, in natural law, 162
Origen, 80
original peoples, 70
ownership, 107, 110, 148, 166, 189, 214

Pacem in terris, 138, 146, 210, 228
Pact of the Catacombs, 60
paideia, 124
palaver, 13, 22, 165, 190
Pāli scriptures, 44
participation, 20–21, 62, 147, 165, 188, 229–31
participative community mediation, 165–66
patriarchy, 82, 199, 211; in Africa, 27
Paul VI, 146
Paulo Freire Institute, 69
peace, 60, 218
Peace Palace, 70
person as social, 209, 213, 217
philosophy of science, 179–81
Philpott, Daniel, 22
Pieper, Josef, 124, 187, 245
Pitso, 21
Pius XI, 47, 141, 144–45, 178, 230, 244, 246
Pius XII, 166
Plato, 134, 197
Pleins, David, 90
politics of difference, 163
popular movements, 141, 148, 167, 230
Populorum progressio, 146, 210
Porpora, Douglas, 182
poverty, 55, 61, 67, 71, 145, 203
power, 39, 84–86, 209, 215; interpretive, 79; moral, 106; practice and theory, in Africa, 15
Prebish, Charles, 43
preferential hiring, 164
preferential option for the poor, 45, 61, 126, 139–40, 143, 147–48, 216, 229–30
preferential treatment, 228
prejudice, 186
priesthood, and gender, 164
privilege, in social structure, 184
property rights. *See* ownership

public good, 120
public reason, 119
publicity, 166, 169
Puebla, 61, 63
punishment, and social status in Hinduism, 39
purity, in Buddhism, 43

Quadragesimo anno, 47, 141, 144, 145, 148, 166, 232
Querida amazônia, 72, 167, 200
quilombos, 58, 72

racism, 56, 58–59, 60, 113, 227; environmental, 94; structural, 90
Raimundo dos Santos, David, 59
Ratzinger, Joseph, 162
Rawls, John, 19, 100, 114, 117–21, 134–36, 185, 197, 214, 226, 233
reciprocity, 119, 166, 168
recognition, 125–27
reconciliation, 21–22, 199
redistribution, 125, 144, 229
redlining, 190
Rerum novarum, 139, 146, 189, 227
respect, 24; for persons, 113; for persons in Aquinas, 103
restitution, 20
restorative justice, *See* justice, restorative
restrictions, in social structure, 183
retribution, 20; karmic, 39
retributive justice, *See* justice, retributive
riberinhos, 72
Richard, Pablo, 61
Ricoeur, Paul, 134
Ṛig Veda, 38
rights, 40, 138; in Hinduism, 36; human, 60; individual, 212; language, 209; natural in Aquinas, 106–12; overemphasis on, 41; subjective, 208

rita, 34, 40
rituals of justice, 13, 22–25
role exclusion, 164–65
Rwanda, 23

sabbath, 89
sabbatical, 189
Salleh, Fatimah, 80
Santo Domingo Conference, 61
Schwantes, Milton, 61
scripture, and justice, 78–96
Second Chance Alliance, 87
Second Vatican Council.
    See Vatican II
Segundo, Juan Luis, 61
self-centeredness, 44
self-criticism, 79
self-interest, 41, 47, 145, 149, 170,
    186; mutual, 43
self-liberation, 61
self-mortification, rejected in
    Buddhism, 41
self-restraint, in Buddhism, 41
Sen, Amartya, 21, 33, 114
sex abuse, 148, 204, 230
sexism, 113, 158, 171
sexual diversity, 211
sharia, 14
Shining World, 44
Sierra Leon, 25
sin, and justice, 215
slavery, 56, 58, 89, 199
Sobrino, Jon, 61
social charity, 143, 145
social class, 227
social contract, 138
social division of labor, 163
social justice. *See* justice,
    social
social ontology; eschatological, 217;
    pluralist, 213, 215
social structures, 134, 148–49, 172–91,
    218, 232, 244

sociality, human, 214
solidarity, 59, 61, 68, 145, 229, 230;
    conflictual, 231; the dark side of,
    231; solidarity fee, 67
Solomon, 81
South Africa, 185
Southern Africa, 21
Special Secretariat for Indigenous
    Health, 58
stratified world, 179
subsidiarity, 141, 145, 167, 213
suffering, 46; in Buddhism, 41
Summi pontificatus, 166
Synod for the Amazon, 71, 149
Synod of Bishops, 146
synodality, 167
systems of domination, 86

Tamez, Elza, 61
Tanzania, 14
Taylor, Charles, 126, 214
teleology, 40
Territorial Management of Indigenous
    Lands, 58
theology of the people, 216
A Theory of Justice, 117, 119
Thompson, Dennis, 165
totalitarianism, 83, 212
tribalism in Africa, 16
Trinity, 217
Truth and Reconciliation Commission,
    18, 24
Tutsis, 23
Tutu, Desmond, 19, 22

U.N. Declaration of Human Rights, 106
Ubuntu, 13, 17–20, 24, 27
Ubupfasoni, 24
Ubushingantahe/bashingantahe,
    24, 203
Uganda, 23
Ukraine, 219
UNESCO, 65, 70

United Nations, 69
universal destination of goods, 217
universal dignity, 229

van Balthasar, Hans Urs, 244
van Velzen, Breana, 91
varna, 36, 38, 39
Vatican II, 60, 62, 139, 146, 158,
    209, 229
Veiga Aranha, Adriana, 66
Villa-Vicencio, Charles, 17
Villa-Vicencio, Fernando, 28
violence, sexual, 211
Virajas, 39
virtue, 228, 231, 232, 244; in
    Buddhism, 42; as disposition,
    227; and justice, 144; of social
    institutions, 234

vocation, 18, 168, 217
voter registration, 188
vyavahāra, 39

wage theft, 88
Walzer, Michael, 214
war, 204, 218
water, in the Bible, 94–95
Watts, James, 90
Weber, Max, 177
Williams Institute, 122
wisdom and justice, 85
World Meeting of Popular Movements,
    230

Young, Iris Marian, 126, 163–65

www.ingramcontent.com/pod-product-compliance
Ingram Content Group UK Ltd.
Pitfield, Milton Keynes, MK11 3LW, UK
UKHW010013050625
2118IPUK00008B/22